Living Labor

CLASS : CULTURE

SERIES EDITORS
Amy Schrager Lang, Syracuse University, Bill V. Mullen, Purdue University, and Kasturi Ray, San Francisco State University

RECENT TITLES IN THE SERIES:

Joseph B. Entin, *Living Labor: Fiction, Film, and Precarious Work*

Sidney Fine, with a new foreword by Kim Moody, *Sit-Down: The General Motors Strike of 1936–1937*

Rebecca Kolins Givan and Amy Schrager Lang, Editors, *Strike for the Common Good: Fighting for the Future of Public Education*

Sylvia Jenkins Cook, *Clothed in Meaning: Literature, Labor, and Cotton in Nineteenth-Century America*

Cedric R. Tolliver, *Of Vagabonds and Fellow Travelers: African Diaspora Literary Culture and the Cultural Cold War*

Ann Mattis, *Dirty Work: Domestic Service in Progressive-Era Women's Fiction*

Marcial González and Carlos Gallego, Editors, *Dialectical Imaginaries: Materialist Approaches to U.S. Latino/a Literature in the Age of Neoliberalism*

Sherry Lee Linkon, *The Half-Life of Deindustrialization: Working-Class Writing about Economic Restructuring*

Mark W. Robbins, *Middle Class Union: Organizing the 'Consuming Public' in Post–World War I America*

Marie A. Failinger and Ezra Rosser, Editors, *The Poverty Law Canon: Exploring the Major Cases*

M. Michelle Robinson, *Dreams for Dead Bodies: Blackness, Labor, and the Corpus of American Detective Fiction*

Benjamin Balthaser, *Anti-Imperialist Modernism: Race and Transnational Radical Culture from the Great Depression to the Cold War*

Clarence Lang, *Black America in the Shadow of the Sixties: Notes on the Civil Rights Movement, Neoliberalism, and Politics*

Andreá N. Williams, *Dividing Lines: Class Anxiety and Postbellum Black Fiction*

Liam Kennedy and Stephen Shapiro, Editors, The Wire: *Race, Class, and Genre*

Mark W. Van Wienen, *American Socialist Triptych: The Literary-Political Work of Charlotte Perkins Gilman, Upton Sinclair, and W. E. B. Du Bois*

Marsh, John, *Hog Butchers, Beggars, and Busboys: Poverty, Labor, and the Making of Modern American Poetry*

Living Labor
Fiction, Film, and Precarious Work

Joseph B. Entin

University of Michigan Press • Ann Arbor

Copyright © 2023 by Joseph B. Entin
Some rights reserved

This work is licensed under a Creative Commons Attribution-NonCommercial-NoDerivatives 4.0 International License. *Note to users*: A Creative Commons license is only valid when it is applied by the person or entity that holds rights to the licensed work. Works may contain components (e.g., photographs, illustrations, or quotations) to which the rightsholder in the work cannot apply the license. It is ultimately your responsibility to independently evaluate the copyright status of any work or component part of a work you use, in light of your intended use. To view a copy of this license, visit http://creativecommons.org/licenses/by-nc-nd/4.0/

For questions or permissions, please contact um.press.perms@umich.edu

Published in the United States of America by the
University of Michigan Press
Manufactured in the United States of America
Printed on acid-free paper
First published February 2023

A CIP catalog record for this book is available from the British Library.

Library of Congress Cataloging-in-Publication data has been applied for.

The University of Michigan Press's open access publishing program is made possible thanks to additional funding from the University of Michigan Office of the Provost and the generous support of contributing libraries.

ISBN 978-0-472-07519-5 (hardcover : alk. paper)
ISBN 978-0-472-05519-7 (paper : alk. paper)
ISBN 978-0-472-90314-6 (open access ebook)

DOI: https://doi.org/10.3998/mpub.11738099

For my students
and
For Miriam and Rachel

Contents

Acknowledgments ix

Introduction: Narratives of Living Labor 1

1 "We Are the Planet": Impossible Solidarities in
Russell Banks's *Continental Drift* 24

2 "Maps of Labor": Globalization, Migration,
and Contemporary Working-Class Literature 50

3 Living Labor, Dead Labor: Cinema, Solidarity,
and Necrocapitalism 86

4 "The Uprooted Worker at the Center of the World":
Labor, Migration, and Precarity on the Urban Underside
of Independent Cinema 125

Coda: Forms of Solidarity in Precarious Times 160

Notes 165

Index 191

Digital materials related to this title can be found on the Fulcrum platform via the following citable URL: https://doi.org/10.3998/mpub.11738099

Acknowledgments

When I look back over the long and at times difficult process of writing this book, I am filled with gratitude. Writing often feels solitary, but it never is. One writes in dialogue with others and with the support of family, friends, colleagues, and comrades. My interest in and understanding of labor can be traced back to my grandparents: my maternal grandmother worked long days in a farm kitchen, feeding and caring for family members and field hands; my maternal grandfather picked, sorted, and sold vegetables, and did everything else to keep a small family farm running; my paternal grandfather, an immigrant from Russia, sold stoves, choir gowns, and hunting camouflage to earn a living; my paternal grandmother worked stints as an executive secretary and a cosmetics and silverware salesperson, and labored as a mother and homemaker. From them all, I inherited a sense that labor makes and remakes the world, and remakes the people who work, too. Thank you to all the Bunces and Entins for their love and their labors.

I wrote *Living Labor* over the course of several years, during which I also collaborated with friends and colleagues on a range of other projects—coedited collections, special journal issues, union and other social justice struggles, coteaching experiments, and student programs. Those acts of collective labor sustained me, even as they took me away from work on this book, and reminded me how fortunate I am to have such stellar people in my orbit. For vital lessons in collective editing and writing, I am grateful to Liz Duclos-Orsello, Rebecca Hill, Jesse Schwartz, Belinda Wallace, Jocelyn Wills, Irvin Hunt, Kinohi Nishikawa, and Clare Callahan. In recent years, several editors, including Ichiro Takayoshi, Kevin McNamara, Christie Launius, Leslie Bow, and Russ Castronovo, have supported my work, providing valuable feedback on my prose and ideas. I am grateful to all of them for their willingness to publish writing about the nexus of literature, class, and labor, which continues to be a neglected scholarly subject. Thanks to Immanuel Ness and Polina Kroik for publishing the first kernel of this book years ago. I am forever thankful for my editorial adventure with Sara Blair and Franny Nudelman, whom I cherish as both friends and mentors; their kindness continues to buoy me.

Many people have expanded and refined my thinking about the intersection of labor and culture, including Nicholas Coles and Paul Lauter, who generously edited an earlier version of chapter 2 and who have contributed so much to the study of working-class literatures; so many others, including but not only Larry Hanley, Janet Zandy, Sherrie Linkon, Michael Denning, Sujatha Fernandez, Sara Appel, Clare Callahan, Sonali Perera, Laura Hapke, Paula Rabinowitz, Bill Mullen, Amy Schrager Lang, Tillie Olsen, and Benjamin Balthaser have directly or indirectly inspired and improved my work. I am especially grateful to Sara Appel, Paula Rabinowitz, Benjamin Balthaser, and Sherrie Linkon for critical readings of versions of the manuscript of this book; their feedback improved it immeasurably. All faults are mine alone.

For funding that provided critical time for reflection, research, and writing, I am grateful to the PSC-CUNY faculty research program, which supported several summers of intellectual labor; the CUNY Graduate Center's Center for the Humanities, through which I participated in a terrific year-long seminar under the direction of Gunja SenGupta and Jessie Daniels, funded by the Andrew W. Mellon Foundation; the CUNY Graduate Center's Committee on Globalization and Social Change, where I spent a generative and genial year in the company of Gary Wilder and several dynamite faculty and student fellows; the Brooklyn College Wolfe Institute of Humanities and its then-director Robert Viscusi for a year-long fellowship during which a substantial portion of this book was drafted; the Brooklyn College Tow Research and Creativity Grant, which provided funds to support this book's completion. An earlier version of chapter 1 appeared in *Working USA*, 15.1 (2012). A condensed version of chapter 2 appeared in *A History of American Working-Class Literature*. Some of the thinking and material included in the introduction first appeared in a chapter I contributed to *The Routledge International Handbook of Working-Class Studies*. My deep thanks go to Sally Stein, Ina Steiner, and the Allan Sekula Studio for permission to include Allan Sekula's photograph, "Shipwreck and worker, Istanbul," on the cover of this book. Sekula's art and criticism have long shaped and inspired my thinking, and I am thrilled to be able to reproduce this image.

I am grateful to have this book published by the University of Michigan Press in the Class: Culture series, which is the only academic book series I know dedicated expressly to scholarship about the crossroads of literature, class, and labor. Thanks to the series editors, Amy Schrager Lang, Bill Mullen, and Kasturi Ray, for backing this book and to LeAnn Fields for early encouragement. Sara Cohen has been a terrific editor—attentive, conscientious, patient, and knowledgeable. I am grateful to her and to Mary Hashman and everyone on the production side at the press who helped bring this book into being.

Teaching at Brooklyn College has been the great thrill of my professional life, and I dedicate this book in part to my students, whose smarts and whose labors both inside and outside the classroom have long inspired me. For care, counsel, and solidarity, I also want to thank a host of Brooklyn College colleagues: faculty and staff in the English department, especially the trio I started alongside in 2003, James Davis, Geoffrey Minter, and Martha Nadell, and our longtime chair Ellen Tremper; and faculty, staff, and students who have been involved in several collective labors that have helped sustain me over the years, including the Brooklyn College Listening Project, the Brooklyn College American Studies Program, the BC documentary group, the BC Anti-Racist Coalition, the BC Native and Indigenous Studies working group, the BC COVID Archive, and the Mellon Transfer Student Research Program. A special shout out to Alan Aja and Jeanne Theoharis for their comradeship and shared vision of what CUNY and the world can be, and to everyone on the Executive Committee of the Brooklyn College chapter of the Professional Staff Congress, which has been the center of so much good and necessary struggle and so much smart and creative thinking about labor. When I arrived at CUNY, I joined a New York City-area writing group that has stood the test of time. I am indebted to its members, Sarah Chinn, Louise Heller, Meg Toth, Jeff Allred, Anna Mae Duane, Sophie Bell, and Jennifer Travis, who have read and supported my work for so long. A particular nod to Sarah, whose steady encouragement and upbeat response to my writing has been a boon for years.

I am indebted to longtime colleagues and friends beyond Brooklyn College, including Kandice Chuh, Jesse Schwartz, Rebecca Schreiber, Alyosha Goldstein, Cynthia Young, Scott Saul, Kathy Newman, Brendan Walsh, Rachel Sulkes, Gaspar González, and the late Richard Ohmann, whose encouragement and intellectual inspiration has propelled me for decades. Thanks to everyone on the *Radical Teacher* editorial board for over two decades of intellectual and political collaboration and comradeship (served up with a healthy dose of perverse humor). Gayle Kirschenbaum, Ira Yankwitt, Gabriel Brownstein, the late Marcia Lerner, Julie Kreinik, Hannah Weyer, Leslie Holt, and Amy Smoucha have provided wondrous forms of kindness and friendship. Eleanor Traubman, Anthony Tassi, Susan Hefner, and Eddie Rosenthal also provided crucial support. Jim McKay has been a good friend and vital interlocutor, sharing insights and the example of his own art. Elis and Josh Kanner make so much so fun, and I am grateful for their friendship and irreverent humor. Will Holshouser and Kathy Belden have listened to me talk for years about my ideas for this book; their personal and intellectual companionship form a key part of my foundation.

I simply could not have completed this book without Audrey Entin, David Entin, and Dorothy Riehm, whose unstinting love and support has made everything else possible. Claudia and Walter Gwardyak, and Dan Ouk, Sam Ouk, and Jill Gustaferri, have likewise offered uninterrupted encouragement and kindness. Living alongside Cathleen Bell and Rick Kahn, and Max and Eliza, has been the greatest adventure; their camaraderie and humor have helped keep me going. My sister, Lena Entin, is quite simply my model for being in—and transforming—the world; she has come to my rescue countless times. Steve O'Neill, Autumn Entin-O'Neill, and Julissa Cañas Reyes have supplied crucial moments of silliness and solidarity. In a life of collaboration, Sophie Bell remains my number one coconspirator, first and last and everywhere in between. Living and working with her makes my world go 'round. Miriam and Rachel Entin-Bell grew up while I was writing this book, and I cannot imagine two more amazing young people. They have supported, humored, inspired, and distracted me in perfect measure. This book is dedicated to them, alongside my students, and to the labors, struggles, and joys to come.

Introduction

Narratives of Living Labor

For much of the twentieth century, and into the twenty-first, the iconic figure of the U.S. working class was a white, male, often hard hat-wearing, lunchbox-toting, blue-collar laborer, personified in popular culture by such characters as Ralph Kramden, Archie Bunker, Homer Simpson, and Joe the Plumber. This image emerged during the long Fordist era, as union membership rates peaked and substantial segments of the U.S. working class, especially white men laboring in industrial manufacturing and eligible for state programs such as the GI Bill and FHA-backed mortgages, achieved a measure of financial stability, even prosperity, that allowed them to purchase houses, send their children to college, and accumulate savings. For these workers, labor was often steady and well-compensated, as the mid-century compact between corporations, the state, and major unions delivered wages that rose consistently with increases in productivity from the 1940s through the early 1970s. At the same time, the prevailing political tendencies of this class shifted, from insurgent CIO proletarians and New Deal supporters who helped facilitate what historian Michael Denning calls "the laboring of American culture," through the post–civil rights, Vietnam-era embrace of Nixonian "law and order" policies, to support for Ronald Reagan's muscular Cold War Americanism.[1] This image of the American working class continues to hold cultural sway, as seen in the media depiction of Donald Trump's election to the U.S. presidency in 2016. In an emblematic headline, the *New York Times* proclaimed, "Why Trump Won: Working-Class Whites."[2] Such coverage frequently raised awareness of workers' struggles and frustrations, but it also reinforced a portrait of the working class as an essentially white male, reactionary formation.

This depiction of the U.S. working class has always obscured at least as much as it illuminated, from the multiracial and multigendered composition of the industrial labor force, to the fact that even during the vaunted heyday of U.S. manufacturing, large segments of the working class labored in nonindustrial jobs, especially in the service and agricultural sectors, as well as in the home and elsewhere outside the traditional wage economy. The landscape of work and workers was always vaster and more variegated than suggested by the association of the U.S. working class with a white guy laboring in a steel or auto plant. More incisively, the dominance of this image reflects the fact that the white working class achieved coherence in part through racial and gendered hierarchies that actively disadvantaged and frequently excluded women, immigrants, and workers of color, who were largely denied access to the stable, well-paying, blue-collar jobs available to many white men during the long Fordist era.[3]

The persistence of this portrait of the working class also tends to conceal the seismic economic, social, and political transformations that, since the 1970s, have altered the shape of global capital, the composition of the labor force, and the labor that many working people perform. Indeed, as Fordism unraveled over the final quarter of the twentieth century in the context of deindustrialization, globalization, and neoliberalism, so did the economic and social basis of the U.S. industrial working class. As these changes took hold, new images of work and workers started to materialize, in both social movements and cultural media, addressed to new conditions of ever more precarious labor and the expanding diversity of the U.S. labor force. The many recent campaigns and uprisings that have helped bring attention to the changing contours of labor and the working class include the nationwide 1997 UPS strike, which underscored the plight of delivery workers being treated by their employers as "independent contractors"; the 1999 protests at the World Trade Organization meeting in Seattle, which saw the convergence of unionists and environmentalists ("teamsters and turtles") alongside anarchists, Indigenous rights activists, and others challenging global elites; the successful campaign of the Coalition of Immokalee Workers (founded in 1993), which exposed the neoslave conditions of migrant farm workers employed by corporate agribusiness; actions by the National Taxi Workers Alliance, including a work stoppage in 2017 to protest President Trump's order to restrict entry to the United States for people from several predominantly Muslim countries and a 2021 hunger strike in New York City against taxi driver debt; the constellation of campaigns coordinated by United Students against Sweatshops (founded in 1998), which brought attention to sweatshop conditions in the multibillion-dollar college apparel industry; the 2006 Immigrant Freedom Rides, which drew support from key labor unions and raised the visibility of immigrant workers in the United States; Occupy Wall Street, which underscored the extreme economic inequalities between the 1 percent and the working majority; the OUR Walmart and "Fight for $15" campaigns, which organized hundreds of walkouts and protests to shine a spotlight on the plight of retail, fast-food, and other low-wage workers; the Black Lives Matter movement, which has brought heightened international attention to the state-sanctioned disposability of Black workers (and those, like Eric Garner, who was executed by police while selling single cigarettes, struggling to earn a living outside the formal economy) under U.S. and global racial capitalism; the June 2020 "Strike for Black Lives," in which tens of thousands of workers walked out to highlight the links between income inequality and structural racism; the unionization drives at an Amazon warehouse in Staten Island and at Starbucks coffee shops across the United States in 2022, which showcased the presence and collective power of distribution and service workers at two of world's largest corporations. All of these campaigns, many of which took place outside union contract negotiations and which addressed non-labor-specific issues such as immigration, race, citizenship, and gender, as well as the intensification of economic precarity, gave prominence to workers outside industrial manufacturing (and at times outside the wage economy) under emergent conditions of post-Fordist globalization.[4]

Writing in the context of these uprisings, several sociologists, historians, and cultural theorists have argued that the old industrial working class is being replaced by a new working-class subject—the multitude, or the precariat—that is taking up the mantle of capital's antagonist from the twentieth-century proletariat.[5] Foregrounding the neoliberal transformation of the U.S. and global economies, and the expansion of the world wage labor market, these narratives depict the postindustrial, primarily service-sector-based class of increasingly precarious "gig" and other low-wage workers—from Uber drivers to home health care aides to fast-food and garment workers—as a multiracial "sleeping giant" that is "awakening" to spark a "global uprising."[6] Recently, the Covid-19 pandemic directed attention to another, postindustrial vision of the working class as "essential workers," composed in large part of immigrant, BIPOC, and women workers laboring across a wide array of fields, from health care and goods delivery to retail and meatpacking.[7]

Living Labor examines the literary and cinematic stories that are emerging to narrate the tumultuous remaking of the U.S. and world working classes in the global present. More specifically, this book directs attention to a largely unrecognized set of narratives about work and workers that has proliferated in post-1980 U.S. fiction and film. These narratives are conflicted and contradictory stories about the challenges and potentialities of working-class life, labor, and collectivity in an age of increasing precarity that undercut twentieth-century assumptions about the U.S. working class as a largely white male industrial labor force with a relatively stable sense of its class identity and values. Stories of perilous life and labor, these tales are organized around motifs of displacement and division in which class consciousness and belonging appear as delicate, often distant prospects, and in which solidarity appears as a tentative, precarious form— a fragile, often speculative process of translation, at times palpable primarily through the contours of its absence.

As an example of such emerging stories, consider the 2017 Oscar-nominated film *The Florida Project*, directed by Sean Baker. A small-budget film starring several nonprofessional actors alongside Hollywood veteran Willem Dafoe, *The Florida Project* centers on a diverse community of working people residing month-to-month and struggling to stay afloat financially in a Florida motel complex a short distance from Disney World. Dafoe's character, Bobby, the motel superintendent, is a grizzled white man, but rather than being resentful and bigoted, he expresses a complex, at times ambivalent but nonetheless palpable sense of camaraderie for the motel residents. The residents themselves constitute a precariously positioned, multiracial, largely female working class that labors, when it can find work, in the service industry or outside the formal economy. The film's protagonist is six-year-old Moonee (Brooklynn Prince), whose wanderings through the capitalist waste-wonderland in the shadow of the Magic Kingdom recall 1930s-era proletarian bildungsromans such as Tillie Olsen's *Yonnondio*, which recounts the meanderings of young Mazie Holbrook through the junkyards of a midwestern city while her mother labors to hold their family together. In an increasingly desperate bid to support Moonee, her mother, Halley (Bria Vinaite), sells perfume to tourists in hotel parking lots and, when that fails, turns to sex work; Halley's best friend, Ashley (Mela Murder), waits tables at a local diner, routinely sneaking food out for her son and her friends.

The Florida Project is a story of working people in continual transition: the motel where the film's primary characters reside is a site of temporary, fleeting stability, a home that is not quite a home; each month, management forces the families to leave their rooms for twenty-four hours to ensure they do not qualify as legal residents. The film offers a volatile tale of precarity and flux that underscores the fluidity of friendships among a mobile and economically distressed group (the film turns on a wrenching split between Halley and Ashley, who suffer a violent falling out, as Halley's efforts to earn a living grow more fraught). In one scene, the film's small gang of children set fire to an abandoned condominium complex; the flames and smoke, which pour into the sky, seem to symbolize the imminent danger that looms over the characters, who live in a harsh, hazardous world beneath the consumer and leisure fantasies manifested by Disney World, without any economic surplus or safety net except for the tenuous relations of mutual support they forge with one another. Despite the dreadful conditions, which seem to demand collective action, there is no revolutionary uprising on the horizon, although the film highlights the fragile potentialities of solidarity among the poor and working-class parents—primarily mothers—trying to feed and house their children, and between the residents and Bobby, who is employed to manage them but frequently bends motel rules to protect them. The film concludes on a deeply unresolved note, as Moonee, having just learned that the Florida Department of Children and Families is going to separate her from her mother, bursts through the gates of Disney World with her best friend and the two dash forward toward the iconic castle. The camera shifts to a handheld cell phone, and the picture becomes unsteady, mirroring the uncertainty of the moment and Moonee's future, as the film abruptly ends.

The Florida Project was a surprise hit, but it didn't come out of nowhere. In fact, the film contributes to a long line of literary and cinematic narratives highlighting the heterogeneity and precarity, more than the uniformity and stability, of the U.S. working class. *Living Labor* excavates this narrative tradition, making visible an alternative cultural history of both the American working class and American literature and film. Focusing on fiction and film produced since 1985, including novels by Russell Banks, Helena Viramontes, Karen Tei Yamashita, and Francisco Goldman, and films by David Riker, Ramin Bahrani, Clint Eastwood, Courtney Hunt, and Ryan Coogler, *Living Labor* argues that new narratives and narrative modes are emerging to reimagine work and working-class collectivity in the contemporary era of global economic restructuring, transnational migration, and precarious labor. The narratives in *Living Labor* represent tales of the working class beyond and after the hegemony of white male industrial labor: stories of jagged, uneven, and incomplete class formation, conflicted social encounters, and difficult, often stalled or blocked transit and migration. These are stories about widely varied workers, some hailing from disparate corners of the planet, facing insecure, perilous, low-wage labor, or coerced labor, or the absence of work; stories about the anxious, often agonized, and usually failed possibilities of solidarity; stories that, while underscoring the structural violence that late capitalism visits on the poor, do not offer a compensatory teleology of proletarian unity, coherence, or rebellion, although there are noteworthy moments of furtive and at times open resistance and revolt. Frequently stretching beyond the geopolitical and cultural boundaries of the United

States, these stories remind us that the "U.S. working class" is and has always been transnational in its origins and affiliations, and that the economic and social conditions that shape its existence have always been global, and linked to empire, imperial war, and colonial dispossession.

Living Labor turns its attention to fiction and film because, despite the claims for their demise or obsolescence in an age of social media saturation, those two forms continue to be crucial modes of contemporary storytelling. Novels and films have a particular capacity for what Fredric Jameson calls "cognitive mapping," that is, for connecting individual stories, details, and sites to world-shaping economic and social forces, and for moving across multiple geographic and temporal scales (for more on cognitive mapping, see chapter 1). The power of fiction and film to juxtapose and combine continuities and discontinuities, to allow for intense and deep characterization as well as sweeping stories, makes them potent mediators of contemporary transformation and struggle. To be sure, the image of the contemporary global working class is being remade in other media—in poetry, photography, and other visual arts, for instance—but fiction and film's narrative capacities, which are at once diachronic and synchronic, chronological and spatial, make them prime modes for depicting change over time and for charting intersecting arcs of decline and emergence, and thus for tracing contemporary stories of American and global labor's long restructuring.[8]

Living Labor advances several interlocking claims about novels and films that grapple with contemporary work and workers. First, it contends that these narratives develop as the social and economic bases of the twentieth-century working class dissolve. Not only have the sites of domestic manufacturing where the core Fordist working class labored (in the steel, mining, and automobile industries, for instance) been relocated or displaced by an economy organized more and more around service and immaterial labor, but also the key institutions, from unions to the welfare state, that helped create a class out of common economic conditions, have been weakened, hollowed out, or destroyed. As historian Gabriel Winant puts it, "The working-class majority still exists, of course, but only as an economic category—not a social one."[9] The books and films examined in *Living Labor* indicate that the contemporary working class is in the midst of an extended process of unmaking and tentative and still indeterminate remaking.[10] Economic conditions of exploitation, dispossession, and precarity may be widely shared, but these stories suggest that coming to class consciousness, never mind concerted action, is an attenuated, uncertain prospect, especially in this prolonged period of economic and political transition and turmoil. These narratives imply that the composition, image, and coherence of the contemporary working class cannot be taken for granted, but have become unsettled, harder to predict, and ever more precarious, as has so much work itself.

Second, *Living Labor* argues that the shifting, fractured nature of working-class collectivity in the global present is visible in narratives of *labor-in-motion*: of working people in transit across spatial, geopolitical, and social borders, in which the primary narrative arc is organized less by the linear development of radical consciousness than by uncertain, often volatile, at times explosive confrontations between differentially positioned segments of the world labor force. Although migrant and itinerant workers make up a small percentage of the U.S. and global labor force, they have become vital emblems for imagining the dynamics of neoliberal globalization, contested border crossing, economic and social instability, and mobile, hyperexploitative production. Sociologists William Robinson and Xuan Santos have asserted that in recent decades, "[*i*]*immigrant workers [have] become the archetype of the new global class relations*[,] *the quintessential workforce of global capitalism.*"[11] *Living Labor* contends that if the male, industrial proletarian was the iconic figure of Fordist labor, a new rhetorical figure is emerging to crystallize and condense the dynamics of post-Fordist flexible production: the worker-in-motion. This figure is not limited to immigrants, but rather refers to broader dimensions of geographic and economic transit and itinerancy that register the precarity of life and labor for workers under emergent conditions of late-capitalist globalization. Much as Stuart Hall argues that race is the modality in which class is lived, *Living Labor* contends that in contemporary U.S. fiction and film, motion is the modality in which labor is most often imagined. Key figures from the films and novels examined in *Living Labor* include Haitian refugees who labor in the underground agricultural and sexual economies of the Caribbean on their way to the United States; a roving family of Chicanx farmworkers in California; a Honduran sailor, forced into virtual slave labor on a ship in Brooklyn; Central American day laborers and sweatshop workers in the Bronx and Queens; a Hmong construction worker in Detroit; a Pakistani coffee cart operator in Manhattan; a Chicanx house cleaner in Los Angeles; a young Latinx auto body shop assistant in Queens, and his sister, a food truck server and sex worker; and a restless, unemployed African American man in Oakland killed by police on a train platform. Not all these figures are migrants or immigrants; some are African American and Chicanx workers with deep historic roots in the United States. Yet even these workers are typically depicted through motifs of displacement, motion, and transit that underscore the uncertainty and precarity of life, labor, citizenship, and class formation for working people across geographic regions, racial categories, and economic sectors. Countering claims by critics and commentators that the current global economy is dominated by disembodied, cognitive, and immaterial work, the narratives at the heart of *Living Labor* underscore the diverse, demanding forms of physical and affective labor, both inside and outside the formal wage economy, that undergird high-tech production and everyday life under late capitalism.

Third, through its examination of literary and cinematic form, *Living Labor* contends that contemporary labor narratives reimagine the working class not as a discrete, stable entity, but rather as a tension-filled coming together of heterogeneous populations in which nascent and uneasy lines of class connection are produced through negotiation, conflict, and translation. These stories suggest that there is no a priori, pre-existing working-class identity waiting to be expressed, but rather a multiplication of working peoples and laboring conditions across global capitalism's expanding horizon. These are not narratives in which tightly grounded class alliances are achieved *despite or above* racial, national, linguistic, and ethnic divisions, but tales in which borders become the very channels through which not-yet-fully-realized class affinities are imagined and tested. These narratives imagine possibilities for class formation and solidarity in a period when the abstract figure of the national citizen-worker, which organized both social policy and political resistance in the United States and across the Global North for much of the twentieth century, no longer prevails. The stories examined in *Living Labor* thus indicate that now more than ever class manifests as a matter of relation rather than identity, of crossing spatial and social boundaries. These texts do not offer tales of consolidation or the overcoming of divisions in the construction of economic and social unity; they are not stories of revolutionary convergence, or of collective coming together in which an underlying working-class identity is realized or reflected. Rather, they are conjunctural stories of uncertain, at times explosive, encounter, intersection, and collision in which unity is most often deferred. The emphasis is not only, or even primarily, on what workers have in common, but on the way both divisions and commonalities between working peoples are translated and experienced across borders of language, culture, nation, and citizenship.

Narratives of living labor *are* a form of proletarian literature, but only when the proletariat is understood not conventionally as the industrial wage labor force, but rather, more fundamentally and capaciously, as people subjected to manifold processes of economic and political dispossession, exploitation, and immiseration, including populations rendered, or on the cusp of being rendered, *surplus* to capital's needs, and thus subject to varied, often extreme forms of economic, social, political, and bodily expropriation, incarceration, abandonment, violence, injury, and death.[12] These narratives depict a working class located not only or even primarily in wage labor, but also in unwaged or coerced labor or confronting the absence of labor, that is, persons without property or reserves, as implied by the originary definition of the term proletariat (from the Roman term *proles*, those with no surplus other than their children), and subject to a foundational precariousness.[13]

These narratives of dispossession take the form of what I call precarious realism: a novelistic and cinematic realism about precarious life, and a realism that is itself precarious, interrupted by and interwoven with other modes, including magical realism, surrealism, and neorealism, in an effort to show the often volatile and perilous state of social life for itinerant workers and the refusal of their stories to resolve into stable forms of class consciousness or composition. The idea of precarious realism is admittedly a kind of redundancy, for realism, like almost all literary forms, is itself precarious and unstable.[14] But in this study it refers to a constellation of novels and films that self-consciously deploy aesthetic techniques of realist representation to render the intimate and interpersonal, as well as the structural and material, dynamics and dimensions of economic, social, and epistemological precarity for working and nonworking poor people under emergent conditions of post-Fordist, global production and empire.[15] In the absence of a coherent radical literary movement of the kind that flourished in the 1930s, these novels and films were not crafted as self-conscious proletarian narratives, and they do not predict for their characters "full consciousness of working-class oppression and a readiness to challenge capitalist structures through the use of force if need be," as one scholar argues proletarian literature typically aimed to do.[16] Rather, contemporary narratives of living labor encourage us to see that many earlier and contemporary examples of proletarian literature are in fact organized around matters of precarity, insecurity, motion, and migration, in which issues of class identification, solidarity, and action are much more uncertain, fluid, and incomplete than we often have presumed.[17] In a similar way, the demise of the image of the white male industrial worker as emblem of the working class, in the face of economic and demographic shifts, reminds us that that figure was never adequate to represent the full range of working-class lives and labors under Fordism—both nonwhite and female industrial workers as well as service, agricultural, and domestic workers, unwaged workers and those in the informal economy—whose experiences fell outside industrial production. In other words, Fordism's ongoing undoing reminds us that Fordism itself was in crucial ways an insufficient hermeneutic, and that, in the long history of capitalism, Fordism, and the relative stability and security it provided though the family wage to many mostly white male workers, was an exception rather than the rule. For most workers throughout history, capitalism has offered little to nothing *but* precarity.[18]

In its focus on deprivation, hardship, and dispossession, as well as a tentative yet persistent emphasis on the potentialities of solidarity in the context of uncertain and underdeveloped class formation and consciousness, the literary and cinematic line of precarious realism that *Living Labor* excavates represents a critically overlooked challenge both to the neoliberal novel and film, and to narratives of finance and market culture, which tend to obscure labor's centrality to the production of value. Accounts of neoliberal literature frequently posit that neoliberalism, which Pierre Bourdieu described helpfully as a project dedicated to "the destruction of collectives," establishes itself as a universal cultural horizon, coming to appear "natural, universal and true," as "normative common sense."[19] Although compelling, these claims tend to overinflate the ubiquity of neoliberalism's influence and thus obscure the zones of literary culture and production that lie beyond, or that actively complicate or offer alternatives to, neoliberal ideology as a form of class struggle. The narratives in *Living Labor*, which recount the travails of low-wage workers, the under- and unemployed, and persons laboring in unwaged and coerced conditions, and the possibilities (typically speculative or distant) of those workers finding common cause, suggest that however multifaceted, neoliberalism is not a totalizing atmosphere, not the "air we breathe," but a contested, contradictory, and partial, if certainly powerful, formation.[20]

Further, the novels and films of contemporary living labor help us to grasp a good deal of contemporary immigrant and multiethnic literature and cinema as stories about labor and class formation, as well as race and ethnicity. Consider, for instance, Ocean Vuong's acclaimed novel *On Earth We're Briefly Gorgeous* (2019), which is organized not only around issues of immigration, race, queer desire, and imperial war, but also by multiple modes of precarious labor: agricultural labor performed predominantly by undocumented workers, sex work during the war in Vietnam, and unwaged immigrant labor in urban nail salons.[21] Vuong's narrator, Little Dog, meets his lover, an opioid-addicted white boy named Trevor, the summer he works on a tobacco farm alongside migrant workers from Central America and Mexico. He describes the labor as a "work of unbreakable links and collaboration.... A work of myriad communications, [in which] I learned to speak to the men not with my tongue, which was useless there, but with smiles, hand gestures, even silences, hesitations."[22] A narrative that underscores the pain, isolation, and violence experienced by Vietnamese American refugees, *On*

Earth We're Briefly Gorgeous also offers imaginative, if still incomplete and fleeting, visions of collective working-class association forged at linguistic and cultural boundaries. Labor is a site where desire, language, race, and ethnicity converge as varied potentialities of class-based connection are explored and tested, making the book one version of what a twenty-first-century proletarian novel looks like.

Anthropologist Anna Tsing has asserted that we must find new images and narratives of work and working people in order to narrate global capitalism's disruptive restructuring. "It is clear," she writes, "that other figurations of labor are needed to tell effective stories about contemporary capitalism."[23] Narratives of living labor provide these "other figurations." They focus on what Tsing describes as "politically ambiguous, liminal figures, caught within the contradictions between varied forms of hierarchy and exclusion"; they suggest that class is something that must always be worked through, actively created, and is never discrete, complete, or closed.[24] Narratives of living labor constitute a previously unrecognized mode of writing and filmmaking that invites us to reimagine what class is, how capitalism operates, and how it might be resisted. Challenging both popular theories of globalization as a process that makes the world "flat," and conceptions of hemispheric literature and culture that, in their emphasis on cultural fluidity, inadequately attend to asymmetries of political and economic force, these are stories of cross-cultural conflict and connection, in which economic inequality, exploitation, and alliance play out across national, racial, and ethnic lines. In these narratives, motion and migration serve as means of and metaphors for class formation as a process of collective identification that is never finished or final. The narratives at the heart of this study suggest *not* that a new universal subject—the multitude, the subaltern, or the precariat—is emerging to unite laboring people in the age of globalization, but rather that working-class belonging is a matter of continual encounter, translation, motion, and struggle.

Post-Fordist Transitions

Narratives of contemporary living labor respond to profound economic and political transformations that have reshaped labor and class relations in the United States and across the planet in several crucial, if uneven, incomplete, and ongoing, ways.[25] First, as capital became ever more transnational and mobile under post-1970s globalization, able to move resources and reorganize production across national borders with unprecedented speed and scale, corporations in the United States and across the Global North began to relocate manufacturing and heavy industrial jobs to regions—many in the Global South—with lower labor costs and fewer regulations. In the United States, this relocation undercut the industrial base of the working class, especially in the traditional "rust belt," as unionized, relatively high-wage manufacturing jobs in auto and steel were moved overseas, and as service-sector jobs in retail, health care, education, and other care work sectors grew.[26] Jobs in the U.S. auto industry were cut almost in half between 1978 and 1982, while up to 70 percent of all jobs generated between 1973 and 1980 were in service and retail, according to one estimate.[27] Service workers rose from 44 percent of the U.S. nonfarm labor force in 1960 to almost 68 percent in 2009.[28] If manufacturing constituted the heart of the mid-twentieth-century U.S. Fordist economy, the focus shifted between 1980 and 2005, as the service sector swelled and as profits in the finance, insurance, and real estate sectors grew an astounding 800 percent.[29]

As capital has reorganized and relocated production, it has undercut the labor stability and economic security that was accessible under Fordism to many mass-production workers, especially white men. Global forms of lean production and "flexploitation" have generated what Andrew Ross describes as "a new landscape of irregular work" across job categories, from seasonal, temporary, and day labor, to part-time retail and service work, to skilled flex- and freelance work in the "creative" and high-tech sectors.[30] Sandro Mezzadra and Brett Neilson argue that post-Fordist globalization has generated what they call *the multiplication of labor* through which the forms and terms of work and labor capture are both diversified and intensified.[31] Across the industrial Global North, this has led to a proliferation of economic and social uncertainty. Historian Joshua Freeman notes, "For working-class Americans, the shift away from manufacturing often meant a move from secure, high-paid, unionized jobs to insecure, nonunion jobs that sometimes paid little more than the minimum wage and lacked benefits or opportunities for promotion."[32] Under these conditions, in which "labor positions are being multiplied from the point of view of tasks and skills," as well as "legal statuses and conditions," Mezzadra and Neilson insist, there is a "widening of the concept of the working class" as the stable wage relation loses its status as an economic norm.[33] Precarity is not only a labor condition, however; it also represents what Ross calls a "new experiential norm," a structure of feeling suffusing what Lauren Berlant terms the contemporary "situation," as insecurity and contingency become more pervasive across social strata.[34] Yet the economic, civic, and subjective conditions of precarity have had disproportionate affects on the most vulnerable workers, whose livelihoods and life chances are diminished as steady labor declines and the population of persons rendered superfluous to economic production grows.[35]

The upheavals wrought by late capitalist globalization have also put millions of people on the move, expanding and diversifying the working population, both in the United States, where post-1965 immigration has brought new immigrants from Latin American, the Caribbean, and Asia into the country, and around the world, where the planet's wage labor force has more than doubled in size and transnational migrations have surged.[36] These conditions have created what Saskia Sassen, Immanuel Ness, David Harvey, and others describe as a new "transnational working class" that lives increasingly, in Harvey's words, "under conditions of poverty, violence, chronic environmental degradation, and fierce repression."[37] "The global proletariat is now far larger than ever," Harvey asserts. "It is also geographically dispersed, culturally heterogeneous and therefore harder to organize into a united labor movement. Yet it is also living under far more exploitative conditions in aggregate than was the case twenty years ago."[38] Workers in the United States are part of this increasingly heterogenous, planetary proletariat. While Europeans constituted more than two-thirds of immigrants to the United States as recently as 1960, immigrants from Europe shrunk to only one-ninth of newcomers by 2000.[39] That year, the United States had the highest proportion of foreign-born residents in the country since the 1920s.[40] More broadly, the U.S. working population has diversified along lines of race, gender, and ethnicity. "Between 1976 and 1988," historian Robin D. G. Kelley notes, "while the nation's overall labor force grew by 26 percent, the percentage of black workers rose by 38 percent, Asian American workers by 103 percent, and Latinos by 110 percent."[41] Women's participation in the U.S. workforce rose from 34 percent in 1954 to 60 percent in 2000, as their share of the total workforce rose from 30 to 47 percent.[42] Noted labor commentator Kim Moody argues that the story of U.S. labor in recent decades is not only the rise of a "gig" economy and precarious work, but also the decline in living standards and changing demographics. He notes that in low-wage production, transportation, and material-moving occupations, as well as in service occupations, workers of color increased from 15 percent of the labor force in 1981 to 40 percent by 2010.[43]

As labor precarity has spread and the working population in the United States has become more diverse, there has also been a divestment in the reproduction of the labor force and an intensification of exploitation. On a planetary scale, the leap in capital accumulation and the expansion of the global wage working population has gone hand-in-hand with, in Silvia Federici's words, "the return of unfree labor, and the increasing criminalization of the working class, through mass incarceration . . . and the formation of an *ex-lege* proletariat made up of undocumented immigrants, under-the-counter workers, producers of illicit goods, sex workers."[44] The conditions of relatively privileged workers across the Global North have also suffered, as neoliberal policies have in many instances hollowed out government-funded welfare, education, housing, and other public goods and services. In the United States, union membership has declined precipitously since its high of over 30 percent in the mid-1950s, to below 10 percent today, and even lower in the private sector. Since 1983, Harold Meyerson notes, "the number of states in which at least 10 percent of private-sector workers have union contracts has shrunk from 42 to 8."[45] Not surprisingly, wages for working people have stagnated or declined since the early 1970s; by the early twenty-first century, roughly one-quarter of U.S. full-time workers held low-wage jobs, the highest percentage of low-wage workers among industrialized countries.[46]

These dynamics have been compounded by, and have in turn intensified, structural inequalities in race and citizenship status. African American unemployment rates have historically been much higher than rates for whites, and Black wages lower.[47] White families average roughly eight times the wealth of Black families and five times the wealth of Latinx families.[48] The post-1965 growth of immigrant labor has coincided with the widespread employment of undocumented workers, who are especially vulnerable to exploitation.[49] The kinds of jobs most accessible to these workers in the service, agricultural, and manufacturing sectors are frequently contingent, informal, and without union protections, intensifying the insecurity these workers already have due to their lack of secure citizenship status.[50] Further, since the 1980s, a concerted expansion of prison construction and mass incarceration has excluded millions of workers—disproportionately Black and Brown—from labor market participation, except at times, as forced prison labor, producing a massive, largely racialized, disposable population.[51] As it has throughout the history of U.S. capitalism, the brutally lopsided state and corporate violence directed at BIPOC workers has served to enforce divisions among working people, to keep substantial segments of the working population under coercive control, and to maintain a steady reserve army of labor.[52]

In sum, since the 1970s, the global and U.S. economies have been reshaped in ways that dismantled the relatively homogeneous, industrial working class that was at the heart of U.S. labor power under Fordism. In its place, a new, increasingly transnational working class is emerging, organized more and more around the contingency, rather than stability, of its labor, and marked by new levels of social and cultural heterogeneity and lower standards of living. The post–World War II era of the citizen-worker that dominated production in the Global North is ending, as more and more workers become more economically, socially, politically vulnerable.[53] As a result, the icon of America's midcentury labor imaginary—a male, unionized, blue-collar worker supporting a family on a single wage—is now almost extinct. At the dawn of the twenty-first century, Freeman notes, "sales clerks, hospital aides, and school teachers were more representative of the working class than the steel workers, coal miners, auto workers, and railroad men who dominated images and notions of twentieth-century labor."[54] *Living Labor* argues that the impact of these roiling transformations, and the unmaking of the twentieth-century industrial working class and unfinished remaking of a new working class, have been rendered with compelling insight in a line of labor literature and cinema that surveys the striated and uneven landscapes of capitalist exploitation, struggle, and resistance in, across, and beyond the United States.

Living Labor

As this book's title suggests, I approach contemporary narratives of precarious work and struggle through the concept of living labor, a term drawn primarily from the work of Karl Marx, where it has multiple valences.[55] At one level, living labor stands opposed to what Marx called the "dead" labor objectified in machines and in capital itself. "Capital," Marx writes, "is dead labor, that, vampire-like, only lives by sucking living labor, and lives the more labor it sucks."[56] Here, drawing on nineteenth-century tropes of gothic horror, Marx invokes living and dead labor to underscore capital's monstrosity, which feeds on the vitality that labor provides. Labor itself embodies the combination of creativity and energy that transforms the world, and without which capital could not exist or survive. If capital and its machines are "dead," they are animated by labor's "life"-generating productive power, which "acts as a fructifying vitality upon [capital's] merely existent and hence dead objectivity."[57] "Labor," Marx asserts in the *Grundrisse*, "is the living, form-giving fire; it is the transitoriness of things, their temporality, as their formation by living time."[58] For Marx, labor is much more than the source of capital's valorization and, through surplus value, of profit; it is the living, ever-fluid, flexible basis for social and world transformation.[59] Capital is monstrously powerful, yet also dead, animated only through labor's life-giving vigor.

Living labor is also composed and managed by capital in part through another form of "dead labor": the threat and production of premature death to which all workers, but especially Black and other racialized workers, are subject under capitalism. In his 1845 study of workers in Manchester, England, Friedrich Engels argued that capitalist society proceeds by "social murder": "it undermines the vital force of these workers gradually, little by little, and so hurries them to the grave before their time."[60] Under capitalism, this social murder is racialized. Ruth Wilson Gilmore defines racism as "the state-sanctioned and/or extra-legal production and exploitation of group-differentiated vulnerability to premature death," and this particular vulnerability is a crucial aspect of capitalist domination.[61] Capital requires and feeds off living labor, but in an effort to divide, shape, and manage living labor, it also produces dead labor; that is, it renders almost all working-class people, but especially workers racialized as Black (and, quite often, Latinx, Asian, and Indigenous), structurally vulnerable to premature death. As Manning Marable contends in his landmark study of U.S. capitalism's racial violence, "Each oppressed person under capitalism must come to the realization that [their] death is a *requirement* for the continued life of the system."[62] Capital disciplines and controls living labor through the threat of premature death to all workers, but especially through the disproportionate threat of arbitrary death to racialized populations. Drawing on Achille Mbembe's definition of necropolitics as "the subjugation of life to the power of death," we can see that capitalism is racial capitalism and also necrocapitalism: a mode of accumulation that exploits living labor by making expendable populations deemed unproductive or redundant.[63] Necrocapitalism refers to the fact that, as James Tyner explains, "profits are increasingly realized though the material death of laborers," and that exposure to death is conditioned by one's position in a racially-structured regime of accumulation.[64]

Living labor is poised not only against dead labor, but also as a counterpart to capital's norm of abstract labor. Abstract labor is capital's measure of general productivity to which all labor can be reduced, independent of specific working persons and their individual capacities. It represents capital's effort to lend homogeneity to the diversity of actual laboring bodies performing concrete tasks, to produce what Marx describes as "a continuity, a uniformity, a regularity, an order . . . of labor."[65] Through its modes of subsumption and labor capture, capital aims to objectify labor as "labor power," to reduce workers' particularities to an abstract and generalizable standard. Abstract labor is thus labor made uniform and productive for capital, capable of being managed and channeled in any direction required during the production process. By contrast, "living labor" is labor "not as an object, but as activity . . . as the *living source* of value"; it is labor as performed and shaped by the bodies, personalities, and energies of individual workers or what, in the *Grundrisse*, Marx calls "labor as subjectivity."[66] This resonant phrase suggests both that labor molds one's sense of self and that workers bring to their labors not only their labor power, but also their specific histories, capacities, limitations, and desires. Capital may have an interest in reducing workers to abstract quantities of pure laboring force, which the capitalist class can direct as it chooses, but in fact workers are always complex and embodied subjects that can never be fully contained, controlled, or subsumed during the accumulation process.

Living labor thus provides a frame to think about class beyond the conventional parameters of class, about the ways economic relations and structures shape, and are in turn shaped by, experiences, vectors of identification, histories, and cultures outside the workplace, beyond the realm of production. Historian Dipesh Chakrabarty argues that the tension between living and abstract labor, between capital's drive to reduce all labor to a quantifiable unit and the individual particularities of the human beings who perform that labor, is one key site where social and cultural differences intersect, and have the capacity to disrupt, capitalism. "Difference," Chakrabarty concludes, "is not something external to capital. Nor is it something subsumed into capital. It lives in intimate and plural relationships to capital."[67] Abstract labor is the norm to which capital attempts to subdue all labor in order to maximize the extraction of surplus value, but there is always a gap that separates abstract and living labor. Capital possesses varied modes of labor subsumption, or capture, many of them far from the normative "free" wage labor relation, which confront the radical multiplicity of living labor. The resulting encounters between labor and capital are by no means uniform, discrete, or predictable.[68]

Chakrabarty's emphasis on the heterogeneity of relationships to capital may underestimate the extent to which capital itself thrives on "differences," exploiting them to expand its markets and divide working people from one another. As Lisa Lowe notes, "in the history of the United States, capital has maximized its profits not through rendering labor 'abstract' but precisely through the social productions of 'difference,' of restrictive particularity and illegitimacy marked by race, nation, geographical origins, and gender."[69] Working-class composition, then, does not occur beyond or above the stubborn particularities of social life and cultural difference. Rather, contradictions, divisions, and inequalities are structured within the working class in the very process of its constitution. Far from rendering the world uniform, capital embraces and exploits already existing social barriers, differences, and divisions, producing "an increasingly heterogenous workforce."[70] David Harvey argues that "[t]he beginning point of class struggle lies with the particularity of the laboring body... the billions [of workers] whose daily existence is shaped through an often traumatic and conflictual relation to the dynamics of capital accumulation."[71] It is the particularities of living labor—of labor as subjectivity—that contemporary fiction and film is so adept at rendering. Literature and film about work and workers, especially what I am calling the literature and film of living labor, is often less interested in depicting the activities and routines of labor itself than in limning what Chakrabarty describes as the "intimate and plural relationships" workers have to capital and to each other.

The focus on living labor, on the everyday life struggles and capacities integral to the production of value under capitalism, also directs us to the processes and politics of social reproduction, which are at the heart of the literary and cinematic tradition this book traces. In *Capital*, Marx insists that the continuation of capitalist production requires incessant *re*production, the perpetuation of workers as workers as well as the terms and conditions of capitalist labor exploitation. As he puts it, "every social process of production is at the same time a process of reproduction."[72] Significantly, social reproduction points us beyond the workplace to the realms of social life through which workers sustain themselves and attend to their own needs. Historically, much of the labor required in these areas—child rearing, educating, and caretaking—has been the province of women. And while much of this labor has traditionally been unwaged, it is in fact crucial to capital accumulation, and therefore a site of capitalist control and resistance, as a long line of Marxist- and socialist-feminist writers have contended.[73]

A focus on reproduction helps us understand the ways in which the literature and film of living labor opens its horizon far beyond the workplace, to conceive manifold conflicts over the reproduction of everyday life—over food, health, housing, and incarceration—*as* class struggles. In the fiction and film of living labor, these struggles over social, personal, and collective reproduction take center stage. In these narratives, living labor refers on the one hand to the experiences of laboring people *beyond* labor—the story of their lives, their *living*. These stories focus not only, or even primarily, on depictions of the work performed, but on the scope and texture of personal, interpersonal, and communal life in, outside, and beyond work. This is in large part what is implied in Marx's notion of "labor as subjectivity": the networks, social and political structures, histories, and communities in which people are embedded that shape how they approach their work as well as their identities and attitudes as workers. At the same time, living labor suggests that living itself *is* labor. Living does not just happen; life needs to be produced, maintained, sustained. These narratives focus on social and personal reproduction, often close to the bone: on staying afloat, on getting housed and fed, on finding safe haven, on keeping the body going under conditions of intense economic, social, and personal vulnerability and duress. These are frequently tales of desperation that underscore the ways in which maintenance of self, family, and community is arduous, intentional, difficult work, carried out within, against, and outside the rule of capital.

Living labor and social reproduction, then, allow an expansive, integrative, relational view of capitalism, class struggle, and working-class formation as, in Marx's words, "a total, connected process."[74] Class is not simply a matter of labor, but also of race, gender, ethnicity; it is not only determined at the conventional workplace—on the shop floor or in the fields—but also in the home, the school, the street; it is not only a question of waged labor, but also of the unwaged labor and all the work entailed in the full and complex reproduction of social life.[75] Capitalism and the reproduction of class power have always been structured by "the unequal valuing of lives" according to race, sex, gender, and other axes of social division.[76] Thinking along these lines allows us to see the false opposition between so-called "identity politics" and class politics; in fact, contemporary struggles around "identity" issues—immigration policies, police killings and mass incarceration, gender- and sexuality-based violence, urban redevelopment and gentrification, the Dakota Access Pipeline, and other environmental injustices and matters of Indigenous sovereignty—can be understood as elements of a larger challenge to the capitalist organization of social, political, and economic life, even as we must realize that the elimination of capitalism will not in and of itself end racist heteropatriarchy. Narratives of living labor foreground the heterogeneity of proletarian populations (including unemployed and unwaged workers), and crucial questions of social, cultural, national, and linguistic division that shape possibilities for working-class formation and belonging.[77]

My analysis builds on work by a range of literary scholars who have productively complicated deterministic, static, organic conceptions of what class is and how it is represented.[78] As Cora Kaplan explained in the introduction to a landmark issue of *PMLA* on the topic, "We tend now to think of class consciousness past and present more polymorphously and perversely: its desires, its object choices, and its antagonisms are neither so straightforward nor so singular as they once seemed."[79] In a similar vein, Sonali Perera has asked how working-class literature from across several national traditions imagines collective identification in an era when globalization is generating not labor unity, but an exacerbation of social, cultural, and geopolitical divisions. Exploding the idea that the working class can be constituted by "alibis of origins and identity," Perera argues productively for class as a "unity-in-dispersal" and defines working-class literature not as a self-evident, stable tradition, but as a serially interrupted form that can "only be understood in terms of its interrelationships and dialogic tensions."[80]

The working class has always been global and heterogeneous, riven with what Perera calls "dialogic tensions." Since its inception, the U.S. working class has been composed of workers from across Europe, Asia, Central and Latin America, and Africa. Even when workers share a common relationship to capital or occupy similar positions in the system of production, their sense of themselves and their place in the economic and social world is shaped by diverse histories, allegiances, and identifications. Discussing the history of the British working class, Richard Hyman observes that class-based forms of consciousness do not emerge organically, but are always produced in dialogue with other, competing forms of knowledge, thought, and belonging:

> The crucial strategic problem confronting labor movements was how to mobilize maximum solidarity from a socially defined constituency which has no essential unity in the sphere of consciousness, but on the contrary a series of particularistic loyalties and preferences and a widely differing experience in everyday life, a mosaic of individual histories. The analyses of working-class politics begins with this dialectic—the contradictory and dynamic intersection of unifying and fragmenting tendencies within the class as a whole.[81]

This dialectic "between unifying and fragmenting tendencies"—or what Marx often termed the tension between competition and association—remains crucial to understanding the way in which the working class is being reformulated in the present, and it constitutes a central concern in narratives about contemporary workers. Political scientist Adam Przeworski has argued that "the process of class formation is a perpetual one: classes are continually organized, disorganized, and reorganized";[82] we are currently in the midst of an extended period of working-class de- and recomposition, in which the work arrangements, collective power, and demographics of the U.S. and global working classes are being reconfigured.[83] Antonio Negri has speculated that "while capital was in the past capable of reducing the multiplicity of singularities to something close to the organic and unitary—a class, a people, a mass, a set—this process has today failed intimately: it no longer works."[84] In this long contemporary context of an emergent, post-Fordist racial capitalism, how do we think about work and exploitation, working-class lives in and beyond labor, and possibilities for working-class collectivity? This is what the narratives of contemporary living labor explore, offering stories of hardship and struggle across widely varied geographic and social locations, and stressing the uneven landscapes and vexing asymmetries of racial, ethnic, linguistic, and cultural power that shape the terms on which working people encounter capital and one another as well.

The Shape of the Book

Let me conclude this introduction by offering a brief overview of the book's chapters. Chapter 1 analyzes Russell Banks's critically acclaimed 1985 novel *Continental Drift* as a form of post-Fordist proletarian literature that allegorizes the demise of the white industrial working class and the emergence of a new, migrant working class. The novel opens with a panoramic meditation on the lives of global refugees and workers, crisscrossing the earth, asserting "we are the planet." The book then zeroes in on the intersection of two migrants: Bob DuBois, who abandons a dead-end job as an oil heater repairman in New Hampshire to start life over in Florida, and Vanise Dorsinville, a young Haitian woman who suffers numerous abuses as she flees to the United States with her young son and nephew. In following migrating workers in an ultimately fruitless search for well-being and wealth, *Continental Drift* stresses the urgency of class consciousness in a neoliberal world, even as it finally insists that the historic legacies and still ongoing dynamics of slavery, colonialism, and the geographically and culturally uneven dimensions of capitalist development make such consciousness in and of itself insufficient to establish a sense of solidarity among laboring peoples from disparate racial and national contexts. This is a novel about the material and ideological *challenges* to the formation of a transnational working class, and about the prevailing precarity of life, labor, and citizenship for workers on the move. It poses the possibility that the emergence of contemporary globalization opens new lines of alliance between the world's poor, migrating peoples, but finally proves unable to imagine how such alliances might come into being.

Chapter 2 analyzes three novels about migrant workers written in the mid-1990s: *Under the Feet of Jesus* (1995), Helena Viramontes's lyrical novel about a Chicanx farm-working family drifting across California; *The Ordinary Seaman* (1997), Francisco Goldman's novel about Central American sailors trapped in slave-labor conditions on a stalled ship in New York harbor; and *Tropic of Orange* (1997), Karen Tei Yamashita's fantastical novel about Los Angeles as a node of intersecting hemispheric migrations. While these three texts are rightly considered works of ethnic or multicultural fiction, they are also, I argue, labor novels, shaped by the upswing in activism and strikes that marked the early and mid-1990s. All three novels chart what one of Yamashita's characters calls a "map of labor," exploring the economic brutality and colonial legacies that shape the circumstances of transnational migratory workers in the United States, as well as nascent forms of mutuality and working-class interconnectedness that contradict capitalism's exploitative imperatives. In underscoring the convergence of neocolonialism and global capitalism's predatory forms of accumulation by dispossession, these three texts update the 1930s novel of proletarian migration for an age of worldwide migrations and undocumented citizenship. In so doing, they not only suggest that contemporary struggles over class and labor manifest in socially, politically, and aesthetically heterogeneous ways, but they also complicate key suppositions of conventional transnational and hemispheric literary studies, which, in foregrounding fluidity and mobility, often fail to address adequately the structural, material forces shaping transborder life under late capitalism.

Chapter 3 examines three films, *Gran Torino* (dir. Clint Eastwood, 2008), *Frozen River* (dir. Courtney Hunt, 2008), and *Fruitvale Station* (dir. Ryan Coogler, 2013), that offer contrasting perspectives on the plight of working-class people and the instability of working-class identity and collectivity in an emergent post-Fordist era of precarious labor. For *Gran Torino*, which recounts the story of a retired Detroit auto worker's relations with his Hmong immigrant neighbors, the crisis of the industrial working class and the emergence of new workers and new social conditions is a source of anxiety as well as possibility, but the film's effort to imagine new lines of transnational, intergeneration alliance founders on its formal and ideological allegiance to an imperialist and deeply racist Hollywood action narrative. In *Frozen River*, which narrates a tentative collaboration between two impoverished women—one white and one Mohawk—the precariousness of working-class life is debilitating for the women and those in their care, yet also generates new avenues of solidarity. In the end, the film suggests that it may be in the realm of social reproduction where some alternatives, however tentative, to capitalism's assault on poor and laboring people might be located. Finally, *Fruitvale Station*—which narrates the story of Oscar Grant, who was executed by Bay Area Rapid Transit police on New Year's Day 2009, and of other working and nonworking Black and Latinx persons whose lives are shadowed by the threat of confinement and death via the targeted violence of state and nonstate actors—offers a trenchant rejoinder to *Gran Torino*'s racist imaginary, suggesting that precarity is not only an economic, but also a biopolitical, category and that capitalism is in fact necrocapitalism, which demands not only living labor, but dead labor, too.

Chapter 4 examines three independent, neorealist films about migrant workers hustling to get by in New York City during the long turn-of-the-twenty-first-century wave of gentrification: *Man Push Cart* (dir. Ramin Bahrani, 2005), about a former Pakistani rock star who scrapes out a living running a breakfast cart in Manhattan; *Chop Shop* (dir. Ramin Bahrani, 2007), which follows an orphaned boy working in an auto body repair shop in the Bronx and his sister, a sex worker, as they save money to purchase a food truck; and *La Ciudad/The City* (dir. David Riker, 1998), a compilation of four stories about Latinx migrants in New York City's informal economy. Focusing on undocumented immigrants, poor women, and young people of color scrambling to find a foothold at the bottom of the economy, these films constitute a realist cinema of precarious labor that underscores the economic, physical, and civic vulnerability of the new working class, hovering on the cusp of wageless life. The aesthetic stress in Bahrani's films on the quotidian details of immigrant workers' lives attends closely and consistently to material and economic concerns, returning again and again to the manner in which the characters' labors and efforts to economize and accumulate some small measure of surplus cash shape their most intimate relations and seemingly innocuous actions. Similarly, Riker's film keeps a steady eye on the material hardships and forms of exploitation that structure migrant lives, even as it explores the potential for social and political transformation through collective action, a possibility raised most potently by *La Cuidad*'s final story, which ends, agonizingly, in the midst of a spontaneous, but perhaps only momentary, labor stoppage by sweatshop workers. This is an appropriate place to end: suspended in tension, uncertain whether collective action will materialize. Stories of precarious motion, encounter, translation, and tentative solidarity, narratives of living labor suggest that while the old working class may be dissolving, the parameters of the new one that may be emerging are still in the process of being imagined and formed.

Finally, the book concludes with a brief coda on solidarity as one way to think about the uneasy forms of working-class connection explored in these novels and films, in which traditional notions of working-class belonging and identity no longer seem to obtain. In these narratives, solidarity is a highly precarious and incomplete process, in which the possibility of collective affiliation is forged not on organic or a priori grounds, but actively created and recreated in and across borders, boundaries, motion, and flux.

1 • "We Are the Planet"

Impossible Solidarities in Russell Banks's *Continental Drift*

In 1986, Mike Davis published his landmark political history of the U.S. working class, *Prisoners of the American Dream*. Writing in the midst of the Reagan era, which had been ushered in with electoral support from substantial numbers of the very working people whose fortunes the former California governor's anti-union, "trickle down" economic policies so brutally undercut, Davis offered a thoroughly bleak assessment of working-class coherence and power in the United States. If the European working class and the labor parties it spawned had proven to be essentially reformist, Davis argued, the U.S. working class has been even weaker, woefully disorganized and depoliticized. Why had there been such a conspicuous absence of class consciousness among American workers and a failure to unify as a class on the political, and quite often the economic, planes? Davis's answer and analysis are complex and multifaceted, but he returns repeatedly to the claim that the political potential of the American working class has been greatly diluted by internal stratification and "the disenfranchisement of large sectors of labor: blacks, immigrants, women, migrant workers, and others."[1] In the 1980s, Davis argues, the unification of the laboring classes across social divisions is as pressing as ever, given the "increasingly one-sidedness of class struggle" manifest in the dismantling of the New Deal compromise and the rise of a new, late-imperial order, in which the U.S. ruling classes "are left with the fantastically dangerous illusion" that they can achieve global economic, political, and military dominance.[2] Any viable challenge to U.S. imperial power, Davis insists, must entail mass solidarity across national and racial lines, in particular between white workers and the "Black and Hispanic working class, fifty million strong ... that alone possesses the numerical and positional strength to undermine American empire from within."[3]

Seen from the twenty-first century, Davis's analysis, especially his emphasis on the muscular, imperial dimensions of Reaganism's response to the contradictions and crises of Fordism, seems especially precocious, appearing well before discussions of "globalization" became commonplace. This chapter asks how novelists addressed the dynamics of economic restructuring and working-class struggle that marked the "late-imperial" moment Davis describes. How did writers imagine working-class lives in a period marked by deindustrialization, wage stagnation, and emerging transborder production? How did fiction take up the potential for and barriers to working-class solidarity, especially across racial, ethnic, and national lines, in an ever-more transnational age dominated by an increasingly integrated world economic system and U.S. empire? Engaging these and other questions, this chapter contends that writers responded to the shifting social, economic, and political conditions of late capitalist globalization by inventing new modes of narrating class and labor that at once built on and departed from the proletarian literary traditions developed in the first half of the twentieth century. As a case in point, I examine one of the Reagan era's most ambitious, yet critically understudied novels: Russell Banks's *Continental Drift*, published in 1985.

Taking the shifting of the earth's plates as its core metaphor, *Continental Drift* traces the paths of several migrants in the context of global flows that span and bind the planet in a pattern of constant motion and explosive encounters. The novel's second chapter opens: "It is as if the creatures residing on this planet in these years, the human creatures, millions of them traveling singly and in families, in clans and tribes, revealing sometimes as entire nations, were a subsystem inside the larger system of currents and tides, of winds and weather, of drifting continents and shifting, uplifting, grinding, cracking land masses."[4] Seen as they are in this passage from an ecological perspective, the movements of millions traveling around the world in response to "war, famine and flood" (38) are akin to the weather patterns swirling the globe. Such a viewpoint provides "a vision of the planet as an organic cell... whose general principle informing that purpose, as if it were a moral imperative, is to keep moving" (43). The agents of this motion are the world's roving poor, from Somali refugees (39) to Afghan migrants trekking across Pakistan (42) to two figures moving across the Americas who serve as the novel's protagonists: Bob DuBois, an oil furnace repair man who moves from New Hampshire to Florida, and Vanise Dorsinville, who leaves Haiti with her infant son Charles and nephew Claude in an attempt to make their way to the United States. By interweaving Bob's and Vanise's stories in alternating chapters, the novel underscores not only their differences, but also their common membership in a hemispheric working class that is itself a segment of a larger, planetary population of migratory workers. "We are the planet," the narrator proclaims, speaking for the drifting millions, who are united not only by the imperative to stay in motion, but also by what the text refers to, without elaboration, as "intricate interdependencies" (43).

Despite the acclaim the novel received, including being nominated for a Pulitzer Prize and winning the Dos Passos award, academic critics have largely overlooked it; a search of the MLA bibliography yields only a handful of entries. When scholars have addressed the book, they have tended to focus, appropriately enough, on its transnational frame. Literary historian J. Michael Dash argues that *Continental Drift* suggests "a remapping of the Americas in which the Caribbean appears as the epicenter of ceaseless change"; political theorist Michael Shapiro contends that the novel "privileges flows of people rather than the consolidation of states through their practice of inclusion and exclusion," thereby challenging nation-based norms of citizenship.[5] And indeed, in expanding its cartographic scope beyond discrete national boundaries, *Continental Drift* anticipates the proliferation during the 1990s of U.S.-focused transnational literature represented by novels such as Leslie Marmon Silko's transborder tale of Indigenous anticolonial resistance, *Almanac of the Dead* (1991), and Karen Te Yamashita's magical realist story of Los Angeles as a hemispheric crossroads, *Tropic of Orange* (1997, discussed in chapter 2), to which critics in recent years have begun to direct substantial attention.[6]

While critics of the novel have successfully identified *Continental Drift*'s transnational ambitions, they have largely neglected to grapple with its meditation on working-class formation and affiliation. It is this dimension of the novel that this chapter takes up. Specifically, I examine *Continental Drift* as a form of transnational working-class fiction, a post-Fordist proletarian novel that, in both its narrative content and its literary form, maps the unmaking of the traditional industrial working class and the emergence of what the cultural historian Michael Denning refers to as "the as yet unorganized and largely uncharted post-Fordist working class," founded on the growing participation in the labor force of women and of immigrants from Asia and Latin America in the wake of the Immigration Act of 1965 and the emergence of the service sector, Sun Belt economy, marked by increasingly contingent, informal, and low-paying forms of work.[7] Banks's novel insists that the story of the white U.S. working class in an increasingly postindustrial, globalized era is also the story of a hemispheric, migratory underclass, composed in large part by poor people of color. Following the fate of questing workers in an ultimately fruitless search for well-being and wealth, *Continental Drift* stresses the urgency of class consciousness in a neoliberal world, even as it finally insists that the historic legacies and ongoing dynamics of slavery, colonialism, and the geographically and culturally uneven dimensions of capitalist development make such consciousness in and of itself insufficient to establish a sense of solidarity among laboring peoples from disparate racial and national contexts. This is a novel about the material and ideological *challenges* to the formation of a transnational working class, about the fragility, even the impossibility, of class coherence. Banks's book poses the possibility that contemporary globalization generates new forms of interdependence, and, potentially, new axes of alliance, among the world's poor, migrating peoples, and it weaves the potentialities as well as the obstacles to such interconnections into its very literary form.

In tracing the transnational contours of working-class lives that have most often historically been rendered in national or regional narratives, *Continental Drift* represents a form of what cultural theorist Fredric Jameson terms cognitive mapping, a concept Jameson publicly articulated two years before Banks's novel was published, at the now-renowned conference on "Marxism and the Interpretation of Culture" held at the University of Illinois. At the conference, Jameson described cognitive mapping as a provisional aesthetic effort to locate individual and collective subjects within the broad horizon of the social, economic, and geopolitical system. He contended that although the totality of capitalist social relations is ultimately unrepresentable, if not conceptually unknowable, progressive political art should aim to connect concrete, individual narratives to the constellation of "class relations on a global ... scale."[8] Cognitive mapping is an active, invariably unfinished process that "involves our insertion as individual subjects into a multidimensional set of radically discontinuous realities," which are, Jameson contends, ultimately parts of a larger, yet never fully representable systemic whole.[9] Jeff Kinkle and Alberto Toscano note that "Jameson's formulation ... does not provide a method"; "rather, it poses a problem which is at once political, economic, aesthetic and existential."[10] In an effort to link local, personal, and experiential dimensions to larger structures, cognitive mapping underscores not the smooth, static, or transparent quality of capitalist, racial, and colonial systems, but their contradictory and uneven lines of power, and Jameson offers no definitive prescriptions for how this might be done.

As a work of cognitive mapping, *Continental Drift* undertakes to link its finely rendered narratives of individual working-class life and struggle to larger hemispheric and planetary dynamics of economic and, significantly, racial and colonial exploitation, displacement, and domination. Strategically adopting conventions from 1930s proletarian literature to a late capitalist context, Banks's novel offers a searing portrait of the *differential yet interconnected* economic and political challenges facing impoverished workers on the move, especially racialized migrants fleeing societies marked by histories and present-day patterns of colonial power. In the process, the text constructs a new, critical narrative geography, incisively mapping the structures of uneven development across the overlapping Sun Belt and Caribbean economies, and insisting on the thorny entanglement of race, class, and empire. In doing so, the novel complicates any hope that cognitive mapping might lead to a transparent view of a singular system; indeed, the novel underscores that structures of economic, racial, gender, and imperial power are interlocking and layered. The novel's discrepant formal registers (realism, allegory, myth) and contrasting, contrapuntal narrative perspectives suggest that mapping such a complex, multifaceted whole requires multiple, heterogenous modes of knowledge and aesthetic representation. The novel fleetingly raises embryonic possibilities for working-class mutuality and solidarity, but its failure to fully develop those possibilities crystallizes the challenge of representing effective interracial, working-class alternatives in the early Reagan era, when working people were under vigorous economic and political attack. *Continental Drift*, I conclude, is an ambitious exemplar of an emergent mode of precarious realism—the transnational proletarian novel—which offers a potent, yet also provisional and partial, critique of neoliberal capitalism and its architecture of deeply uneven economic and racial power.

"Wages acceptable only to someone who would otherwise starve"

Neoliberal globalization, and the concomitant demographic, social, and political transformations that shaped the second half of the twentieth century, transfigured the U.S. and global working class. In the United States, the blue-collar, industrial working class, which achieved unprecedented coherence and power in the 1930s, and peak wages in the 1960s on the basis of the post–World War II settlement between corporations and the major labor unions, was largely dismantled and reorganized into what sociologists and historians have described as a new American working class made up increasingly of women; immigrants from Latin America, Asia, and the Caribbean; and people of color laboring in service-sector jobs.[11] Several factors drove the recomposition of the U.S. proletariat. Perhaps the most important was the beginning of a shift from Fordist, welfare capitalism that depended on the relative stability of its workforce, to a post-Fordist economy of flexible accumulation, organized around ever more informalized, low-wage labor conditions. In the 1970s, deregulation, privatization, and the increasing mobility of capital facilitated by the move away from Keynesian economic policies created grounds for a massive deindustrialization of the U.S. economy, as companies moved their production sites to the Global South in an effort to cut labor costs. These economic changes were accompanied by demographic shifts, most notably the surge in immigration from Latin America, Asia, and the Caribbean after the Immigration Act of 1965, which accelerated the growing racial, cultural, and linguistic heterogeneity of the American workforce. These transformations produced a working class increasingly organized around the contingency rather than stability of its labor and the racial and ethnic and gender diversity of its membership. It is a class less stable and discrete, not bounded by the occupational, gender, or racial expectations that had structured the prevailing image of the twentieth-century working class, which was most often represented in the cultural sphere by a white man in industrial work gear.

Hailed by James Atlas in *The Atlantic* as "the most convincing portrait I know of contemporary America," *Continental Drift* is a resolutely working-class novel, centered on the lives of laboring people traversing what Davis, in *Prisoners of the American Dream*, called "a new social and cultural landscape of intensifying class and racial polarizations."[12] The narrator of Banks's text identifies Bob as "one of those who makes their livings with their hands" (408), and traces the impetus for his journey to Florida directly to his economic frustration. Leaving work with his paycheck in hand, Bob thinks, "a man does his work, does it for eight long years, and for that he gets to take home to his wife and two kids a weekly paycheck for one hundred thirty-seven dollars and forty-four cents. Dirt money. Chump change. Money gone before it's got" (4). Haunted by television ads extolling wealth and consumer glamour, Bob feels trapped in a dead-end job, "inert and shackled" (22), living out the same life of quiet desperation and futility as his father and grandfather who ran lathes at the local mill. "Only difference now," Bob explains to his wife Elaine, is that "the mill is turned into a fucking pea cannery where only women work, so I'm fixing broken oil burners for Fred Turner, crawling in and out of boiler rooms and basements *my* whole livelong life!" (26). Caught in an economy marked by industrial decline and the feminization of labor, Bob figures his inadequacy—feeling "shackled," a term that invokes slavery—in implicitly racialized terms. As a narrative of Bob's sense of confinement and resentment, Banks's novel takes its place in a post-Vietnam-era canon of texts, ranging from the Joel Schumacher–Michael Douglas film *Falling Down*, to the TV series *Hung* and *Breaking Bad*, that narrate the travails of white working men coming to grips with their economic vulnerability, even obsolescence, in a deindustrializing world. As an allegory for white working men in the United States, whose wages were dropping in the 1970s as union membership plunged and women entered the workforce in greater numbers (the factory where his father labored is now a cannery populated by female workers), Bob's story is, appropriately, a tale of decline, as he moves from a position of relative economic security (a steady job, ownership of a house, car, and boat) to a state of accelerating insecurity, destitution, and desperation (living in a trailer at the end of a dirt road, Bob turns to smuggling in a doomed effort to improve his economic lot). This is a story of Bob's coming to understand his subordinate place in the economic hierarchy and his common cause with other poor and working people, but it is not, like many proletarian novels from the 1930s, a narrative of growing up. Rather, it is a narrative of growing old, of crisis, of death. It is also a story of race: of white anxiety and grievance as well as the ultimately unfulfilled prospect of cross-racial alliance. (It is also worth noting that Bob's economic descent is accompanied by his wife Elaine's entry into the workforce; she takes a waitressing job that symbolizes the transition from male, industrial labor to feminized, service-sector work.)

Indeed, Bob's arc of decline and failure echoes the weakening of the white male industrial working class as a whole during the 1970s. As Jefferson Cowie has argued, the 1970s started brightly for the traditional working class, as laborers undertook an array of assertive job actions, signaling their collective intent to put their stamp on the period. But by decade's end, the modern prospect of a "conscious, diverse, and unified working class acting as a powerful agenda in political, social, and economic life" had effectively disappeared from the landscape of cultural possibility.[13] Bob's move from a position of relative economic, social, and personal stability to a life of uncertainty and worry echoes the national transition, during the 1970s, from "a republic of security" to a "republic of anxiety," as Cowie puts it.[14] Further, Bob's death on the streets of a major Sun Belt city, Miami, might be seen as an allegorical figure for the demise of the New Deal proletariat, and the end of the long postwar boom (and the accompanying accord between unions and corporations) that had raised the living standards of many industrial workers in the United States to unprecedented heights.

The novel devotes fewer pages to Vanise and Claude than to Bob, but they, too, are working people, neo-slaves, in fact, who labor in the Caribbean's underground agricultural and sexual economies. In New Providence, Vanise is held captive by club owner Jimmy Grabow who sells her sexual services to local seamen, while Claude joins an invisible force of Black workers who perform the menial labor that keeps the Global North's leisure economy moving. The novel underscores the status of Vanise and Claude as modern-day slaves by invoking rhetoric of the middle passage to describe their journey across the Caribbean, especially the leg from North Caicos to Nassau. The trip, in which the two are confined for several days to the fetid hold of a small vessel described as a "pit of darkness" (201) is a figurative, if not quite literal, death. During the journey, both Vanise and Claude are raped repeatedly. They are "surrounded by darkness, as if buried" (197); "all of time was gone" (201). "They did not sleep, but, like small animals in shock... were not awake either" (205). Lying on pallets just above the bilge water into which they are forced to defecate and urinate, they "were rats now" (204), reduced to a state akin to what Georgio Agamben has called bare life, although here bare life is not imagined as an exception that grounds normative political subjectivity, but rather as a form of terror, exploitation, and virtual death that is internal to and constitutive of racial capitalism. "They had come," the narrator explains, "over three hundred miles as if chained in darkness, a middle passage" (207). Evoking transnational slave narratives, such as Olaudah Equiano's *Narrative* and Martin Delaney's *Blake* that were among the Americas' first working-class stories, Banks insists that slavery is not a vestige of the past, but an integral aspect of the human trafficking and labor regimes that shape the contemporary Caribbean and American world. Seen through this narrative, contemporary capitalism is not only racial capitalism, but also what I described in the introduction as necrocapitalism, a mode of economic accumulation that deploys and produces the social and physical death of racialized workers as forms of biopolitical control and labor discipline. Vanise and Claude are vulnerable to hyperexploitation because the intersecting systems of colonialism and capitalism render them figuratively and literally disposable, subject to premature, arbitrary death at almost any moment. Vanise and Claude are subject to the prospect of death at every stage of their journey across the novel's landscape, from Haiti, to the wider Caribbean, to the United States. They are never free from the threat of premature death; indeed, their early deaths are almost a foregone conclusion. Their stories suggest that under late capitalist, colonial globalization, death and exploitation intertwine to form an unending, deeply violent structure of racialized economic extraction.[15]

Banks's depiction of Vanise and Claude's journey is remarkable not only for the detailed descriptions of the brutality they suffer, but also for the way the novel links their journey and their labor to a larger economy of First World consumer pleasure. Indeed, the novel deftly connects their enslavement to the infrastructure of capitalist development, implying that the two forms of exploitation are interwoven. When Vanise and Claude emerge from the hold of the boat in which they were smuggled, the first things they see are "high, rectangular hotels on Cable Beach... glittery casinos, crowded restaurants, strings of streetlights, beacons blinking off North Cay at the entrance to the harbor, a jet plane taking off" (207). As they move along the waterfront, they see "two Scandinavian cruise ships tied up... sleek, white and huge, with strings of lights running up the masts and stacks like Christmas tree decorations, and... downtown Nassau off the starboard, where taxis cruised through Rawson Square, turned and headed off to the casinos or cross-island to the airport for late-night arrivals from London, New York and Miami" (208). Here, in a paradigmatic moment of cognitive mapping, the novel ties the fate of these two destitute, abused, socially invisible migrants to the imperial economic and cultural circuits that link the Bahamas to major European and U.S. metropolises.

In several remarkable passages, the novel traces the trans-Caribbean structures of what geographer Neil Smith calls uneven development, the spatial patterns of capitalist accumulation that create immense wealth for a few and corresponding wretchedness for many others. After Vanise and Claude are deposited in the Bahamas, Claude finds and joins a community of people forcibly hidden in the shadows:

> [P]eople from the outskirts of towns, the squatters and shack people, whose lives are official secrets. They are off-islanders, most of them, illegal immigrants from Haiti, wandering foreigners whose presence on the island is officially forbidden and unofficially tolerated, for they provide a considerable part of the huge, underpaid, unprotected labor force that is required by the tourist industry on New Providence. They wash the dishes, scrub the pots, clean the toilets, clip the grass and haul the trash for the managers of the enormous glass, steel and concrete hotels and casinos... for wages acceptable only to someone who would otherwise starve. (230)

Here, as elsewhere, the novel insists that the members of the Haitian diaspora are not only political refugees, but also vital members of a suppressed pan-Caribbean working class, caught in the unforgiving gears of capitalist exploitation: there are "whole communities" of Haitians living in the bushes (225), "working in the kitchens of the hotels and in private homes as maids and gardeners" (225).

The portrait of these underground, "unofficial" workers suggests that late-industrial globalization, for which cognitive and symbolic labor are often taken as emblematic forms of work, is in fact founded on the brutal subjugation and exploitation of manual and physical workers "who would otherwise starve." Silvia Federici, in her critique of Hardt and Negri's insistence on the dominance of immaterial labor in contemporary capitalism, asserts that the emerging post-Fordist era has witnessed a widespread "deregulat[ion] of labor relations" which has facilitated "the return on a massive scale of un-free forms of labor," "an immense leap in the exploitation and devaluation of labor, and the deepening of divisions within the world proletariat."[16] There is, she continues, "a multitude of proletarians working in the shadow, reminding us that the existence of a population of rightless workers—whether slaves, colonial subjects, peons, convicts, or *sans papiers*—remains a structural necessity of capital accumulation."[17] In a spirit quite similar to Federici's trenchant remarks, Banks's narrative underscores the devaluation of labor in the Global North, the incorporation of dispossessed colonial peoples into the global proletariat, and prevalence of unfree forms of labor in the so-called modern era. Significantly, if *Continental Drift* stresses the shared *desperation* of workers across contexts, it also underscores the *heterogeneity* of working populations and laboring situations, the *asymmetry* of their positions in the global economic and racial system. As I indicate below, the novel illustrates the translocal web of economic accumulation linking disparate geographic regions and human populations, but it also depicts contemporary capitalism as a system of widely varied forms of exploitation and dispossession, founded on the differentiation and proliferation rather than the homogenization of labor.[18]

The novel is quite clear that, relative to Vanise and Claude, who lack the most basic physical, economic, and civil freedoms, Bob is immensely privileged. As Bob himself realizes when he finally meets them, the Haitians "are not trying merely to improve their lot; they're trying to obtain one" (335). The novel does not underplay Bob's substantially more fortunate position in the global economy, but its narrative arc does follow the erosion of the position of the working classes in the advanced capitalist countries relative to the conditions of labor in the rest of the world. The decline is epitomized in Bob's downward spiral: leaving behind his small house in Catamount, he ends up on a "bumpy dirt road not much wider than a path," at the end of which sit "three rusting, flaking house trailers situated on cinder blocks . . . [surrounded by] rusted car chassis, old tires, [and] tossed-out kitchen appliances." (251). Moreover, Bob eventually comes to see himself, like millions of other workers roaming the planet, as a poor person who "has as much chance of becoming rich as he had of becoming Ted Williams" (342) and whose interests are fundamentally at odds with the interests of the wealthy. "In the past," we are told, "he sometimes regarded poor people through the cracked lens of liberal guilt, but that was before he discovered that he was poor himself and stopped envying the rich and started hating them. That was before he learned that what was wrong with the rich was not that they had something he wanted, but that they were unconscious, often deliberately so, of the power they wielded over the lives of others" (341–42).

The novel's frank insistence on the opposition between rich and poor runs hand-in-hand with its assertion that the American Dream—"the dream of a new life, the dream of starting over" (314)—has been purchased by elite financial powers that have turned the lure of upward mobility into a hollow fantasy. All the novel's U.S. characters are floating on debt, living in paper houses, scrambling to stay one step ahead of their creditors. Bob's pal Avery Boone, who owns the boat that Bob uses to smuggle the Haitians and who Bob thinks has successfully catapulted himself into genuine economic independence, is in fact living on overextended loans. "The bank's got me by the nuts," he tells Bob, using the inflated masculinist rhetoric that the novel indicates is at once compensation for deepening economic insecurity and an assertion of enduring male authority. "Why the hell do you think everyone with a boat is running dope? It's not to live good, pal. It's just to live. It all ends up going back to the banks" (313). By the time Bob is standing on the deck of the *Belinda Blue* with Vanise's nephew Claude, imagining that the young Haitian must be drawn by the American Dream, he thinks to himself, "like Columbus and all those guys looking for the Fountain of Youth, when you finally get to America, you get something else. You get Disney World and land deals and fast-moving high-interest bank loans, and if you don't get the hell out of the way, they'll knock you down . . . so they can throw some condos up on top of you or maybe a parking lot or maybe an orange grove" (348). "It's *never a fair exchange,* [Bob] thinks, never an even swap" (349). The novel's demonization of banks—crafted just as the savings and loan crisis of the 1980s was starting to crest—culminates in a throwback image on the text's final page of "*men in three-piece suits behind desks in the banks [who] grow fatter and more secure and skillful in their work*" while a new generation of working people "*go on breaking their lives trying to bend them around the wheel of commerce*" (410, italics in original).

In underscoring the way Bob comes to understand his subordinate position in the economic hierarchy and, subsequently, the interests he has in common with other poor people against social, financial, and political elites, *Continental Drift* echoes the narrative logic of a more traditional proletarian novel. In addition, the novel's focus on work and the "diverse values, vernaculars, and daily lives of laboring and jobless people," its critique of possessive individualism, and its depiction of Bob's growing destitution, alongside the concluding image of fat cat bankers that recalls turn-of-the-century prolabor cartoons and graphics, suggest Banks's debts to, and conscious recasting of the long history of anticapitalist, prolabor art and literature and his desire to fit *Continental Drift* into that venerable and diverse canon.[19] Yet, importantly, the motifs and tropes from earlier radical literary forms have been substantially recast. While proletarian literature regularly revolved around a tension between unity and difference, solidarity and separation, it typically tended toward a logic of consolidation and climax, in which isolation and alienation might be overcome through the emergence of a socialist imperative, consciousness, or movement. By contrast, *Continental Drift* bears no trace of the culminating strike or revolutionary commitment that marked many left texts from the 1930s, when a sense of radical possibility shaped much art and thinking. Indeed, as I argue below, the possibility of working-class affiliation and collectivity—a recognition of shared circumstances and intertwined futures—is visible in Banks's novel largely as a missed opportunity.

The novel thus allegorizes the dissolution of Fordist-era social relations, aesthetic forms, and political subjectivities, and it suggests that transformation has a dialectical edge. On one hand, globalization constitutes an opening up, as new lines of flight and motion put figures previously separated by geopolitical boundaries in motion and contact. The novel thus raises the possibility that globalization can establish greater recognition of the multiplicity of lives and the multitude of others, especially among the planet's poor and exploited populations. Both in the story it tells, and in its very form of twinned and intersecting narrative threads, the book posits the contemporary as a ground for the potential emergence of new beginnings, new social projects, new forms of self-determination and subjectivity, new collectivities among and across the world's subordinated and subaltern inhabitants. At the same time, and even more powerfully, the novel depicts globalization as a deeply destructive process, in which new populations in motion become additional grist for the exploitative violence of racialized, necrocapitalist processes, which overwhelm and destroy the tentative, incipient, all-too-fragile forms of alliance and interdependence coming into being.

"Exposed, revealed to the world for what he is"

Much as the novel indicates that the social topography of the Bahamas is organized by the contrast between wealthy tourists and destitute vagabonds, so Florida has been shaped by the unmistakable and virtually unmediated imperatives of corporate, consumer capitalism.[20] Continuing its close attention to the conjunction of natural landscape, built environment, and capitalist accumulation, the novel stresses the way Florida's integration into a burgeoning Sun Belt economy has molded its terrain. Driving into central Florida, the DuBois family is surrounded by

> McDonald's and Burger Kings, Kentucky Fried Chickens and Pizza Huts, a long, straight tunnel of franchises broken intermittently by storefront loan companies and paved lots crammed with glistening Corvettes, T-Birds, Cameos and Trans Ams, and beyond the car dealerships, surrounded by chain link fences, automobile graveyards, vast and disordered, dreary, colorless and indestructible. On the outskirts of every town they pass through are miles of trailer parks laid out in grids, like the orange groves beyond them, with a geometric precision determined by the logic of ledgers instead of the logic of land, water, and sky. (59–60)

Dominated by industrial agriculture (geometric grids of orange groves) and service-sector capitalism (car dealerships and fast-food joints), Florida is a prefabricated, planned environment, built according to the demands of profit. After the trailer parks, the DuBois family passes "tracts of pastel-colored cinderblock bungalows," "instant, isolated neighborhoods, suburbs of the suburbs, reflecting not the inhabitants' needs so much as the builders' and landowners' greed" (60). The landscape of consumerism and geometry of economic efficiency continues unabated as an "endless barrage of billboards, neon signs, flapping plastic banners and flags, arrows, and huge profiled fingers pointed at them through the windshield, shrilling at them to Buy, buy, buy me now!" (60). This is a one-dimensional landscape, without subtlety or variation, that stands as a blunt expression of the economic forces shaping the historic moment of the novel's present, when the Sun Belt economies and corresponding geometries of sprawl were rising, while the older industrial segments of the U.S. economy, such as former factory towns in New England, were in corresponding decline.

Crucially, the novel insists that the anxieties Bob and Elaine might otherwise have about the dubious financial implications of their move to the Sunshine State are filtered through the prism of race. As "they near Oleander Park, Florida, their new home, after Bob's having quit his job, after having sold everything they could sell . . . after having said and waved goodbye forever to everything familiar, known, understood, they come up against and are forced to see many people of color, more of them, so it seems, than there are white people" (61–62). The "newness" of Florida, its strangeness to Bob and Elaine, and the fragility of their predicament as migrants, are profoundly racialized: "These black- and brown-skinned people, the American blacks in the department stores and supermarkets, the Jamaicans and Haitians in the fields, the Cubans in the filling stations—these working people, who got here first, belong here, not Bob and Elaine DuBois and their daughters Ruthie and Emma" (62). The sight of Black people working makes Bob (whose last name in this context takes on an ironic reference to W. E. B. DuBois) self-conscious about his poverty as well as his whiteness; he feels "exposed, revealed to the world for what he is," "ugly in his winter-gray skin ... poor and ignorant in his noisy, dented station wagon" (62). Race and labor converge here, as Bob's economic and social insecurities manifest as racial anxieties. Bob's worries about leaving behind the familiar culture in which he grew up, and his fears about having leveraged all of his meager financial assets to plunge his family into an uncertain future in unfamiliar territory, acquire tangibility when he is confronted with "these working people" of color, whose position in the economy and whose presence in the social body make him feel "exposed, revealed."

Written before the rise to prominence of whiteness studies in academe, *Continental Drift* underscores Bob as a racialized subject, indicating both that race is central to his position in the world and that his lack of understanding about race as a structural dynamic of power and as a mode of social understanding obstructs his relations with others. In an interview, Banks asserted his view that "in the United States, race is first and foremost an excellent means to conceal class. In the end, the omnipresence of race protects the myth of a classless society. . . . It is very useful to have the screen of race to protect a society of capitalist exploitation."[21] As if echoing Stuart Hall, whose landmark essay "Race, Class and Societies Structured in Dominance" was published in 1981, the novel seems to be suggesting not so much that race obscures the visibility of class, but that that race is the modality in which class is lived.[22] Bob's anxieties about his economic status as a white worker relative to workers of color reflect a certain demographic reality about the U.S. workforce in the late twentieth century. Indeed, several factors, including the demise of industrial employment, the explosion of the service sector, growing female employment, and the increase in immigration meant that by the end of the twentieth century, as Joshua Freeman explains, "white men no longer constituted a majority of the waged labor force."[23] "Between 1976 and 1988," Robin Kelley notes, "while the nation's overall labor force grew by 26 percent, the percentage of black workers rose by 38 percent, Asian American workers by 103 percent, and Latinos by 110 percent."[24] Bob's racial apprehensions, so closely bound up with his economic fears, forcefully register the changing status of the white proletariat in the United States.

Race continues to shape Bob's life in Florida, most notably in his affair with Marguerite Dill. In charting this relationship, the novel indicates that Bob is unable to fully or finally eliminate what Banks calls "the screen of race," the sedimented layers of projection and stereotype that inform, if not entirely govern, his conception of African Americans. We are told that Bob "has never seen an attractive black woman up close before" (86) and that his desires for women of color have been, until his relationship with Marguerite, "impersonal, abstract, pornographic, and racist" (86). Yet despite the sexual intimacy he and Marguerite share, his conception of her never moves entirely beyond his pre-existing primitivist frames. We are told that he loves her, yet when having sex with her, he has a baldly colonial "vision of himself as a white boat . . . sliding easily onto the hot golden sands of a tropical beach, with dark, lush jungle ahead of him" (108). Marguerite remains an abstract idea to Bob, a generalizable Other, as much as a singular human being. After their relationship has ended, Bob finds himself "once again thinking of them both in term of color, which he cannot seem to avoid doing, even though every time he does it, he loses sight of her face and voice and almost forgets her name" (304). Bob seems unaware that his preconceptions about race interfere with his capacity to see Marguerite as a unique individual, and the novel gives no indication that Bob can work through this interference. Marguerite "is not at all as he imagines and supposes her to be" (97), but Bob's relationship with Marguerite fails finally to dereify race, to undermine or destabilize the racist fantasies that Bob brought to the relationship in the first place. The novel thus incisively anatomizes and illustrates the durability of Bob's racial (and racist) fantasies and the way such fantasies limit his capacity to see Marguerite for who she is. Yet significantly, the text does not offer a countervailing perspective; it does not render Marguerite's point of view (or even explain why she finds Bob attractive in the first place), and it does not provide evidence of the relationship's capacity to shake the preconceptions that inform and impoverish Bob's view of Marguerite. As if reflecting Bob's inability to move beyond his rudimentary, indeed imperialist, ideas about race, the plot with Marguerite is cut short, oddly abandoned. This failure to more fully and directly engage and confront the dimensions and dynamics of race, even as the narrative acknowledges the utter centrality of race to U.S. society and working-class experience, foreshadows the novel's climactic scene, which I discuss in detail below, when a failure of transracial communication and connection effectively dooms the text's protagonists.

"The kind of map you must keep moving into, if you want to read it"

The novel's deterritorialization, its move beyond a purely or primarily national narrative frame, occurs not only at the level of the plot, but also at the level of literary form and narrative voice, which extend and complicate the Euro-American literary traditions within which Banks is primarily working. As the book urges us to adopt a planetary perspective in order to look past the differences in locale, culture, and political predicament that distinguish (and ultimately divide) migrants from one another, it also asks its U.S. readership to see through another set of eyes. At one level, the novel's narrator, who is omniscient and looks down from afar as he narrates the characters' struggles, springs from the Dreiserian mode of American literary naturalism. Yet the book opens in a very different vein, with an "Invocation," in which the narrator summons a Haitian loa, the god Legba, to help tell the story. While the narrator acknowledges that the story stems from a "white Christian man's entwined obsession with race and sex and a proper middle-class American's shame for his nation's history" (2), he also insists that this "is an American story of the late twentieth century and you don't need a muse to tell it, you need something more like a loa, or mouth man, a voice that makes speech stand in front of you and not behind" (2); "you must see it with eyes not your own and must tell it with a mouth not your own. Let Legba come forward, then, come forward and bring this middle-aging, white mouth man into speech again" (2). This is an "American" story in the hemispheric sense, the telling of which demands voices from across the Americas. Accordingly, the novel not only references such canonical works of U.S. literature as Melville's "Benito Cereno," Twain's *The Adventures of Huckleberry Finn*, and Hemingway's *To Have and Have Not*, but also draws from Haitian Vodun.[25] As Banks explained in an interview, he aimed to "invoke a narrator the way you invoke a loa in Haitian Vodun. Which is to say, I'll allow myself, if I can, to be possessed: I'll let this voice speak through me, and it'll be of a specific character—the loa will be Legba."[26] Moreover, Legba, considered the guardian of the crossroads, is not only a model for the text's narrative voice, but a figure of the novel itself, which is set at the juncture of the Caribbean and New England, and of its form, which is woven of strands drawn from inside and outside the Euro-American realist tradition. As Christopher Douglas contends, the presence of Legba has the effect of "decentering" the tale "away from [the United States]. The double tale of the American dream is thus simultaneously told from within and without the United States."[27] If this is a quintessential "American" story, it is framed by, and in some measure narrated through, a Caribbean voice.

The invocation of Haitian traditions could be seen as a form of literary imperialism, of cultural poaching and ventriloquism that is dependent on, and reinforces, colonial relations of power between North and South, white and Black, First and Third Worlds. It is, after all, Bob's book first and foremost, and Vanise and Claude are secondary, if not background, figures. Yet the novel shows immense respect for its Haitian characters, their value systems, and for Vodun ritual. Indeed, the narrator expressly defends Vanise's religious convictions as a rational response to her circumstances: "[W]hen, like Vanise, you have no control over your destiny, it's reasonable to assume that someone or something else does, which is why it's reasonable, not irrational, for Vanise to believe that the bizarre fact of her survival, her destiny now, is due to a loa's intervention" (358). What's more, the novel blends her faith into the realistic fabric of the text, lending her spiritual visions literary authority. For instance, when she sees a three-legged dog on North Caicos, and insists that it is Legba, the novel gives us every reason to believe she is right. When the dog talks to her, we are not told that it *seemed* to talk to her, or that she *thought* the dog talked to her. The dog *talks* to her (131).[28] Similarly, when Ghede and Agwé meet in Miami to discuss Vanise's fate, it is rendered not as a spiritual vision or a religious delusion, but as an actual, real event (364–67).

Even more significant, while Vanise remains a relatively opaque figure, much less accessible to readers than Bob, she becomes the moral center of the novel. Certainly, the text underscores the precarious nature of Vanise's life, the abuse and abjection she suffers. She is a single mother, a former sex worker, once favored and then rejected by the police constable in Allanche, who impregnated and then abandoned her. She "stood on the further side of resignation" (57), we are told, "emptied out" (57). The novel draws attention to her particular vulnerability as a woman, constantly prey to male sexual violence, and as a mother, who stays at Jimmy Grabow's club in part because it provides a secure, relatively stable location for her infant son. Unlike Bob, who is chasing a commercially formulated and socially sanctioned fantasy of upwardly mobile, white male American success, Vanise swims against the current, in the face of a social system set up not only to exploit, but also to belittle and abuse her. In the novel's moral economy, Vanise's struggles endow her with integrity, so that at the end, she is positioned to judge Bob's efforts to redeem himself by returning the migrants' money, a gesture she refuses. Critic J. Michael Dash contends that Vanise "holds the key to [Bob's] urge to find a better life."[29] "In the novel," Dash contends, "the tough, enduring, female face of Haiti sits in judgment over the naïve, earnest experience of the male protagonist."[30] For Dash, that Banks lends Vanise such moral force distinguishes the novel from so many other European and U.S. texts in which Haitian characters pose as mere foils or shadowy, alien stereotypes.

Further, from the point of view of the novel's form, one could argue that there is a politics in refusing to render Vanise's interior consciousness more fully, even as she takes on a substantial moral role in the text. Bob is exposed to readers, and we see the deeply contradictory and confused quality of much of his thinking about his own predicament and the world he inhabits. By contrast, through a complex play of presence and absence, in which Vanise assumes a growing importance to the novel's plot and perspective, she is granted a measure of literary autonomy, as readers are not given the same kind of access to her interior consciousness as they are to Bob's. This could be a symptom of literary or imaginative "failure," but it could also represent a sign of the novel's unwillingness to render Vanise fully legible, to offer her protection from the novel's anticipated white U.S. readership, whose literary access to Vanise is at some level rebuffed or denied.

Shortly before its tragic conclusion, when Bob and the Haitians meet aboard the *Belinda Blue*, the novel offers its most ambitious, if incomplete, rhetoric of transnational proletarian relation.[31] While Bob is fairly clear-eyed about the pragmatic nature of his relationship with the Haitians he is transporting—"They need him to carry them to where starvation and degradation are unlikely; he needs them to help him stay there" (343)—he also senses the possibility that he and they have something more substantial in common, and much to tell each other. For his part, Bob tries to let Claude know that, for poor people, the American dream is "always . . . worth less than what you gave away for it. Because in the land of the free, nothing's free" (348). In turn, he senses that the Haitians know something that could illuminate, perhaps even redeem, his own existence (it's worth noting that like Vanise, Bob, whose family roots are French-Canadian, is indirectly a product of the French colonial system). Bob thinks, "The Haitians know something about themselves, about history, about human life that he doesn't know" (341). The novel acknowledges the alterity of the Haitians, the "mystery" (343) they represent to Bob, to whom they appear as "silent, dark-skinned, utterly foreign people" (343). Yet the book also underscores the prospect of relation and exchange, of dialogue and mutuality: Bob "can't stop himself... from believing that [the refugees] know something that, if he learns it himself, will make his mere survival more than possible" (343). This is the novel's most imaginatively and politically ambitious moment, when the personification of U.S. labor and racial privilege senses that his existence can perhaps only be grasped through the lives of these Black refugees, who appear to know something about him which, he realizes, "I don't know myself, something crucial, something that basically defines me" (345). In opening up the prospect of exchange, in which we come to see that both Bob and the Haitians have something vital to offer one another, the novel creates—if only for an instant—a space of interracial, transhemispheric, working-class reciprocity, or solidarity.

That this possibility occurs on a boat is entirely fitting. As chronotropes, ships often stand for transit, transition, and change. Ships are metaphors for circulation, symbols of modernity's restless energies of motion and transformation. Ships have often been engines of capitalism and imperialism, carrying colonial explorers and conquerors, commodities, raw materials, and slaves between sites of empire. At the same time, ships have also been crucial to the formation of various countermodernities. Paul Gilroy has argued that ships brought into being the fluid countercultures of the Black Atlantic and its emphasis on routes over roots.[32] Peter Linebaugh and Marcus Rediker argue that during the seventeenth and eighteenth centuries, Atlantic ships served as sites of transnational working-class contact and communication, vehicles through which a polyglot maritime proletariat "built an autonomous, democratic, egalitarian social order of their own."[33] In *Moby-Dick*, Herman Melville imagined that even as the *Pequod* served as the vessel of Ahab's mad venture, it was also a site in which the transnational, multiracial crew established subversive forms of interdependence and fellow-feeling. In this book, I argue that contemporary globalization has undercut the relatively stable forms of working-class life and culture forged in the United States during the long Fordist era, and that contemporary literature about working peoples figures class *not through metaphors of identity, but rather through metaphors of contested space*. It is no surprise that the ocean, figured as a space of mobility, encounter, and contact, represents a crucial site in several of the texts examined in this book. In *Continental Drift*, the sea serves as a space of convergence, where the novel's characters meet and interact, gaining a sense of the interdependencies that link them. Yet as the novel's earlier descriptions of ships—both the cruise ships as embodiments of metropolitan, capitalist power, and the boat on which Vanise and Claude travel from

Haiti as virtual slaves—make clear, the sea is by no means free of the brutal forces of economic and racial power.

And indeed, the asymmetrical lines of social division and power that come close to being broached in the scene on Bob's boat are reimposed with a vengeance. While the novel indicates that Bob and the Haitians are bound, at least momentarily, in a relation of mutuality, or solidarity, the narrator gives no insight into the knowledge the Haitians carry with them and informs us that sharing this wisdom would in any event be impossible: "even if [the Haitians] spoke English or [Bob] spoke Creole," the substance of what the Haitians know "could never be told" (343). Moments later, the novel reaches its terrible denouement, as Bob and Tyrone, in an effort to save themselves from arrest by the Coast Guard, force the refugees into the swirling sea, dissolving the fragile prospect of transhemispheric working-class understanding and support that the novel had tentatively, fleetingly raised. In effect, the novel invokes what we might call the specter of solidarity—a version of what Tillie Olsen refers to as "the not yet in the now," the ghost of a hope that these characters could find common cause despite (and to some extent because of) their differences—only to underscore the social and political impediments to cross-cultural identification and mutual aid.[34] The resulting disaster is comprehensive: Claude and the other Haitians except Vanise drown; Vanise survives, but at the cost of her soul, which the loa Agwé takes to protect her drowning infant; and Bob is killed by robbers in Miami who steal the money he had tried to return to Vanise. Whatever counterhegemonic potentialities are raised in the scene of oceanic encounter are shattered; solidarity proves impossible, a distant, fleeting, doomed prospect.

The scene on the boat deserves close attention, and one of the most disturbing elements is the role that Tyrone plays in the incident. Tyrone is an itinerant figure, another of the novel's roving, unsettled laborers, who, like the novel's core characters, is chasing the fantasy of American promise (as a boy, "his head [was] full of dreams of someday going to America and becoming a millionaire" (319)). Born in Jamaica, Tyrone worked as a teenager in "a migrant work camp in the cane fields west of Miami," which he fled and "drifted across the Everglades and down the Keys, putting to good use everything he'd learned as a boy working for white American yachtsmen back in Port Antonio" (246). Having spent his adult life crewing for charter boats on the Keys, Tyrone has knowledge of the area's currents and fish that are essential to Bob and Avery, and their dependence on him "gives Tyrone power in a world in which he is otherwise powerless" (246). The novel recognizes Tyrone's tenuous economic and social position as an undocumented, Black immigrant working for whites, and underscores the prejudicial treatment he receives from Bob's clients, who call him a "n——r" behind his back. Yet his relations with the Haitians, and his knowledge of Creole, do not create grounds for an alliance; the novel foregrounds the fact that it is Tyrone who "is bodily hurling the Haitians into the sea, one after the other," as the Coast Guard approaches and Bob looks on in horror (353). Bob may have felt some stirring of connection with refugees, but Tyrone, whose own status as a Caribbean migrant struggling to stay afloat in a world controlled by wealthier whites is similar to the Haitians, seems unmoved by their plight, and he shows no hint of solidarity with, or even pity for, them. The cruel irony of race, the novel suggests, is that while it organizes relations of exploitation, it does not in turn provide a reliable basis for collective action among racially subjugated characters. Race seems to be both too much and too little, durable and powerful as an axis of subordination, yet in this case too thin as a political or social category to establish bonds of collective resistance among subordinated persons.

Class, which the novel suggests is inseparable from race, has a similar status. Working-classness is not a stable, organic identity waiting to be embraced, the expression of a determinate economic status or condition. Rather, class is rendered here as a fluid, deeply uncertain relation, a vexing process of struggle, conflict, misidentification. The novel suggests that class is crucial to contemporary social life in the trans-American landscape: Bob, Vanise, and Claude are connected by their shared, yet differentiated, position as exploited laborers in a global system of capital accumulation. Yet class in the novel is also an unreliable and undeveloped form of affiliation and collectivity. Common conditions, similar circumstances, analogous desires may create a nascent basis for collectivity, but whether such conditions create a sense of shared commitment and identity is a matter of history and politics, not ontology. *Continental Drift* suggests that from a planetary perspective the millions, even billions, of migrating poor and working people circling the globe form a common flow; more specifically, it suggests that the fates of Bob and Vanise and Claude are linked in material, historical, perhaps even metaphysical, ways. Yet the characters (and the narrator) are unable to fully grasp or articulate the ties that link them. Class is here visible negatively, through the absence or impossibility of solidarity.

The moment and idea toward which the novel turns, both in content and form, is the intersection of Bob, Vanise, and Claude on the midocean boat, and the suggestion that their fates are intertwined. But how are we to theorize this? On one level, I have been suggesting, the novel insists that their relation is a class relation, a product of their adjacent, if deeply differentiated, positions in a hemispheric, indeed global, economic system. Yet as much as the novel stresses the importance of economic structures in bringing the three characters together, it also suggests that class, as a form of collective identification, common cause, and intersubjective understanding, fails. Class, the novel suggests, is simultaneously indispensable and inadequate.[35] If we are to imagine Bob, Claude, and Vanise as members of the same class, as the novel encourages us to do, we need to think beyond categorical oppositions often used to conceptualize working-class labor and collectivity (formal/informal, industrial/peasant, unity/division); indeed, we need to overhaul and revise the concept itself. As a term that speaks to the position of human subjects under the regime of an expanding global capitalist system, class is crucial. At the same time, the novel suggests we need to understand class in a way that undercuts or clears away many of the accumulated connotations embedded in the term.

One frame for understanding the presence of class as a category of social, economic, and subjective organization in this scene, and in *Continental Drift* more generally, is Jean-Paul Sartre's notion of seriality, adapted via the work of Iris Marion Young and Sonya Rose. Seriality denotes a loose or passive form of social collectivity that does not rise to the level of self-conscious identity that marks what Sartre calls a group, which is united by a common project and shared commitments. Unlike a group, a series refers to a social collective whose members are placed in shared circumstances by historically sedimented material objects and social forces, which Sartre calls the "practico-inert reality," or "milieu of action." A series is not an identity, but a more open configuration; membership in a series is defined not by one's being, but by the fact that one's "diverse existences and actions are oriented" around a common set of forces and structures.[36] Sartre contends that class as a series constitutes a "unity ... which is ever present but always elsewhere."[37] In response to changing conditions, a series may become animated by a common project and unified by a set of collective aims, but it would then be a group, an integrated collective in which members adopt deliberate membership. "There is *identity*," Sartre explains, "when the *common* interest ... is made manifest, and when the plurality is defined just *in relation to this interest*."[38] The shared conditions that create serial relations establish a "complex of possibilities"; group unity, or identity, is created out of these possibilities only through "praxis."[39] Seriality is an experience of being with others in isolation that comes *before* identity.

Seriality is helpful for reading the scene on the boat because it is a relation defined by a tension between commonality and separation. Indeed, seriality refers to the loose and unstable, even unconscious, unity of a collective that is felt largely through isolation. As opposed to the group, seriality is "a plurality of isolations" that demonstrates "the impossibility of uniting with Others in an organic totality."[40] As a serial relation, Sartre explains, class is an "indefinite series" that can expand to include all waged, and indeed unwaged, laborers.[41] The conditions of wage labor, specifically the necessity of participating in the competitive labor market, have a paradoxical effect on workers, uniting them in competition with one another. Members of a class, Young notes, encounter one another as "alienated others," paradoxically separated from one another by many of the material objects, structures, and relations that shape class existence.[42] Sartre puts it this way: "[T]he existence of a labour market create[s] a link of *antagonistic reciprocity* between workers."[43] The idea of "antagonistic reciprocity" approaches the thorny, uneven, anxiety-ridden interdependence that Bob and Vanise and Claude seem to experience. Elsewhere, in a turn of phrase especially fitting for the scene on the boat, Sartre refers to seriality as "the unity of a flight."[44] Young describes it as "a collective gathering that slips away at the edges, whose qualities are impossible to pin down because they are an inert result of the confluence of actions."[45] Rose notes that Sartre's ideas about class "do not presume that one level of practice leads to another in any simple way or in any predefined narrative of class development."[46]

As a concept, seriality allows for the notion that individuals may belong to, or participate in, several series simultaneously. Multiple series may overlap or contradict one another, creating layered or conflicting lines of social allegiance and possibility. As *Continental Drift* implies, the flows that bring Bob and Vanise and Claude into proximity are not only economic. Indeed, their interconnection is, at the deepest historical level, a product of the histories and ongoing processes of imperialism and colonialism: the French conquest of North America and the Caribbean (Bob's French-Canadian roots and Vanise and Claude's Haitian origins represent another form of differential commonality, or "antagonistic reciprocity," that they share). In *Prisoners of the American Dream*, Davis argues that given the endemic, enduring, and damaging history of race in the United States, and the production of national unity through racialized warfare and conquest, working-class and Left movements can only succeed to the extent that they confront American empire. "It is a central thesis of this book," Davis asserted, "that the future of the Left in the United States is more than ever bound up with its ability to organize solidarity with revolutionary struggles against American imperialism."[47] Capitalism—especially in its imperial mode—thrives not by creating a smooth social and economic landscape, or homogeneous class subjects, but rather through differentiation and the proliferation of boundaries and divisions.[48] *Continental Drift* suggests that in this global world, class is forged at borders and in border zones shaped by colonial and imperial histories, politics, and processes.[49]

How are we to understand the novel's simultaneous adoption of a transnational, working-class perspective and its pessimism about the possibilities for hemispheric proletarian solidarity? In significant measure, the novel's insights and limitations register the imaginary climate of the Reagan era in which it was produced. During the early 1980s, when Banks was writing the novel, the reality of postindustrialization, outsourcing, and manufacturing competition with other capital-intensive economies, most notably Japan, fostered a new awareness in the United States of the international context of labor and production. The increasing interdependency of world economics became palpable in a new way in everyday life, and the term "globalization" was coined. In a sense, in this period the transnational dimensions of working-class life, and links between working people in the United States and other nations, were more legible than they had been before. At the same time, Reagan led an aggressive assault on unions and working people, most famously in his mass firing of air traffic controllers in 1981, even as workers' electoral support helped propel him to power. Reagan responded to the growing realities of global interdependency and economic competition with a reinvigorated national exceptionalism, the assertion of ostensibly pure and essential "American" values to combat the presumed threats from abroad, whether those threats were perceived to be Soviet totalitarianism, Japanese automakers, or Central American or Haitian refugees, whom Reagan's administration treated with great prejudice, and in whose home countries his administration intervened vigorously. In sum, it was a moment when the rise of a global, postindustrial economy became visible, yet when the political fates of working people in the United States, and across Central America and the Caribbean, were under new forms of political and economic pressure. *Continental Drift*'s conflicted mixture of ideological elements echoes, even as the novel tries to push beyond, the period's prevailing socio- and geopolitical parameters.

Continental Drift offers bold rebukes to several of the ideological shibboleths that prevailed at the moment of its publication: binding Haitian and American characters in a single story, the novel challenges the period's rejuvenated Cold War American exceptionalism, insisting on the history and contemporary force of colonialism; tracing the hemispheric structure of uneven development, it indicts multinational capitalism's penchant to produce poverty on a continental scale; making the specter of slavery and the problematics of race central to the politics of the white North American working class, it undermines the presumed innocence of whiteness; foregrounding the struggles of working people, it offers a deep critique of the American Dream and the ideologies of acquisitive individualism that dominated the Reagan-led "me" decade of the 1980s. Yet both the novel's critique of prevailing ideological narratives and its aesthetic form are profoundly uneven. Its narrative structure grants substantially more ink to Bob than to Vanise and Claude, and while it affords readers a fine-grained view of events from his perspective, it only allows us to see the Haitians' lives from outside. Although the novel offers a searing account of the abuse the Haitians suffer and the courage they show, and lends them a moral legitimacy in the text that Bob lacks, it does not provide a view of the final encounter on the boat through the Haitians' eyes; we have a sense of what Bob thinks about Claude, but not what Claude or Vanise think about him. Similarly, while the novel underscores Tyrone's status as an especially vulnerable member of the transnational proletariat, it also insists that he, rather than Bob, forces the Haitians into the ocean, even as it refuses to fully explain his mindset and motives. These lacunae, or imaginary limitations, represent the novel's conceptual boundaries, the horizon beyond which it seems unable to imagine its story. As a work of precarious realism, this is a novel about varied, interrelated, and at times quite violent forms of economic, social, and physical precarity under late, neocolonial capitalism; it is also a text the very literary structure of which is precarious: uneven, multiplicitous (vernacular realism crosscut by myth and magical realism), marked by contradictory, unresolved perspectives.

In his descriptions of cognitive mapping, Jameson acknowledges that a comprehensive or fully accurate tracing of the contemporary world's social totality is ultimately unachievable. Cognitive mapping's attempts to traverse the "gap," or "rift," between knowledge of the world system and its representation are always in some measure unfulfilled.[50] Furthermore, mapping is a process rather than a product; it produces narratives, rather than static images, that forge connections between seemingly disarticulated realities in an effort to imagine the relation between individual subjectivities and the "ensemble of society's structures as whole."[51] Banks's novel likewise questions the validity of fixed maps, underscoring that they are often faulty or false. At one point, the novel offers a diagram of Vanise's imagined map of her trip, which is inaccurate, based on her belief that the Florida coast is much closer to Haiti than it actually is. Yet as she moves, her map shifts: "her map is a living, coiling and uncoiling thing, moving in undulant waves before her the way a manta ray sweeps the bottom of the sea. Her map is a process, the kind of map you must keep moving into, if you want to read it."[52] Like Vanise's fluid understanding of her own location, the novel itself is not a fixed map, but a mapping, an unfolding, finally unfinished and unevenly rendered story organized around the explosive encounter of characters from radically different sectors of American geopolitical terrain whose understanding of their own locations in the world cultural system are in continual flux. As noted earlier, Jameson contends that cognitive mapping "involves our insertion as individual subjects into a multidimensional set of radically discontinuous realities"; *Continental Drift*'s intersecting and at times conflicting cartographies and narrative threads—centered on uncertain migrations across a transnational social space striated by brutally violent forms of economic, racial, and political power—provide a tentative, if resoundingly incomplete, mapping of the larger social and economic forces buffeting the book's cast of migrants as they skitter across the landscape of late 1970s America. All novels, all representations, all exercises in cognitive mapping fail. Yet their failures illuminate the ways in which a culture's prevailing ideologies mark a text, even one that boldly brushes accepted ideas against the grain, opening space to consider new, as yet unrealized forms of social being, seeing, and relating.

2 • "Maps of Labor"

Globalization, Migration, and Contemporary Working-Class Literature

Manzanar Murakami, one of the seven protagonists of Karen Tei Yamashita's cacophonous, apocalyptic novel about Los Angeles, *Tropic of Orange* (1997), conducts symphonies of traffic from a freeway overpass. Standing with a baton in hand above Route 110, the city's primary transportation artery, Murakami imagines a range of ways "the great flow of humanity [that] ran below his feet in every direction" might be mapped.[1] One of these is what the narrator calls "his map of labor" (237) traced by following the patterns of people commuting to work, "divvying themselves up into the garment district, the entertainment industry, the tourist business, the military machine, the service sector, the automotive industry, the education industry, federal, county, and city employees, union workers, domestics, and day labor. It was work that defined each person in the city, despite the fact that almost everyone wanted to be defined by their leisure" (238). The city's vast swirl of morning motion, Murakami realizes, is animated and organized by labor, filtering people into the industries and economies that structure the vast metropolis.

This chapter examines three novels—Helena María Viramontes's *Under the Feet of Jesus* (1995), Francisco Goldman's *The Ordinary Seaman* (1997), and *Tropic of Orange*—that map U.S. and hemispheric labor, foregrounding the struggles of working, unemployed, and poor people in a society in which "almost everyone want[s] to be defined by their leisure," as Yamashita puts it. More specifically, these novels generate imaginary, cognitive cartographies of American border zones through stories of migrants living and laboring on the bottom layers of the economic hierarchy: seasonal farm workers, stateless sailors, immigrant janitors, and unhoused and unemployed persons. Published during the mid-1990s, when the contemporary age of neoliberal globalization was accelerating—and being widely celebrated in mainstream political discourse—all three novels highlight the flow of migrants and migrant cultures across and within U.S. national borders. Yet in addition to being works of hemispheric literature, written at the crossroads of Latin and North America (and in the case of *Tropic of Orange*, the Pacific as well), they are also working-class texts, oriented toward the precarity of labor and laboring peoples, inside and outside the formal economy, struggling to scrape by on the underside of an evolving post-Fordist system of multinational capitalism. While these texts possess resonant differences of story, form, and politics, they also share some key commonalities: all three texts prioritize the stories of "new" immigrants from Latin America and/or Asia; all three foreground the manner in which race and citizenship status shape working-class existence; and all three highlight the creative, if often provisional, ways that transnational migrants resist, refuse, and challenge economic injustice as well as the ideologies of national exceptionalism, white supremacy, and market freedom that prevail in North America's late capitalist society. All three novels are about the Global South in the Global North, about Latin American and Asian immigrants in the United States, about the reliance of the North American economy on the exploited labor of migrant workers. They are stories of violence and abuse in which colonial and neocolonial relations between the United States and its Latin American neighbors are played out in the fields of California, on a ship docked in Brooklyn, and in Los Angeles, where, in Yamashita's novel, a mystical figure representing downtrodden and dispossessed citizens from across the Americas emerges to challenge the forces of U.S. capitalist hegemony in a magical realist wrestling match.

This chapter makes several interlocking arguments about these texts and the broader tradition of trans-American migration fiction to which they belong. First, I argue that migration narratives have become a primary genre of working-class literature in the emergent post-Fordist era, much as the proletarian bildungsroman, which traced the emergence of the young artist as worker and revolutionary, was for the CIO working class during the era of the cultural front.[2] Many of the proletarian novels penned during the Depression about young working-class people coming of age—Jack Conroy's *The Disinherited*, Richard Wright's *American Hunger*, Tillie Olsen's *Yonnondio*, Meridel LeSueur's *The Girl*, and Carlos Bulosan's *America Is in the Heart*, among others—were also stories of wandering and migration, of workers adrift in search of work. Indeed, Michael Denning argues that the migrant narrative, represented most famously by *The Grapes of Wrath*, was "one of the forms that 'proletarian literature' took in the United States."[3] The three texts I examine here extend this tradition, adopting it for the age of late capitalist globalization, in which the migrations are increasingly international and in which the condition of many migrants, moving into or through the United States, often without official citizenship status, is marked by a political precariousness that did not obtain in most of the stories of migration from the 1930s. These are stories of precarious-labor-in-motion: narratives of working people engaged in informal, contingent, unpaid, or forced work, who lack secure political and social standing, traveling across spatial, geopolitical, and social borders. As such, these texts return to a more originary definition of the proletariat, which referred not to the mass industrial worker or the wage laborer, but, derived from the Roman legal term for the lowest class of citizens, *proles*, those without reserves, those who had been expropriated and cast off the land, and whose only recourse was to seek out whatever labor and compensation they could find. As stories of labor, they defy the image of stable industrial work, instead featuring figures in search of work, or working outside the formal labor market, scrambling, struggling, hustling to get by. Together, these novels chart an expansive, unorthodox vision of the working class, centering on racialized workers whose labor is tenuous, unregulated, or coerced, and whose social and political status makes them vulnerable to varied forms of extreme exploitation, including laboring under threat of imminent, arbitrary death.

Second, these texts confirm that in the contemporary era of flexible accumulation, struggles over class and labor manifest in socially, politically, and aesthetically heterogeneous ways, and that narratives about class and labor often look quite different than they did in the long Fordist era, when industrial manufacturing performed by white men served as the normative image of work in the United States.[4] Indeed, in the present economic and literary conjuncture, much of what is typically considered multicultural and ethnic literature is *also* working-class literature, dedicated to narrating the struggles of America's most vulnerable laborers to carve out a living and shape the world in which they live. Walter Benn Michaels has argued that contemporary American novels tend to displace attention to class conflict in favor of ethnic and racial identity. No move is more characteristic of what Michaels calls the neoliberal novel than the "substitution of cultural difference for ... class difference."[5] These three novels, in suggesting that stories of racially subordinated and ethnically marked peoples in the United States *are also* often stories of working-class struggle and formation, constitute a countertradition to the line of neoliberal novels that Michaels describes. In these texts, economic, racial, ethnic, and colonial systems prove inextricable and interdependent. These texts suggest that in the contemporary era, when the industrial forms and images of working-class life and labor that prevailed in the

United States since at least the 1930s have been largely dismantled, class often defies our expectations. The working class—increasingly made up of a heterogeneous population laboring in low-wage, no benefit, contingent, service-sector jobs—doesn't look the way it did in an earlier era, when a white man laboring on an assembly line was the iconic image of labor, and class as a salient cultural category doesn't seem to have the solidity, stability, or currency it did in a putatively less fluid, flexible age. On the one hand, the novels examined here echo this uncertainty: class does *not* constitute a self-evident or stable category of identity, something around which characters can gather or even join forces and fight. If these are stories of coming to class consciousness—and to some extent, as I argue below, they are—that consciousness does not produce strikes or organized resistance to the forces of economic dominance and does not take precedence or priority over other axes of cultural and social identification and struggle. Yet at the same time, while the question of whether and how class may serve as a collective form of identification for working people remains open, these novels are deeply and persistently focused on economic structures and processes; they foreground the perspectives and experiences of low-wage laborers, struggling against economic exploitation, racial injustice, and immigration policies that cast them in highly vulnerable social positions. These texts locate capitalist production and exploitation at the heart of contemporary global society, yet they also suggest that countercapitalist ideas and movements will have to account for the complexities of "living labor"—the irreducible heterogeneity of laboring populations and positions, waged and unwaged, citizen and noncitizen. These novels are highly critical of contemporary capitalism, and they try to delineate—in fragile, embryonic forms—modes of knowledge, social relation, and collective belonging that could, if elaborated more fully, constitute alternative structures of feeling, being, and relating.

In focusing on working people and labor exploitation, these novels register the growing militancy on the part of many workers during the early and mid-1990s, when—in the midst of a decades-long decline in labor movement power—a series of strikes and other labor mobilizations spread around the globe. Indeed, the 1990s saw a spike in labor unrest across continents as workers reacted against the rise in job insecurity, the stagnation of wages, and the undermining of social welfare protections that unions in the Global North had won in earlier decades. In the United States, the Clinton administration was greasing the wheels of globalization, steering the Democratic Party, and the nation, along neoliberal policy lines by deregulating the finance industry, signing NAFTA, and dismantling welfare. But after the defeats and relative quiescence of the 1980s, labor in the 1990s fought back in a widespread series of job actions across Europe, South America, Asia, and the United States. As labor journalist Kim Moody explains,

> Strikes and struggles from Staley [a large corn-processing plant in Decatur, Illinois] to the Detroit News Agency, from Yale to casualized or contract jobs in Los Angeles' construction, building, service and waterfront trucking industries had all made America a war zone by the mid-1990s in the minds of millions of working-class people, whose lives and futures seemed more and more impossible ... words like 'working-class' and 'class war' were back in the American vocabulary by the mid-1990s.[6]

Although only one of the three novels discussed below—*Tropic of Orange*—culminates in a scene of class warfare, all three novels can fruitfully be read in part as responses to the upsurge of anger and action in working-class communities across the Americas against the ascendant neoliberal regime.

Third, in focusing on the plight of proletarianized migrants and their labors, these narratives complicate and challenge key suppositions of conventional transnational and hemispheric literary studies, which are often organized around notions of fluidity and mobility and often offer salutary readings of the ostensible demise of borders and boundaries.[7] For instance, in her study of American culture through a hemispheric lens, Rachel Adams reads the continent in a way that complicates established geopolitical boundaries. The continent, she argues, is best seen as a "heuristic frame designed to enable comparative perspectives and to bring into view alternative histories and cultural formations that might be obscured by an exclusive emphasis on the nation-state, or by too-close attention to any one region. These alternatives become apparent only by approaching North America as a shifting geographical assemblage with multiple vectors extending outward across the globe."[8] This is a nuanced and persuasive claim, but one that the novels examined below suggest inadequately attends to the deeply asymmetrical lines of geopolitical, economic, and racial power that shape the continent's cultural and social terrain. These texts underscore not only the motility and flexibility of lives and ideas moving across national and cultural borders, but also the trenchant material limitations, coercions, and restrictions under which many migrants live and labor. More than merely exposing the transnational fluidity of cultural traditions, these novels attend to the hard labor and the systemic, economic, and political inequalities that shape the flow of global circulations.[9]

At the level of literary form, these novels encode the dynamics of division, collision, and conflict in a variety of ways. All of them foreground multiple languages, raising translation not only as a necessary literary act, but also as a metaphor for the process of class formation in the context of global cultural gaps. Like translation, class formation is figured as a process of navigating commonalities and incommensurabilities, of extending and proliferating meanings across borders while also underscoring the inevitable limitations of that endeavor. Each text makes these dynamics of connection and fracture visible formally in different ways, as they take up tactics associated with literary postmodernism to varied ends. In particular, all three blend elements of social realism, traditionally associated with the proletarian literary tradition, with other literary modes, including magical realism and epic poetry (*Tropic of Orange*), pastoralism (*Under the Feet of Jesus*), and maritime adventure (*The Ordinary Seaman*). Each novel constitutes a literary assemblage, a tale about the intersecting dynamics of ethnicity, race, and labor that is itself, at the level of literary style and form, manifold and uneven. As narratives that blend forms of critical, social realism from the long proletarian tradition with other modes of late-modern literary experimentalism to focus on precarious labor and the political, social, and civic precarity of migrant workers, nonworkers, and the poor, these books represent examples of what I am calling precarious realism.

"It was always a question of work": *Under the Feet of Jesus*

Under the Feet of Jesus narrates the story of Estrella, a fifteen-year-old farmworker following the harvest with her three younger siblings, her mother Petra, and her seventy-three-year-old stepfather, Perfecto, whom Petra married after she was abandoned by Estrella's father several years before. Shortly after her family arrives on a fruit farm, Estrella develops a friendship, and eventually a romance, with Alejo, a sixteen-year-old migrant worker traveling with his cousin Gumecindo. While sneaking peaches from the orchards one evening, Alejo is sprayed with toxic pesticides and eventually becomes extremely ill. He has no parents to care for him, and Petra agrees to take him in and nurse him. When the family finally drives him to a medical clinic, the white nurse on duty charges them nine dollars to examine him, only to tell them that he needs to go to the local hospital for care. Outraged, and knowing her family needs the nine dollars for gas, Estrella threatens the nurse with a crowbar and reclaims the money, and the family transports Alejo to a hospital, presumably to die.

Viramontes's novel is, as critics have observed, a feminist, Chicanx novel about environmental racism.[10] It is also a searing, lyrical tale about work and workers.[11] In fact, I contend, it is a latter-day proletarian novel that evokes and rewrites earlier novels about migratory laborers, including Tillie Olsen's *Yonnondio* (1932–36/1974), which follows the young daughter in a destitute family on the move for work; John Steinbeck's *The Grapes of Wrath* (1939), which narrates the journey of the Joad family from Oklahoma to the fields and orchards of California's Central Valley; Carlos Bulosan's *America Is in the Heart* (1946), which centers on a young Filipino migrant working in farms along the West Coast; and *. . . y no se lo tragó la tierra / . . . And the Earth Did Not Devour Him* (1971), Tomás Rivera's episodic novel about Chicanx farm workers. While my focus is on labor, the deeply exploitative conditions under which the protagonists of Viramontes's novel work are not only a matter of economics, but also a function of racial and gender stratification, as the text makes clear. In what follows, I examine the novel's labor-based epistemology, its suggestion that work is a cognitive, political, and literary lens for imagining and understanding the text's protagonists, their struggles, and the possibilities for their liberation.

Viramontes has described herself as a social realist, and her novel emphasizes the perilousness of lives on the edge of destitution, stressing the links between migration, work, poverty, and hunger. Living under transient conditions shaped by hard labor and economic desperation, these workers travel in what Saskia Sassen calls "survival circuits," routes of desperation and subsistence running along the underside of economic well-being.[12] In the opening pages, the novel underlines the way in which labor shapes their lives, molding the very meanings they assign to the world and their existence: "The silence and the barn and the clouds meant many things. It was always a question of work, and work depended on the harvest, the car running, their health, the conditions of the road, how long the money held out, and the weather, which meant they could depend on nothing."[13] There is an almost tautological quality to these migratory lives, which are organized around finding work ("It was always a question of work"), which itself is contingent on several other unpredictable and volatile factors. To be migrant workers, the novel suggests, is thus to rely on what is utterly unreliable, to be in an ongoing state of economic, social, physical, epistemological insecurity.

The attention that *Under the Feet of Jesus* gives to physical labor marks it as an exception to much contemporary American literature. "Morning, noon or night," Estrella thinks to herself as she fills a basket of grapes, "four or fourteen or forty it was all the same" (53). In its description of Estrella picking grapes, the novel deconstructs the consumer-friendly version of farm work that shoppers find depicted on iconic images like the label of the Sun Maid raisin box: "Carrying the full basket was not like the picture on the red raisin boxes Estrella saw in the markets, not like the woman wearing a fluffy bonnet, holding out the grapes with her smiling, ruby lips, the sun a flat orange behind her. The sun was white and it make Estrella's eyes sting like an onion, and the baskets of grapes resisted her muscles, pulling their magnetic weight back to the earth" (49–50). Like Esther Hernandez's 1981 *detournement* of the Sun Maid raisin logo as Sun *Mad* Raisins—"unnaturally grown with pesticides, miticides, herbicides, and fungicides," and featuring a skeleton in place of the smiling white woman on the original box—Viramontes's text cuts through commodity fetishism, exposing the way in which advertisements efface the hard, at times deadly labor required to bring commodities to market. Indeed, this work demands painful measures of exertion, which the text details. Carrying a full basket of grapes, the "muscles of [Estrella's] back coiled like barbed wire and clawed against whatever movement she made" (53). The description of the pain she experiences indicates that labor, like barbed wire and a clawed animal, confines and wounds; migrant field work is coercive, violent, debilitating, and carried out under conditions in which "every job is not enough wage" (14).

The most piercing example of labor's dangers is Alejo's likely death by pesticide poisoning, around which the plot revolves. When the pesticide rains down on him from the crop duster, Viramontes delineates the way the toxic chemicals puncture his body: "a hole ripped in his stomach like a match to paper, spreading into a deeper and bigger black hole that wanted to swallow him completely" (77). While Estrella feels that she is being undone by her labors, Alejo here feels as if he is being set ablaze; physical labor performed under these conditions, the novel suggests, is a form of violence with great risks to individual health and bodily integrity. In the California fields, living labor is converted to dead labor, both metaphorically, as it is extracted and congealed in capitalist value, and literally, as workers' health is sacrificed for profit.[14]

Elsewhere, the novel highlights the persistent, if at times subtle, brutality of everyday life for migrant laborers, who are treated as interchangeable and expendable instruments of production. Workers in the back of a truck are compared to "loose change in a pocket" (67), an apt metaphor for individuals who are paid a pittance for long hours of physical labor in the harsh California sun. Arriving in the field for a day's work, "the piscadores were herded out of the corralled flatbed" like cattle (67). A "drowned, bloated dog" floating in a canal serves as a metaphor for farm workers who are treated as disposable and who risk their lives to bring produce to gleaming corporate supermarkets. The rich metaphoricity of Viramontes's descriptions of the precariousness and hardship of migrant existence lends aesthetic power to lives that are treated with calculated indifference by employers and the society at large. The lyricism of her prose, which cuts against the social realist grain of much of the text, counters the degradation the migrants suffer by endowing their struggles with a literary beauty and significance that is denied by their employers and the dominant culture of the United States.

The text places special emphasis on the double labors, and particular vulnerabilities, of migrant women, blending a Chicanx feminist focus on the burdens and creative capacities of "Third World" women with a labor-based attention to physical work, both paid and unpaid. In its focus on the labors of children and mothers, both productive and reproductive, the novel expands the very definition of "worker." Estrella remembers accompanying her mother to the fields at the age of four; although pregnant, Petra "hauled pounds and pounds of cotton by the pull of her back" (51), eventually laying an exhausted Estrella on top of her cotton sack "as she dragged the bag slowly between the rows of cotton plants" (52). Viramontes provides delicate, detailed descriptions of Petra washing clothes with soap made from ground yucca, "her knuckles raw white ... against coffee skin" (61), and making tortillas, which she could do "in the dark, ill or healthy, near some trees, by a road, on a door made into a table or while birds flew past her with twigs between their beaks because tortillas filled her children's stomachs and made their stomachs hungry for more" (120). Much like the metaphoric renderings of migrant travails, these passages counteract the devaluation of women's work in patriarchal society. Although the novel foregrounds the fields and farm work as the primary sites of harm and struggle, *Under the Feet of Jesus* is also a testament to the intelligence, skill, and strength of Petra and other migrant women, whose labors both in and outside the fields are essential to social reproduction and, Viramontes's attentive renderings suggest, possess a beauty and power that deserves our attention.

To live as a migrant—even migrants like Estrella and her family, who have citizenship or legal residence—is to be rendered criminal, outside and in violation of the law, which the novel suggests serves to protect dominant interests and efface the traces of labor and the presence of laboring people from national consciousness.[15] "Perfecto," the narrator explains, "lived a travesty of laws. He knew nothing of their source but it seemed his very existence contradicted the laws of others, so that everything he did like eat and sleep and work and love was prohibited" (83). Rather than serving as a source of protection, the state reinforces the social marginality of these vulnerable workers who find themselves fearing the federal agents, which their citizenship status in fact gives them no reason to fear. Perfecto, Estrella, and other migrants in the book are thus part of a transborder population of field workers that Mae Ngai describes as "a Mexican migratory agricultural proletariat, a racialized, transnational workforce comprising various legal status categories across the U.S.-Mexico boundary—Mexican Americans, legal immigrants, undocumented migrants, and imported contract workers (braceros)."[16] As a whole, this transnational workforce, Ngai asserts, has "remained external to definitions of the American working class and national body," even though their labors have driven a major sector of the U.S. economy.[17] Viramontes's novel, like Yamashita's, which I discuss below, aims to rewrite the proletarian novel to foreground these migrant workers and the questions of civic belonging that their status raises.

But *Under the Feet of Jesus* is not only a record of displacement, discrimination, and exploitation; it does more than "map a geography of oppression within the gendered, racialized spaces of a capitalist system."[18] The novel also traces the fragile forms of shared imagination and solidarity that the migrants create to endure and in some vital measure resist the colonial, racial capitalist system within which they are caught. Viramontes's novel is thus both a critical, realist text dedicated to narrating the injuries and injustices migrant farm workers suffer *and* an experimental novel of working-class consciousness that outlines the incipient, emergent forms of knowledge, beauty, and togetherness with which its migrant protagonists respond to the often oppressive circumstances they face. More specifically, the novel outlines two crucial ideological and ethical counterpoints to the systemic forces of labor, racial, and gender domination that govern much of the migrants' lives. While lacking the power to challenge the oppressive forces arrayed against the migrants, these alternative epistemologies constitute immanent potentialities, kernels of what might become larger, oppositional ideas and practices.

The first of these counterpoints is a planetary labor citizenship that contradicts the political disenfranchisement and sense of criminality that is imposed on the novels' migrant farm workers. When Petra tells Estrella how to respond if she is stopped by immigration officers, she insists, "Don't run scared. You stay there and look them in the eye. Don't let them make you feel you did a crime for picking the vegetables they'll be eating for dinner. If they stop you, if they try to tell you to pull into the green vans, you tell them the birth certificates are under the feet of Jesus, just tell them" (63). While reminding Estrella that she is a U.S. citizen by virtue of her nativity and thus has no legal reason to fear La Migra, Petra also makes a secondary, and more elemental, claim to political status based on the labor that the members of family have performed, harvesting the food that the officers—and millions of others in the United States and around the world—take for granted. Indeed, regardless of national origin, the piscadores have a sense of belonging based on their work in the fields, their cultivation of the earth: "You are not an orphan, and [Petra] pointed a red finger to the earth, Aqui" (63). Migrants may be treated as criminals, intimidated and threatened by the border police, but Petra insists that among these migrant workers, there are no "illegals"; the labor they perform gives them social and political validity as well as ties to the earth that supersede the claims of a particular nation. It is important to stress that this labor-based claim is *also* an anticolonial, Chicanx claim to belonging; Petra's assertion carries an implicit claim that she and her children cannot be "illegal" on land inhabited by Indigenous and Mexican peoples long before it was expropriated by the United States after the U.S.-Mexico War (an event alluded to in Alejo's surname, Hidalgo, which references the Treaty of Guadalupe Hildago). Ethnicity and labor converge here, as Petra articulates a form of belonging that blends transnational, Chicanx claims to the land of the Southwest with claims based on the significance of the labor performed by farm workers to the economy of the very nation that threatens to expel them. This is another dimension of "living labor," not only recognition that labor makes possible the lives of others (in this case, through the food consumers eat), but also that labor itself justifies life beyond the claims of any geopolitical entity.

And in fact, this labor-based, planetary citizenship is part of a more expansive labor-based epistemology, which is captured in the novel's key geological metaphor: the La Brea tar pits. The pits are bubbling pools of tar formed by fossilized animal bones and plant matter that were compressed over millions of years into oil and asphalt. Alejo, who describes the pits to Estrella, imagines himself being swallowed by the tar as he is poisoned by the crop-dusting plane: "He thought first of his feet sinking [. . .] Black bubbles erasing him, Finally the eyes. Blankness. Thousands of bones, the bleached white marrow of bones [. . .] No fingerprint of history, bone. No lava stone. No story or family, bone" (78). For Alejo, the pits signify annihilation and erasure from history, the "bleaching" and disappearance of the Chicanx presence. The images of suffocation and effacement he associates with the pits reflect the concern that his work and his struggles will not be granted the social recognition they deserve. It is a worry that Petra, "who often feared that she would die and no one would know who she was" (166), shares.

For Estrella, however, the geology lesson of the tar pits provides inspiration for subversive action. When the nurse at the medical clinic, who is unable to help Alejo and merely refers him to a local hospital, demands a payment for the appointment that would consume the family's remaining cash, Estrella:

> remembered the tar pits.... How bones made oil and oil made gasoline. The oil was made from their bones, and it was their bones that kept the nurse's car from not halting on some highway somewhere.... It was their bones that kept the air conditioning in the cars humming.... Their bones. Why couldn't the nurse see that? Estrella had figured it out: the nurse owed *them* as much as they owed her. (148)

Through the image of the tar pits, which here serves as a metaphor of primitive accumulation, Estrella understands that society is in fact an extension of the bodies of exploited laborers; civilization is literally founded on the violent appropriation of the bodily skills and energies of working people.[19] Without the labor of farm workers and other dispossessed and exploited working people, society would grind to a halt: cars and air conditioners would not run, fruits and vegetables would not reach kitchen tables. Labor, she realizes, is the living source, what Marx called the creative "fire," that animates and makes possible human community.[20] Turning inside-out the logic of capitalist society—in which the workers who perform the most demanding acts of physical labor are typically accorded the least respect and lowest pay—Estrella realizes that the nurse, and U.S. society as a whole, are in fact indebted to the farm workers. Enraged by the unfairness of their predicament, Estrella uses a crowbar to threaten the nurse and reclaim the money they had paid her, which allows them to buy gas to drive Alejo to the hospital.

As the scene at the clinic suggests, labor for Estrella is more than the work that she and her family perform, more than the object of their migratory journey across California, more than the source of Alejo's toxic contamination; it is a cognitive lens through which she learns to read the social world.[21] The novel references this labor-as-cognition early on. Shortly after Perfecto joined the family, Estrella discovered his toolbox:

> Perfecto Flores taught her the names that went with the tools: a claw hammer, he said with authority, miming its function; screwdrivers . . . crescent wrenches . . . old wood saw, new hacksaw, a sledge hammer, pry bar, chisel, axe, names that gave meanings to the tools. Tools to build, bury, tear down, rearrange and repair.... She lifted the pry bar in her hand, felt the coolness of iron and power of func-

tion, weighed the significance it awarded her, and soon came to understand how essential it was to know these things. This was when she began to read. (26)

Perfecto's naming of the tools and demonstration of their capacities teaches Estrella that labor produces the world. Tools are extensions of the body's power to shape its environment, to "build, bury, tear down, rearrange and repair." To understand these tools is to unlock the power of human beings to shape their futures; it is to learn to read in the most comprehensive sense.

In illustrating both the power of the migrants' labor, as well as their disposability in the eyes of their employers and their vulnerability to death on the job, the novel underscores their status as both living and dead labor. On one hand, the piscadores' labor literally sustains the United States, providing the food the nation consumes and powering and producing the society more generally. On the other hand, their labor figuratively and literally consumes and kills them, crushing their bones, maiming and poisoning their bodies. Exposing the contradiction at the heart of migrant labor, the novel "makes vivid the violence of the value form [under capitalism]," in Dennis López's words, which transforms "concrete, living labor into abstract dead labor."[22]

Having learned to see the world through the lens of labor—through what Janet Zandy calls "an epistemology that comes out of physical work and the use value of tools"—Estrella and other migrants forge forms of mutuality to counter the indifference and violence with which they are treated by capitalist agriculture, the U.S. political system, and American society more generally.[23] Two examples are particularly telling. First, when it becomes evident that Alejo does not have parents or other adults to care for him, Petra insists to Perfecto that they take Alejo in, even though they are living in cramped quarters on the narrowest of economic margins. "If we don't take care of each other, who would take care of us? Petra asked" (96). Perfecto initially objects, but then assents when he grasps how determined Petra is. Perfecto himself then supports Alejo by backing Estrella in her confrontation with the nurse and driving them to the hospital. As they deliver Alejo to the emergency room, Estrella thanks Perfecto and her simple words of gratitude move him: "He had given this country his all, and in this land that used his bones for kindling, in this land that never once said thank you, this young woman who could be his granddaughter had said the words with such honest gratitude, he was struck by how deeply those words touched him" (155). Her simple gesture to acknowledge Perfecto represents a balm, a small yet potent antidote to the disrespect he has suffered for decades. Her words, and Petra's opening of her house to Alejo, are, if not exactly expressions of class consciousness, acknowledgments of labor-inflected solidarity, of a commitment to respect and care for one another as members of a fluid collective of Chicanx workers whose "bones" have been used to fuel the U.S. economy for generations. While these gestures do not facilitate a strike or lead to direct opposition to the forces of capital, they are significant nonetheless as forms of shared feeling, belief, and action that counter the denigration and domination these workers face, engendering what in another context Aiwa Ong describes as "a new sense of self and community."[24]

The novel concludes as Estrella climbs the dilapidated barn that Perfecto was hired to dismantle. Ascending to the peak of the roof, she "remained as immobile as an angel standing on the verge of faith. Like the chiming bells of the great cathedrals, she believed her heart powerful enough to summon home all those who strayed" (176). Here the religious and spiritual iconography—an angel, the bells of a cathedral—strike a transcendental note, as if to suggest that the harm and isolation the migrants suffer could be overcome or resolved, and the exiles brought "home." But the angel stands "on the verge of faith," not quite fully committed to the sacred ideal, and the emphasis on "all those who strayed" reminds us of Alejo, Perfecto, and other Chicanx workers whose lives and (living and dead) labor have been sacrificed to the imperatives of American capitalist production. It is, finally, the enduring tensions between the dynamics of isolation and collectivity, transcendence and materiality, injury and repair that the novel refuses to—indeed cannot—resolve. The images of solidarity, community, and dignity that the novel provides are potent, but fleeting and fragile, incipient sparks rather than fully developed or realized alternatives.

These tensions are woven into the novel's form, which on the one hand echoes the displacements, discrepancies, and disorientations of migrant life. The novel moves back and forth between flashbacks and present time, punctuated by breaks and gaps of indeterminate chronological duration. Refusing a consistent, linear progression, the novel is structured by vignettes and short scenes. The narrative progresses in fits and starts, with detours through the past, and often without clear signposts to indicate the time elapsed between one scene and the next, and at times without clear indications of location. It is purposely disorienting for readers. Yet the novel is cast in a classic five-part, Aristotelian arc, which lends literary gravitas and significance to the story of socially disenfranchised peoples. Furthermore, the novel's lyrical beauty, which stresses the aesthetic force of the migrant's experience, stands as a rejoinder to the contingency, exploitation, and anguish that pervades their lives. Viramontes models her writing on her mother's reproductive labors, a form of work that transformed lack into sustenance.[25] Echoing the dialectical dynamics of fracture and collectivity that are at the heart of both class formation and migrant belonging, the shape and texture of *Under the Feet of Jesus* likewise revolve around a tension between fragmentation and an urge toward an impossible wholeness.

A "fucked up iron pirate ship that's made a bunch of poor men even poorer": *The Ordinary Seaman*

A novel based on actual events, Francisco Goldman's *The Ordinary Seaman* narrates the story of a group of Central American men (nine Hondurans, five Nicaraguans, and one Guatemalan) who are recruited to crew a ship under Panamanian registry, the *Urus*, that is docked in Brooklyn, New York. The ship, however, is not seaworthy: it has no electricity, running water, or plumbing and its engine does not work. Having flown to New York for the job, yet having no legal status on U.S. shores and no way to get home, the crew members are trapped on the dilapidated vessel. They labor futilely for several months without pay to repair the ship under the direction of Elias Tureen and Mark Baker, the Anglo captain and first officer who are also, unbeknownst to the crew, its owners and who purchased the ship in Canada as it was about to be sold for scrap. They plan to use the Central Americans' cheap labor to renovate the freighter before selling it at a sizeable profit. The story is narrated largely from the point of view of two crew members: Bernardo Puyano, the ship's waiter and eldest crew member, and Esteban Gaitan, a nineteen-year-old veteran of a special brigade of the Sandinista army, who accepts the job in an attempt to escape the grief of losing his lover, Marta, in the war in Nicaragua. As the crew members are all but abandoned by the ship's owners, who stop coming to the ship regularly when the restoration proves too difficult, Esteban begins taking nightly journeys onto shore and slowly joins Brooklyn's Latinx community, finding a job at a chair factory, which allows him to buy basic necessities for the starving crew, and falling in love with a Mexican manicurist. In December, six months after arriving in New York, the crew is discovered by a Ship Visitor from a seafarer's charity, who secures funding for crew members to return home, but several follow Esteban, who decides to stay in Brooklyn.

Critics have read *The Ordinary Seaman* as a text about Central Americans in the U.S. Latinx imaginary, about the possibility of panethnic Latinx identity, and as an expression of a utopian temporality at the heart of Latinx studies.[26] Here I want to underscore the novel as a working-class text that explores the dynamics of hemispheric neocolonialism and neoliberal globalization through the lens of labor. A tale of what Michael Templeton calls "United States capital gone rogue" that is told largely from the point of view of Central American migrant workers, Goldman's novel is at once a lyrical story of loss and love, a dark tale of captivity and corruption, a meditation on emergent possibilities of solidarity and community, and a critical realist narrative about the exploitation of migrant workers, as living and dead labor, in the age of late capitalist globalization.[27]

The Ordinary Seaman is a multifaceted text that interweaves several narrative threads, but its central tale concerns Esteban's attempt to "start a new life" (3) in the wake of war and the death of his lover, Marta. As he boards his flight to the United States in Tegucigalpa, however, the novel suggests that his effort to escape the horrors of the country's conflict will not be easy: looking out the plane window, he "saw five green military ambulances parked in a row [. . .] So helicopters and planes were still flying mangled and bullet-punctured bodies in heated, vibrating pools of blood over jungles, mountains, and plains. Despite the cease-fire and all the talk of peace" (7). Esteban has paid the fee for the job and his plane ticket with money borrowed from his uncles, assuming that "After two months on the *Urus*, he'd be able to pay them back and there'd still be four months to go; then he'd be able to sign on for a whole other year, provided his capitàn was happy with his work" (8–9). Work, he hopes, will pave the way for a new life, providing direction, stability, and upward mobility. But after traveling to New York to sail on a ship that cannot sail and which is docked in "a deserted and apparently defunct end of the port" (19), Esteban and the other sailors become trapped on the *Urus*—a ship for which Tureen and Baker, it turns out, never filed proper registration papers.

The seamen thus undertake hard labor for money they are never paid on a ship that proves utterly resistant to repair in a country where they do not have legal status as citizens or guests. The water they drink is poisoned by rat remains and they are brought food only intermittently, leaving them famished and malnourished while the weather turns colder and colder. Under these brutal conditions, none of the crew "is quite the same person he was when he arrived in June, not on the outside and certainly on the inside" (38). When Baker and Tureen realize that the vessel's repair may be beyond the knowledge and resources they have at their disposal, they stop visiting the ship regularly, leaving the crew disoriented and increasingly desperate, as cold weather sets in. With little to do but "dream of previous lives" and recall "imagined and reimagined pleasures" (38), several of the seamen start to inhale paint fumes to numb themselves against the hardship and despair they face. Soon they begin to deteriorate into zombie-like creatures: "sad eyed, shaggy, and dirty as young corpses risen from graves" (46). Karl Marx suggested that the proletariat are the gravediggers of the bourgeoisie, but in Goldman's novel, the workers are the undead: starved, forgotten, left to die, the energy sucked out of them; without rights or security, they are specters of migratory labor's precarious predicament in the world of neoliberal globalization. The crew members become "barely living labor," labor on the edge of bare life, labor subject to death through capitalist value production, which renders living labor "dead" through its transformation into capital, through a form of social death precipitated by the migrants' civic "illegality" in the United States, and through forced exposure to working and living conditions that threaten their very lives.

While, as noted in chapter 1, ships often serve as chronotopes of modernity's motion and opportunity, oceanic metaphors of possibility and progress, the *Urus* is a ship that does not move, a "fathomless expanse of floating iron" (28), "a ghost ship" (107), "a dead ship, a mass of inert iron provocatively shaped like a ship" (38). As Bernardo explains to two people he encounters during his lone sojourn on shore, "I think this ship is in violation of every conceivable maritime law and regulation. The truth is, we're stranded here, as much as any shipwrecked sailors on some remote island" (120). A floating sweatshop, the *Urus* is, in Esteban's words, "a fucked up iron pirate ship that's made a bunch of poor men even poorer" (363). Goldman's novel is thus not only, as Ana Rodríguez asserts, "an allegory of homelessness and abandonment in the (post)modern world";[28] it is also a narrative of extreme exploitation, in which a group of political and economic refugees are forced into virtual slave labor. Goldman's novel grounds itself in the fact that the "advances" of globalization have been perversely facilitated by the proliferation of informal, unwaged, and forced labor.[29] Living and dead labor are intertwined, as the harsh physical work the sailors perform renders them vulnerable to social as well as literal death.

During the steamy summer after the crew arrives, a group of young people from the adjacent neighborhood, referred to by Captain Elias and then the crew as "los blacks," holds impromptu dance parties on the dock next to the ship. The young people are at first unaware that the *Urus* is inhabited, but soon one of them spots the crew members, who had been standing surreptitiously at the edge of the ship's deck in the dark, watching the party. The result is a strange form of rapprochement:

> once they'd been discovered, los blacks grew more and more interested in the crew, actually seeming to absorb the crew's silent, furtive

presence up there on a darkened ship into what they came to the pier to do at night. Almost nightly at least someone took a turn shouting taunts up at them, usually incomprehensibly, though sometimes they understood, "*You fucked you fucked you po mothuhfucks fucked...*," and on and on like a chant. (49)

The crew wonders if the young Black people are insulting them, or perhaps describing—even identifying with—the crew's miserable predicament: "Los blacks seemed to know something about the *Urus*; it was as if they'd somehow figured out what the crew's situation was" (49). Esteban notes that the young partiers seem to find the crew's situation funny, but "it also seems to make them angry. Why?" (50). Recalling the lessons in Marxian theory he had been given by his commander in the Sandinista army, Esteban contends that "los blacks" recognize their own misery in the plight of the stateless crew forced to labor without pay: they are all—young Black Americans and stranded Central American workers—members of what Marx called the lumpenproletariat. "'Vos, son lumpen!' Esteban suddenly exclaimed," adding "Lumpen jodido ... Fucked lumpen, just like us." (51). The novel does not pursue the relation between the teenagers from the poor neighborhoods and housing projects of Brooklyn and the trapped Latinx workers, yet in using the nebulous term "lumpen" as a placeholder for a never-fully-articulated relation between these impoverished Black and Brown peoples, natives and immigrants, the novel suggests they share and recognize affinities based on similar conditions of destitution and despair, of being "fucked," as Esteban puts it, by larger social structures of discrimination and injustice.[30]

The prospect, however faint, of a multiracial, Atlantic lumpenproletariat underscores Goldman's knowledge of the history of seafaring labor and his debts to Herman Melville. In their magisterial history of the working-class Atlantic, Peter Linebaugh and Marcus Rediker argue that during the seventeenth and eighteenth centuries, Atlantic ships and seaports served as sites of transnational working-class intersection, "meeting place[s] where various traditions were jammed together in a forcing house of internationalism."[31] Seaports served as nodes of contact and communication where workers and ideas from around the Atlantic basin mingled and mixed, producing a "multinational, multicultural, and multiracial" proletariat, figured symbolically in the image of the many-headed hydra.[32] Sailors and maritime workers, Linebaugh and Rediker contend, "self-consciously built an autonomous, democratic, egalitarian social order of their own," "a counterculture to the civilization of Atlantic capitalism."[33] Limning these laborers into literature in *Moby-Dick*, Melville depicted the nineteenth-century whaling ship as home to a motley crew of "mariners, renegades, and castaways," as C. L. R. James put it, bonded by their labor, yet misled and manipulated by a monomaniacal captain (a plot that echoes the basic narrative of Goldman's novel). In an ironic twist, of course, the ship in Goldman's sea novel remains moored to the dock until the final scene, when its engine is hotwired by the crew and it lurches forward, only to run aground in the harbor a short distance from the pier. This is a maritime tale about a vessel that never hits the open seas, although unlike the crew of *The Pequod*, all of whom except Ishmael are destroyed in the confrontation with the great white whale, sacrificed to Ahab's myopic desire for revenge, several—although significantly not all—of the men working on the *Urus* eventually escape the ship, finding their way back home or into New York's Latinx diaspora.[34]

Indeed, the story's basic scenario, in which two aspiring entrepreneurs, Mark Baker and Elias Tureen, who met while attending an elite liberal arts college, are able to leverage a modest amount of family money to buy a dilapidated ship and hire fifteen central Americans to repair it, offers an allegorical critique of the inequalities of hemispheric political economics, in which wealthy North Americans exploit impoverished Central American workers fleeing U.S.-funded civil wars in their home countries. On its face, Baker and Tureen's plan is simple: "[g]et one of those cheap flag of convenience registries and incorporations. Import the cheapest possible crew, even have them pay their own airfare. Work night and day, repair the ship fast. . . . Keep expenses to a minimum, pile up debts. And then decide if they want to sell her: should be able to get half a million dollars at least" (276). When it turns out, however, that the two Anglos don't have sufficient knowledge or resources to complete the repair job, it is the workers who pay the heaviest price, toiling under extreme physical and emotional duress for months without any compensation. "One of the great things about sea stories," Goldman notes, "is that they lend themselves to all sorts of metaphorical suggestions." His novel is, he asserts, "an economic fable, a '90s story that happened in the '80s—a businesses-going-to-Honduras-and-opening-sweatshops type of situation."[35] As Goldman suggests, the *Urus* is a (barely) floating sweatshop, and its crew are emblems of the most vulnerable ranks of contemporary workers: undocumented, unpaid, without benefits or rights. The Ship Visitor, who ultimately helps the crew leave the *Urus*, makes clear the relation of the crew to the larger bureaucratic and economic structures of global finance and consumerism. As he explains to his girlfriend, the get-rich-quick scheme that Baker and Tureen are following, which relies on phantom owners and flag of convenience registration to protect the two friends from liability, is enabled by international legal codes and economic inequities that serve the interests of U.S. consumer capitalism. "[We] know [phantom owners] exist because if they didn't," he observes, "and if the flag of convenience ships they own didn't, if cheap Third World crews and low registration, incorporation fees, and tonnage taxes and every other related convenience didn't exist, exports would lag... and imported products would be much more expensive and not so abundant" (136–137).[36]

Rather than stock villains, however, the ship's owners are nuanced characters. Elias Tureen, in particular, is a complex figure. A white liberal who has spent time in Latin America, Tureen is not unsympathetic to the crew. He was raised in Mexico City by an English father and Greek mother, speaks Spanish, has traveled widely in the Amazon basin, often works alongside the crew, and proclaims his opposition to the United States's "illegal war" in Nicaragua (80). But his deception, manipulation, and mistreatment of the seamen repeats rather than reverses the imperialist policies he seems to critique (his role in the novel seems to be to expose the cruelty and hardheartedness that in fact subtends the white North American liberal position). "What did they need cash for in Brooklyn?" Tureen asks himself, trying to justify not paying the crew. "They were illegal once they went off the ship anyway" (68). The apex of Tureen's criminal negligence is his refusal to take Puyano to a hospital after the older man's leg is severely burned in a cooking accident. Puyano's fate—initially left on the ship to suffer because Elias fears that if the old waiter is taken to a hospital, police will discover the illegal arrangement on the *Urus*, and finally brought to the hospital when it is too late to save his life—signifies the way Central Americans are sacrificed for the sake of Anglo American wealth, transformed into dead labor not only through the process of value production, but quite literally through intense exploitation and deliberate neglect.

The neocolonial structures of thought and practice that make possible and shape the two Anglos' exploitative scheme are exposed most clearly in Mark Baker's interior monologue near the end of the novel as the failure of the ship owners' plan becomes evident. In a burst of "self-mocking irony" (305), Baker imagines himself writing a humorous magazine piece, based on Tureen's exploits, that would explain "How to comport your soul at a dinner party with wealthy young artistes, liberal do-nothings and the really wonderful, remarkable girl innocently seated next to you when you happen to own a secret slave ship in New York harbor" (304). Referring to the crew as "little brown guys, property of Capitán Elias Cortés and First Mate Mark Pizzaro" (305), Baker makes plain the imperialist history that his own contemporary venture evokes and replays. Scornfully deriding his partner, Baker notes that Tureen thinks "he's fucking Indiana Jones (a jungle explorer! born in the wrong century, he likes to say)" (205–6). Linking sixteenth-century colonial exploration (and forms of mercenary adventuring glorified by Hollywood) to the abuse of present-day Latin American labor, the novel, as Kirsten Silva Gruesz has argued, "means to indict not only the structures of a globalized economy in which Third-World workers are used as interchangeable and expendable labor, but the entire course of hemispheric history leading up to this moment."[37] *The Ordinary Seaman* suggests that in the contemporary Americas, labor, immigration, and colonialism are inextricably intertwined: Central American workers are crucial to North American profits, yet immigration policies and imperialist structures make those workers vulnerable to forms of hyperexploitation from which North American workers are generally protected. The narrative explodes the idea of the abstract worker, of workers without history, and of capitalism without colonialism and racism. The crew may be treated as abstract units of labor power by Baker and Tureen, who are indifferent to the fact that Puyano needs medical attention, but the novel underscores their "living"—the complex, transnational histories and relationships in which they are embedded and the individual personalities and proclivities they each bring to their labors.

The novel does offer a counternarrative to the neocolonial tale of deception and abuse suffered by the Central American labor refugees: the story of Esteban's entrance into Brooklyn's panethnic Latinx community. Esteban's escape from the *Urus* and his survival are made possible by several small but crucial gestures of generosity extended by persons he does not initially know. Joaquina, a Mexican manicurist with whom Esteban falls in love, serves him tea when she first encounters him prowling outside the hair salon where she works, even though Esteban, having just stumbled off the ship, looks "like one of those boys raised by wolves" (213); Marilu, a Dominican waitress, feeds Esteban for free and offers to let him sleep in her cramped apartment after hearing the story of the *Urus*; Gonzalo, Joaquina's Cuban boss, allows Esteban to sleep in the back of the hair salon; a fellow "Nica" whom Esteban meets at a Friday night dance helps him find a job at a chair factory, where he labors alongside other "refugees from the Salvadoran and Guatemalan wars and death squads" (361). Buoyed by the generosity of other exiles and migrants, Esteban uses his earnings from work at the chair factory to purchase food for the crew, still stranded on the *Urus*, which costs him "almost as much money as renting out a share of a plywood room would" (356).

The Brooklyn-based inter-Latinx community that Esteban enters is a heterogeneous conglomeration of peoples from across Latin America. A fluid, transnational society, it represents the promise of something new: an open-ended, diasporic community of working people that is in the process of emergence. As such, it might be considered a form of what Michael Templeton describes as "transnationalism from below that is, in Deleuzian spirit, very much in a state of 'becoming' rather than 'arrival.'"[38] Yet while Goldman's novel concludes on a hopeful note, intimating that Esteban's new life in Nueva York, and especially the love he shares with Joaquina, will heal, perhaps even redeem, the trauma he has suffered ("Joaquina loves Esteban with a solicitous tenderness and exacting passion that dissolve his self-doubts and fears or startle them away like a flock of crows" (360)), it ultimately casts doubt on a purely rhizomatic reading of social change. Kirsten Silva Gruesz argues that the novel's delineation and endorsement of this community-in-becoming has a utopian dimension that anticipates a truly hemispheric America, in which the histories of domination and injustice might be surpassed. Yet the novel also refuses to allow readers to forget, or even look past, those histories; after escaping the horrors onboard the *Urus* and finding love, Esteban nonetheless awakens one morning "trying to comprehend or imagine this mysterious abyss that has somehow swallowed Bernardo" (369). Moreover, he "suddenly realizes that it isn't something that has been done only to Bernardo. It's something that's been done to all of them.... And makes it also too much like what happened to la Marta and to how many compas, everyone he's lost so far" (369). Here the ghost of dead labor, of laborers who died on the job and in war, emerges to cast a shadow over the novel's conclusion. Bernardo's death by neglect and Marta's death in the war, and more generally the "abyss" Esteban sees, symbolize the bloody histories of colonial conquest, military intervention, and neoliberal exploitation that continue to haunt and actively shape the lives of Esteban and other Central American refugees.[39] In this way, the novel underscores the status of these workers as both living labor and dead labor, alive and with access to modes of being, believing, and relating that capital is unable to fully or finally capture or contain and yet also ultimately and acutely vulnerable to early death at the hands of the interlocking systems of exploitation, extraction, and war that dominate the globe.

"Always working. Hustling. Moving": *Tropic of Orange*

A challenging text to describe, Yamashita's novel is an aesthetic mash-up of various genres and styles, including postmodern metafiction, magical realism, detective noir, and reality television. At the level of both form and plot, the text is a pastiche in which, in the words of one character, "Everything's colliding into everything" (192). The novel's action centers on a massive pileup of cars on the freeway in Los Angeles. Traffic grinds to a halt and the cars are abandoned by their drivers, only to be claimed by the city's homeless residents, who form a makeshift community on the frozen freeway (112–13), a tenuous congregation that might serve as an allegory for the novel itself.[40] The accident is blamed on a driver's ingestion of a mysterious orange, one of a larger shipment rumored to be spiked with cocaine.

The novel contains forty-nine chapters narrated from the points of view—and in the distinct voices—of seven characters over the course of seven days. The characters include Gabriel Balboa, a Chicanx newspaper reporter specializing in human-interest stories; Gabriel's girlfriend, Emi, a Japanese American television weather reporter who ends up producing coverage of the freeway accident and its aftermath; Bobby Ngu, a Singaporean immigrant who speaks Spanish-inflected English; Rafaela Cortes, Bobby's partner who has left Los Angeles with their son Sol to care for a house that Gabriel is renovating in Mexico; Manzanar Murakami, a homeless former surgeon who conducts symphonies of traffic from a freeway overpass; Buzzworm, a homeless African American veteran who, working with a journalism crew assigned to cover the freeway disaster, creates an impromptu reality television show about the indigent community that blossoms in the midst of the disaster; and Arcangel, a five-hundred-year-old mythical figure—part poet, part performance artist—traveling North from Mexico to challenge the First World forces of free market capital in the name of Latin America's oppressed peoples.

Alongside the freeway stoppage, a series of other plot lines emerge: as Arcangel journeys north, he picks up an orange that is attached to the Tropic of Cancer and literally drags the geographical marker with him to Los Angeles, bringing the Southern Hemisphere into the Northern one; Bobby ventures to Tijuana to help his niece cross into the United States after a journey from China; Gabriel investigates a child-organ-smuggling ring run by the son of the woman living next door to Gabriel's second house in Mexico; Rafaela battles with a serpent-like monster that assaults her as she and Sol begin to make their way back to Los Angeles from Mexico. As it builds, the chaotic, fantastical sequence of events takes on a potentially apocalyptic cast ("I think the world we know is coming to an end," Emi asserts), and a fleet of military and police helicopters finally swoops down to attack and disperse the encampment of homeless people on the freeway ("The coordinated might of the Army, Navy, Air Force, Marines, the Coast and National Guards, federal, state, and local police forces of the most militaristic of nations looked down [on the homeless community] as it had in the past on tiny islands and puny countries the size of San Bernadino and descended in a single storm" (239)). The novel ends after the explosive—and mutually destructive—

wrestling match between Arcangel (as "El Grand Mojado," the Big Wetback) and SuperNAFTA, as Bobby, who was holding and then finally releases the orange attached to the Tropic of Cancer, lurches across the crowded auditorium toward a reunion with Rafaela and Sol.

Critics have given Yamashita's novel a good deal of attention in recent years, and they have tended to read it as a challenge to both identitarian and nation-state-centered forms of ethnic fiction. Rather than focusing on the history and identity claims of a discrete ethnic group, scholars argue, the novel offers an expansively hemispheric, indeed global, lens for understanding the intersection of multiple migratory cultural and social strands on and across geopolitical borders; rather than locating the story of contemporary Los Angeles in a national frame, the text provides a decidedly post- or transnational reading of the city, linking its cultural and economic flows to Latin America, the Pacific, Africa.[41] Yet few critics have read *Tropic of Orange* as a labor novel, focused on the historical significance of subaltern workers in the growth of North American capitalism and on the socially productive capacity of migrant workers and the poor to remap and remake the city and its global contexts.[42] Here I examine the novel's focus on a range of characters who labor at the edges and outside the formal wage system, but whose material, affective, social, and reproductive work is paradoxically central both to economic accumulation and to emergent forms of counterknowledge around which alternatives and resistance to racial and colonial capitalism might potentially be organized.

In re-envisioning Los Angeles, the United States, and the hemisphere more broadly, *Tropic of Orange* suggests that the power to imagine alternative forms of social being is less likely to come from its upwardly mobile characters, Gabriel and Emi—media-information workers who are on the cutting edge of the new economy—than from its unhoused and migratory working poor characters, who undermine the totalizing aspirations of official maps and make possible new, if ultimately not fully realized, modes of counterhegemonic belonging and connection. The novel is remarkably attendant to labor and the material inequalities that structure Los Angeles and the hemisphere, and it posits that, more than Emi, who is shot by an errant bullet fired when the military attack the homeless encampment, or Gabriel, who remains driven and distracted by professional ambitions, it is the loose collective of indigent and proletarian characters who, through their practice of an art of making do, provide resources for hope and equipment for living in a "social and economic construct that nobody knew how to change" (254).

As a book that undertakes to rechart Los Angeles and its relation to hemispheric and global flows of capital movement and human migration,

Tropic of Orange takes mapping as a crucial metaphor. Several of the characters are social cartographers of one form or another, and the novel itself is an effort to combine several different, and at times competing, maps of Los Angeles and its geocultural contexts. As Jameson argues of cognitive mapping, the mapping in *Tropic* is an ongoing process that links individual and local stories to global capitalist and colonial forces and histories. The two most incisive cartographers in the book are the two homeless characters, Murakami and Buzzworm, whose positions on the edges of Los Angeles give them unorthodox vantage points for understanding the shape and contours of the city.[43]

As a cartographer, Murakami is a figure of the artist as gatherer, collator, and arranger, blending multiple frames into a multilayered whole (his mapmaking is akin to his conducting, through which he brings manifold musical strains into a multifaceted symphony). "*There are maps and there are maps and there are maps*," the narrator notes. "The uncanny thing was that [Manzanar] could see all of them at once, filter some, pick them out like transparent windows and place them even delicately and consecutively in a complex grid of pattern, spatial discernment, body politic" (56). Manzanar realizes that a truly comprehensive map would have to be dense, layered, and rigorously materialist, stretching from the "geology" (57) of underground rivers, rock formations and fault lines, to the system of utility pipes, wires and cables, to the "historic grid of land usage and property, the great overlays of transport—sidewalks, bicycle paths, roads, freeways, systems of transit both ground and air, a thousand natural and man-made divisions . . . from the distribution of wealth to race, from the patterns of climate to the curious blueprint of skies" (57). The ideal map would thus be not only spatial, but historical as well, focused on strata of earth, strata of power, the embedded structures of inequality and exploitation layered over time into the landscape, the streets, and the built environment.

Of course, no matter how multifaceted, no cognitive or physical map is objective, and the prospect of crafting a definitive map is remote, if not impossible. Urban space is a palimpsest, the novel implies, and every framing obscures other, overlapping grids. Examining a 1972 map of gang territory in Los Angeles, Buzzworm, whose starting point is not a freeway overpass but the streets of the largely impoverished neighborhoods he walks, reflects that it "[m]ight as well show which police departments covered which beats; which local, state and federal politicians claimed which constituents; which kind of colored people (brown, black, yellow) lived where. . . . If someone could put down all the layers of the real map, maybe he could get the real picture" (81). But conventional maps are two-dimensional, without three-dimensional depth, and each new mapping effaces historical traces of earlier eras. Looking at a contemporary map of the area in which he grew up, Buzzworm wonders, "Where was his [childhood] house on this map? Between Mrs. Field's and the Footlocker? Somebody's parking lot? Somebody's tennis court?" (82). The map, which presents its landscape as singular and final, contains no trace of his boyhood abode or the larger communities that have been displaced to make way for the chain stores and consumer infrastructure.

The city, Buzzworm knows, is a tangle of perspectives, and one's angle of vision shapes what one can see and understand. Maps are not politically innocent. Growing up, he realized that his own neighborhood was largely invisible from the city's central artery, the freeway: "One day, Buzzworm got taken for a ride on the freeway.... He realized that you could just skip out over his house, his streets, his part of town. You never had to see it ever" (33). In contrast to the urban renewal plan promoted by the city, which ran the freeway and an exit ramp through the neighborhood where he grew up, and to the commercial upscaling of urban neighborhoods for the wealthy, Buzzworm advances a plan for bottom-up urban development: "self-gentrification by a self-made set of standards and respectability. Do-it-yourself gentrification. Latinos had this word, *gente*. Something translated like *us*. Like *folks*. That sort of gente-fication. Restore the neighborhood. Clean up the streets. Take care of the people" (83). Buzzworm's business card identifies him as an "Angel of Mercy" (26), linking him to Arcangel, who also represents the oppressed, and to Walter Benjamin's Angel of History, swept forward by the catastrophe called "progress." Buzzworm walks the streets of his neighborhood providing advice and steering people in need to forms of assistance: "He was walking social services.... Some poor nobody in trouble paged him at three A.M., and he was there long before anyone, especially the police" (26). Compensating for the lack of attention and support his impoverished community receives from public agencies and institutions, Buzzworm literally keeps his neighbors alive: "Weren't for him, been more dead people on the street" (26). Buzzworm is formally unemployed, but he performs critical reproductive and social labor.

The dynamics of insight and obfuscation that characterize maps extend to modes of seeing the city more generally. One's social and economic position shapes what one can see, masking or illuminating cultural, social, and material contradictions. As Buzzworm notes at one point, the culture of enclosure, division, and isolation in Los Angeles prevents many people from seeing beyond their own comfort zone: "All these people living in their cars. The cars living in garages. The garages living inside guarded walls.... Meantime people going through the garbage at McDonald's looking for a crust of bread" (43). In a discussion with Emi, who hails from the upscale Westside, Buzzworm notes that inequalities are structured by the built environment. Not only does his neighborhood lack the luxury infrastructure of wealthier neighborhoods, including "sidewalk bistros, tanning parlors, pillowed weenie-dogs, [and] golf courses" (175), it is also without such basic institutions as "major supermarkets, department stores, pharmacies, medical and dental clinics, hospitals, banks, factories and industry" (175). "In this city," he concludes, "you have to risk your life, go farther, and pay more to be poor" (175). Yamashita's novel not only stresses the manner in which a particular map, even as it enables one to navigate the city, *limits* one's capacity to see, but also writes largely from the point of view of figures who have historically been mapped out of the prevailing portrait of Los Angeles as a shining city of Hollywood-style glamour: poor and homeless people, migrant and immigrant workers laboring in the informal economy.

More than merely highlighting the innately ideological nature of all maps, Murakami's and Buzzworm's countercartography underscores the productivity of unhoused and unemployed persons, especially their capacity to perform aesthetic, social, and political work that shapes and transforms urban communities. Indeed, Yamashita's novel emphasizes that the labors of those rendered "surplus" to the formal wage economy are in fact crucial to the maintenance of, and possible resistance to, the engine of capitalist accumulation. *Tropic* shows that Murakami's and Buzzworm's labors are not below or beyond political economy, but in fact expand traditional notions of the "workforce," evoking the originary sense of proletarians not as industrial wage laborers, but as persons *without reserves*. Their labor, the novel insists, is vital, world-shaping. Manzanar's conducting synthesizes and coordinates the flow of bodies and sounds on the freeways coursing through Los Angeles, producing a unity out of seeming chaos: "standing there, he bore and raised each note, joined them, united families, creating a community, a great society, an entire civilization of sound. The great flow of humanity ran below and beyond his feet in every direction, pumping and pulsating, that blood connection, the great heartbeat of a great city uniting" (35). Like writers and other artists, whose aesthetic productions allow access to new ways of imagining the world and new possibilities for surviving (and surviving *differently* or in other modes), Murakami's conducting underscores the harmonic possibilities composed by a rush of atomized individuals in isolated vehicles, the possibility that singularities could be articulated in a collectivity. Likewise, the novel itself is a jagged symphony of competing, at times converging, voices, marked by both harmony and dissonance, unity and fracture.

Murakami's symphonic labors echo the work of other indigent residents to realize the cultural promise in what most people would see as a cultural or economic void. In an allegory of the improvisational, revisionary powers of the poor, the city's homeless citizens forge a makeshift community among the stalled cars in the wake of the catastrophe and chaos of the freeway crash, transforming an emergency into a site of cultural, social, and political emergence. Descending from their encampment under a freeway overpass that had been destroyed by the conflagration caused by the crashing semis, homeless men and women take over the field of abandoned vehicles. "In a matter of minutes, life filled a vacuum, reorganizing itself in predictable and unpredictable ways" (121). A food stand and a recycling station open as stalled delivery vans, commercial trucks, and cars are reappropriated in what Manzanar describes as "one of those happy riots" (122), a phrase that alludes to the more tumultuous and violent Los Angeles "riots" in Watts in 1965 and after the Rodney King verdict in 1992. In a carnivalesque spirit, cars are repurposed as miniature houses, someone opens a convenience store out of the back of a truck, and "People [are] busting out singing. Just busting out" (156). Neither the "happy riot" nor the improvised community founded in the field of stalled cars last long, however. Manzanar realizes that those watching the spectacle unfold on TV likely shared one "utterly violent assumption": "that the homeless were expendable, that citizens had a right to protect their property with firearms" (123). Accordingly, the military eventually storms the freeway, scattering and killing the homeless, while all the airbags in the abandoned vehicles burst in unison as if to protest (263).

The novel's focus on the social and aesthetic work performed by Manzanar and Buzzworm is part of a larger emphasis on labor—especially the labor (physical, intellectual, and affective; reproductive and unproductive) of immigrants and migrants—that pervades the text. If Buzzworm and Murakami personify informal, unwaged labor, the two most prominent representatives of physical work and working people in the novel are Bobby and Arcangel. Bobby personifies the flow of migrant labor from across the Pacific, although, like many figures in the novel, he cannot be easily or discretely categorized: "Bobby's Chinese. Chinese from Singapore with a Vietnam name speaking like a Mexican living in Koreatown" (15). The clipped prose in which his section is written reflects the frenetic pace of his life, which is organized by work. Bobby "don't have time to tell stories. Too busy. Never stops. Got only a little time to sleep even. Always working. Hustling. Moving. . . . Daytime, works the mailroom at a big-time newspaper. Sorts mail nonstop. Tons of it. Nighttime got his own business. Him and his wife [Rafaela]. Cleaning buildings" (16). Indeed, Bobby's life is a litany of immigrant labor:

Ever since he's been here, never stopped working. Always working. Washing dishes. Chopping vegetables. Cleaning floors. Flipping hamburgers. Painting walls. Laying brick. Cutting hedges. Mowing lawns. Digging ditches. Sweeping trash. Fixing pipes. Pumping toilets. Scrubbing urinals. Washing clothes. Pressing clothes. Sewing clothes. Planting trees. Changing tires. Changing oil and filters. Stocking shelves. Lifting sacks. Loading trucks. Smashing trash. Recycling plastic. Recycling aluminum. Recycling cans and glass. Drilling asphalt. Pouring cement. Building up. Tearing down. Fixing up. Cleaning up. Keeping up. (79)

Bobby's labors are varied, menial, and low-paying, a catalogue of emblematic immigrant work, performed in the cultural shadows to maintain the infrastructure of consumerism and leisure for which postmodern Los Angeles is famous. In outlining Bobby's cycle of hectic, near-perpetual labors ("Always working. Hustling. Moving"), Yamashita's novel reminds readers that the city's shiny surfaces are kept clean by the hard work of immigrants who take out the trash, wash the clothes, and restock the shelves. Set alongside the narratives of cultural knowledge workers like Gabriel and Emi, embedded in an emerging system of immaterial production organized around the internet and the virtual circulation of images and ideas, Bobby's story is a reminder of the physical work that subtends the supposedly postindustrial, immaterial, knowledge economy. As a migrant who is "always working" and who defies discrete categories of identity and language, Bobby personifies what I am calling *labor-in-motion*: labor that is on the move between places, that exceeds the political economic and cultural containers that are typically used to limn its power, that is at once critical to contemporary capitalism, yet performed by workers who have been rendered expendable.

If Bobby embodies the immigrant labor present, its history is personified by Arcangel. A character inspired by poet Pablo Neruda, border performance artist Guillermo Gómez-Peña, and historian Eduardo Galeano, Arcangel is a walking condemnation of colonialism who knows that "Everybody's labor got occupied in the / industry of draining their / homeland of its natural wealth. In exchange / they got progress, / technology, / loans, and / loaded guns" (146). Scanning five centuries of hemispheric history, his mind's eye sees the working populations: enslaved persons, indentured workers, impoverished field hands, fruit harvesters, miners, builders, and others who extracted the natural resources and agricultural products of Latin America for the profit of First World countries and companies. He "could see: / Haitian farmers burning and slashing cane, / workers stirring molasses into white gold. / Guatemalans loading trucks with crates of bananas and corn. / Indians, who mined tin in the Cerro Rico / and saltpeter from the Atacama desert" (145). The history of labor, Arcangel reminds us, is synonymous with the history of settler colonialism and slave capitalism, which in turn form the foundation of contemporary Los Angeles and the Americas.

Viewing history and current events from the perspective of Latin America's laboring peoples, Arcangel offers a scathing critique of neoliberal trade policies such as NAFTA. At one point, he chants that free-market-inspired structural adjustments imposed on the economies of the developing nations by institutions like the IMF and World Bank expand rather than alleviate Latin American poverty: "A twenty-eight billion dollar trade deficit? / Devaluate the peso. / A miracle! / No more debt for the country. Instead, / personal debt for all its people. / Free trade" (147). In fact, Arcangel insists, the immense profit-making and world-spanning powers of global finance and multinational capitalism are built on the backs of exploited and colonized workers from the Global South. The "graceful movement of free capital, at least 45 billion of it," across the U.S.-Mexico border in the wake of NAFTA's implementation, is "carried across by hidden and cheap labor" (200).

In an attempt to strike a measure of restitution for low-wage workers, Arcangel transforms himself into a "motley personage: part superhero, part professional wrestler, part Subcomandante Marcos" (132) called "El Grand Mojado" ("The Big Wetback"), who champions "all of you Californianos who were already there [when the United States annexed California in 1848] / and all of you indigenas who crossed / and still cross the new border" (133). He announces his intention to keep moving north to challenge the champion of the imperialist-capitalist North, "SuperNAFTA," in a contest "being billed as the Fight of the Century" (134).

The novel ends on a note of pervasive uncertainty. The allegorical battle between the forces of the Global South and Global North ends in reciprocal destruction: El Grand Mojado destroys SuperNAFTA, but dies from the wounds he suffers in the confrontation. Emi is killed by an errant bullet fired by the military forces that descend on the homeless people camped on the freeway to disperse the alternative community that had briefly taken root. Unaware that Emi has died, Gabriel continues to track the organ-transplant circuit, although he insists, "I no longer looked for a resolution to the loose threads hanging off my storylines" (248). The future seems to belong to Rafaela, Bobby, and Sol, who are reunited in the final pages. Hailing from Latin America and Asia, they are migrant laborers who have worked a range of jobs across the informal and formal economies. Immigrant workers who are woven into the social and economic fabric of Los Angeles, they will remain "working. Hustling. Moving." "They could pass all the propositions [like California Proposition 187] they want," Bobby thinks. "People like him and Rafaela weren't gonna just disappear" (161).

Yamashita's novel does not offer a viable vision of revolutionary possibility, and indeed its images of counterhegemonic collectivity are fantastical elements of a magical realist fable. The freeway takeover does not produce an uprising; rather, it is quashed by the coercive forces of the state's military-police apparatus. Arcangel, the crusading superhero of aggrieved colonial peoples, meets his match in SuperNAFTA, and the two destroy each other. What the text does offer, however, is a series of alternative mappings of U.S. hemispheric space that collectively foreground the cultural, social, economic, and aesthetic centrality of migrant, homeless, and working people. The novel leaves the shape of the future unclear, but it suggests that working people, carrying the history of colonial conflicts, will have a primary role in shaping it.

• • •

In the early 1990s, in the years shortly before the three novels examined in this chapter were published, Edward Said argued for the emergence of migratory ideas and art as a new paradigm for cultural analysis in an increasingly globalized age, in which prevailing strategies of political, economic, and geographical containment are being weakened. "[L]iberation as an intellectual mission," Said asserted, "has now shifted from the settled, established, and domesticated dynamics of culture to its unhoused, decentered, and exilic energies whose incarnation today is the migrant, and whose consciousness is that of the intellectual and artist in exile, the political figure between domains, between forms, between homes, and between languages."[44] Said's assertion is typically eloquent, but anchored in a problematic discrepancy. In his formulation, migrants embody the "energies," but migrant "consciousness" finds expression in exilic intellectuals and artists. Ordinary peoples and workers, indeed the realm of economics and material life more generally, are thus implicitly relegated to the realm *below* culture and ideas, the sphere of the body—"incarnation," the carnal.

The three texts examined in this chapter were written by transnational artists whose allegiances, identifications, and influences span geocultural traditions and borders, but they privilege the perspectives and experiences of migrant workers, drawing attention to the social, economic, and geopolitical divides cutting through the striated global landscape. These texts thus work across the division between what Zygmunt Bauman calls tourists and vagabonds, indicating the ways in which the privileges of a few are produced through the misery of many. They draw our attention to the travails of migratory working people on the periphery of the formal waged economy, underscoring the paradoxical centrality of those rendered "surplus" by capitalist accumulation. In this, they indict neoliberal globalization's foundational structures of violence, dispossession, and inequality. These texts are alive both to the emergent cultural and political possibilities spawned by the growing fluidity and interconnections across the hemisphere in the age of globalization, as well as the pervasive forms of structural harm and power that define the period's prevailing economic and political regimes. It may be true, as Henry Yu argues in his powerful case for transnational approaches to cultural study, that "[m]igrants create geographic space," but they do not do so under conditions of their own choosing.[45] If Yu's analysis underemphasizes the systemic, structural forces that shape such movements, the three novels discussed in this chapter suggest that, as radical geographer Don Mitchell puts it, "[m]obility—or really the control over the conditions of mobility—is thus an aspect of class power and struggle."[46]

By stressing the structural, material hardships and constraints marking migrant life, these texts pose a challenge to rhizomatic conceptions of transnational transit and culture articulated, among other places, in the work of Antonio Negri and Michael Hardt, who propose the migratory poor as representative figures of the multitude. For Hardt and Negri, migrants represent a special category of the poor that demonstrate the multitude's status as the very basis of productive life, wealth, and social commonality. Hardt and Negri acknowledge that migrants are often driven by hunger and desperation, but they contend that migrants "treat the globe as one common space, serving as living testimony to the irreversible fact of globalization. Migrants demonstrate (and help construct) the general commonality of the multitude by crossing and thus partially undermining every geographical barrier."[47] While Hardt and Negri see a steady, inexorable dissolution of social and political boundaries among the planetary poor in the age of global capital, the novels discussed suggest that divisions of race, nation, and language are remarkably durable. In different ways, these texts do imagine moments or gestures of solidarity and commonality in which prevailing social and political boundaries are, in some measure, breached, as potentially subversive cross-cultural connections within the migrant community, and between migrants and nonmigrants, are forged. But these moments are fleeting and underdeveloped, glimpses rather than fully realized alternatives. Possibilities of solidarity along and across lines of class and ethnicity exist, but these novels imply that such possibilities would come to fruition—if at all—through social struggle rather than through the inevitable commonalities formed by an ontological condition of poverty or migrancy, as Hardt and Negri imply. These texts foreground the structural violence and the everyday, slow violence that enforces the asymmetries of social, cultural, and political power across the Americas and beyond.[48] In narrating stories of migration, these texts thus do more than challenge or undermine national narratives; they trace the structures of economic and political power that shape the contemporary transnational landscape, in which global migration is driven largely by poor people's search for increasingly precarious forms of labor under ever more exploitative conditions.

As critical concepts, labor and class often seem out of place in academic discussions of hemispheric studies and transnationalism, in which poststructuralist metaphors of fluidity, flow, and transit tend to obscure and deflect attention from the materiality of work and working-class critique.[49] The novels by Yamashita, Goldman, and Viramontes, however, foreground the *violence* that structures and gives force to the asymmetries of social, cultural, and political power across the Americas and beyond. The violence they stress is at once neocolonial, racial, and economic; it renders large sectors of the racialized and colonized working population disposable, vulnerable to premature death. In tracing stories of migration, then, these texts do more than challenge or undermine national narratives; they map lines of economic and political force that govern the contemporary global terrain, in which migration is animated largely by poor people's pursuit of labor across a geography of racial, ethnic, and financial stratification. They are thus more attuned to Rodrigo Lazo's description of hemispheric novels as texts that encourage readers to "conceptualize a new space of economic interaction and abuse that brings together different parts of the hemisphere."[50] Hemispheric novels, Lazo insists, are thus not merely sites where interactions, exchanges, and spatial relations within and across the Americas can be represented in a way that moves beyond national and local frames; such texts can also highlight the forms of deep colonial violence and economic exploitation that have marked the history of the Americas.

These novels insist that what animates transnational culture, the circuits of labor migration, and the subsequent remapping of the world that such migrations demand, are economic imperatives, specifically capital's drive to find a vulnerable work force. The large-scale movements of people across national borders in the Americas (and beyond) are thus responses to corporate capital's need for labor, and the political conditions—from the history of colonialism and well-established patterns of racism to immigration policies that categorize many workers as "illegal" persons without state protection and labor rights—that make certain sectors of the population especially susceptible to exploitation, abuse, even death.[51] Mexican, Central American, and Caribbean workers are especially vulnerable because they are often, under U.S. immigration policy, rendered stateless, stripped of most legal and political rights and protections.[52] They are also isolated, due to language, immigration status, and cultural segregation, from native-born workers, and subject, due to the historical and ongoing dynamics of colonialism and racist discrimination, to forms of prejudice and abuse from which many U.S. workers are protected. In their efforts to render the contemporary world and its most compelling and emblematic dynamics, Yamashita, Viramontes, and Goldman all turn to migrant workers whose civil rights have been stripped or are endangered.

Conceptually, these novels revolve around key issues at the heart of working-class formation, including displacement and belonging, competition and association, abstraction and particularity. These novels focus on migrant populations roving in search of work, uprooted and on the road (or, in the case of *The Ordinary Seaman*, adrift in the harbor). Yet, in the tradition of migrant novels like Steinbeck's *The Grapes of Wrath*, which returns continually to the roadside camps where migrant congregate to form provisional communities, these three novels also emphasize the forms of imaginative connection and collectivity that migrant workers create in the fields and farm camps of California, in a panethnic Latinx neighborhood in Brooklyn, and in Los Angeles, where a group of unhoused men and women craft a temporary city amidst a sea of abandoned cars. (It is worth underscoring, however, that these three transnational texts expose and trouble the racial and national homogeneity of Steinbeck's Okie refugees, whose shared sense of "American" belonging is in significant measure a function of their white citizenship.)

In addition, all three novels are about workers treated by capital as fungible sources of productive power that can be sacrificed figuratively and literally as dead labor. The thematics of invisibility that unite the three texts stem not only from dynamics of racial subjugation, but also from the dynamics of wage- (and *unwaged-*) labor: these stories recount, each in a different way, the demands of workers for recognition and respect, and the forms of denial with which such demands are met by employers and by "American" society at large, which relies on immigrant and racialized workers yet is organized to efface any trace of that reliance. These novels suggest that capital's desire to homogenize workers as interchangeable units of labor power continually runs up against the stubborn facts of particularity: the histories and traditions, and the social, cultural, and individual specificities, relations, habits, and entanglements that workers always bring to their encounters with capital and with one another. Even in the midst of capital's drive to render it abstract and uniform, labor is always living labor, always in motion, never fixed, always embedded in histories, contexts, and circumstances that shape and exceed the relations and meaning of work as a category of experience and activity. Together, these novels demonstrate both the centrality of capitalism to what is often framed as "ethnic literature" and also the limitations of capitalism as an analytic frame for thinking through the heterogeneity of working-class life, labor, and resistance. These stories suggest that workers from varied ethnic, national, cultural, and linguistic traditions bring with them non-Western, and resolutely non- and anticapitalist, traditions, ideas, and practices, even as capitalism shapes their prospects, expectations, and journeys. These novels indicate that capitalism is open, not closed—what Cedric Robinson describes as "a rather more complex capitalist world system"—and that the working class, too, is and always has been a porous, multifarious formation, never just a matter of industrial workers in the Global North.[53]

Much of the most compelling historical and theoretical work on the working class—by scholars such as Peter Linebaugh and Marcus Rediker, Silvia Federici, Dipesh Chakrabarty, George Lipsitz, Robin Kelley, and so many others—reminds us that the process of capital accumulation not only entails the consolidation and expansion of capital and exploitable workers, but also, as Federici explains, "an accumulation of differences and divisions within the working class."[54] As Nathan Brown has put it, "the proletariat is constitutively divided, in the first instance: the very process of its constitution is also the creation of internal contradictions and inequalities within the proletariat itself."[55] The proletariat, he continues, "is never stable or cohesive as a class: it is always already divided in and through the continual process of its constitution."[56] In the age of neoliberal globalization and planetary migration—when the extension of what Marx called the "world market" is wider than ever and the working population is in remarkable flux—now, more than ever, we need to take seriously, these novels imply, the differences, divisions, and diversities of traditions and histories, the heterogeneities of working peoples and the unfinished, always contested quality of class formation, even as we insist on the acute centrality of capitalist accumulation and exploitation to the shaping of contemporary world experience and the significance of class as a category of analysis.

Finally, as these novels direct our attention to the convergence of migration, colonialism, and capitalist exploitation, they also remind us why literature remains a significant resource for imagining the contemporary world, even in this age of high-tech information culture and spectacle. Two things in particular about literature strike me as crucial. First, literary narrative is a spatially symbolic act, a form of mapping that orients and connects.[57] This act is especially valuable in an age of accelerated global capitalist accumulation characterized by, in Saskia Sassen's words, "contestation, internal differentiation, and continuous border crossings."[58] Literature can span space, time, and tradition, render intimate distant interior worlds, limn scenarios that stage the states of emergency linking disparate global locations and peoples. In the course of mapping the world, of organizing and structuring space, people, and ideas, novels locate their readers, helping us begin to grasp, in Fredric Jameson's words, "that vaster and properly unrepresentable totality which is the ensemble of society's structures as a whole."[59] The narrative and cognitive mappings these texts provide are, as such mappings always are, partial and provisional, but each in its various ways tries to link individual characters to encompassing systems of colonial and capitalist dispossession, exploitation, and accumulation and resistance to them. And in contrast to mappings that insist on the smooth or flattened nature of global culture in the age of transnational capital, these three novels stress the borders, barriers, and boundaries that limit, block, or enclose the movements of subaltern, proletarianized peoples across the Americas.

The second reason why the novel in particular remains vital is its formal complexity, its capacity to combine multiple forms and styles, to render divergent voices, rhetorical and stylistic registers, and points of view. Examples of what I have termed precarious realism, the three texts discussed in this chapter blend varieties of critical, social realism, focused on the quotidian (as well as extraordinary) struggles of politically discounted working peoples, with other aesthetic threads: from Yamashita's postmodern irony and magical realism, to Viramontes's lyrical fragmentation, to Goldman's perverse stalling of the sea novel in an unseaworthy ship and his subtly shifting experiment in point of view. As an innately polyglossic form, the novel contains contradictory elements of fracture and coherence, universalizing aspirations and detailed particulars, historical legacies and speculative futures, bringing into dialogue multiple and conflicting perspectives as well as competing social forms, feelings, structures, and traditions. Literary narrative's abilities to render the heterogeneous struggles of working and nonworking people constitute crucial capacities in our contemporary transnational age. Literature about labor and working people is alive and well, but it often takes forms we may not easily or instantly recognize. We need to continue to develop the critical flexibility it demands and deserves.

3 • Living Labor, Dead Labor

Cinema, Solidarity, and Necrocapitalism

This chapter examines two films released in 2008, Clint Eastwood's *Gran Torino* and Courtney Hunt's *Frozen River*, and a third film, Ryan Coogler's *Fruitvale Station*, released in 2013 but set in the final hours of December 31, 2008, and first few hours of January 1, 2009. All three films address the struggles of working-class people in an emergent post-Fordist era of precarious labor, but they strike up an uneasy dialogue, in which some of the central social, ideological, and political ambitions of the first film I discuss, *Gran Torino*, are complicated by the second, *Frozen River*, and bluntly challenged by the third, *Fruitvale Station*. *Gran Torino* and *Frozen River* narrate the development of fragile, and in crucial ways uneven, relationships of economic and emotional solidarity between white and, respectively, immigrant and Indigenous working-class characters in social landscapes marked by economic disinvestment and proliferating national, ethnic, and racial heterogeneity. By contrast, *Fruitvale Station* narrates a story about working and unemployed Black and Latinx persons under carceral capitalism, in which living labor is shadowed by the ever-present threat of confinement and death via the targeted violence of state and nonstate actors.[1] *Gran Torino* imagines transethnic, intergenerational working-class collaboration, but only as predicated on the demonization and violent expulsion of Black figures; *Frozen River* offers a more expansive vision of feminist working-class cooperation across lines of race and nation; *Fruitvale Station* offers a robust counterpoint to *Gran Torino*'s racist imaginary, suggesting that precarity is not only an economic, but also a biopolitical category, and that capitalism is always necrocapitalism, organized around the disposability and social and literal death of working and nonworking, racialized, especially Black, populations.[2]

This chapter is thus organized around a conversation between three films that offer contrasting perspectives on the economic fates, social relations, and biopolitical vulnerabilities of working and unemployed peoples in the years surrounding the 2008 economic recession. I begin with *Gran Torino*, the most widely distributed of the three films, and then discuss in turn how the other two films expand, question, and contest the terms on which Eastwood's film imagines the plight of the global working class. *Gran Torino*, set in Detroit, revolves around an unlikely friendship between retired white autoworker Walt Kowalski (Clint Eastwood), a personification of the declining industrial proletariat, and two of his Hmong immigrant neighbors, Thao and Sue Lor (Vee Bang and Ahney Her); *Frozen River*, set in upstate New York, centers on an alliance between Ray Eddy (Melissa Leo), a white single mother and discount store worker, and Lila Littlewolf (Misty Upham), a Mohawk single mother and bingo palace employee, who join forces to smuggle South and East Asian immigrants across the U.S.-Canadian border through the Mohawk reservation where Littlewolf lives; *Fruitvale Station* fictionalizes the final twenty-four hours of the life of Oscar Grant (Michael B. Jordan), who was murdered by a Bay Area Rapid Transit (BART) police officer early in the morning of January 1, 2009, as Grant, his girlfriend Sophina Mesa (Melonie Diaz), and some friends were on the way home to Hayward, California, after spending New Year's Eve in San Francisco.

All three films are narratives of destruction set against the backdrop of deindustrialization and the rise of contingent labor that explore possibilities of social relation and solidarity within a multiracial global working class.[3] *Gran Torino* and *Frozen River* take as their starting point the decline of Fordism as an era of white working-class stability and well-being, and both address the end of the white male industrial worker as the iconic emblem of the American working class. In *Gran Torino*, elderly autoworker Walt Kowalski—whose name echoes another iconic working-class character, Stanley Kowalski, from Tennessee Williams's *A Streetcar Named Desire*—wakes up to find himself living in what he perceives as a dystopian Detroit, in which the formerly well-kept single-family homes in his neighborhood have crumbled and his white neighbors, who fled the area in the wake of deindustrialization, have been replaced by "Third World" immigrants. In *Frozen River*, set in an economically depressed area of upstate New York, the husbands of the two protagonists have fled or been killed and have left behind women struggling to scrape together a living and feed their children in a wasteland of low-wage service work. *Fruitvale Station*, set in the gentrifying East Bay, focuses mostly on employed and unemployed Black and Latinx service workers, caught in the riptides of contingent labor and also the explosive violence of a racist police state. Coogler's film is acutely attuned to issues of labor, class, and economic struggle, and it imagines possibilities for cross-racial alliance and harmony, but within the film those potentialities possess little power against the social, political, and economic forces that render Black persons not only exploitable, but also brutally expendable. The film reminds us that capitalist accumulation demands both exploitation and expropriation, both living labor and dead labor.

Together, these three films depict the unraveling of mid-twentieth-century industrial working-class identities, relations, and traditions, and the instability and uncertainty of working-class composition and labor in an age of flexible accumulation and global migrations. Indeed, if the twentieth-century working class was imagined in relatively settled and homogeneous terms as a class of male, predominantly white industrial workers, the array of characters in *Gran Torino*, *Frozen River*, and *Fruitvale Station* suggest the economic and social heterogeneity of blue-collar life and labor in the contemporary United States and beyond: from Walt Kowalski, an icon of the CIO working class who profited from the post–World War II era of prosperity, earning enough as a factory worker to purchase a single-family house, send his children to college, and retire in relative comfort; to Ray Eddy, a native-born white worker like Kowalski, but a woman whose gender status and location in an economically depressed region prevent her from earning enough to adequately feed her children; to Lila Littlewolf, a Mohawk woman with so few economic options that she has turned to smuggling undocumented immigrants to earn a (modest, even meager) living; to Thao and Sue Lor, immigrants coming of age in a postindustrial city with a collapsed economy and decimated infrastructure; to Oscar Grant and Sophina Mesa, young Black and Latinx workers on the fringes of the service economy, struggling to pay rent in the outer districts of a gentrifying city, San Francisco, that is an epicenter of the expanding digital economy. Together, these films suggest that in the early twenty-first century, the lineaments of class and working-class identity have been thrown into flux. These are films about workers without jobs, or struggling to find jobs, or with jobs that do not pay the bills. What it means to be working class can no longer be taken for granted, if it ever could. Working-class identity, these films suggest, is not stable, but shifting, and very much a matter of social relations, in particular, uneasy relations between social groups from substantially different social and geopolitical locations.

Indeed, all three films address *challenges* to working-class formation and reproduction in the age of labor's "multiplication," as work becomes more precarious and the working class more heterogeneous.[4] Under these fluctuating conditions, the question of how, by whom, and on what terms the working-class will be constituted after Fordism remains an open question.

Gran Torino asks how working-classness will be transmitted primarily between men from different generations, from the Fordist working class to an emergent, still undefined, and culturally more variegated post-Fordist class; *Frozen River* asks how class might be formed and forged across lines of nation and culture between women, as figures relegated to the margins of the formal economy find common ground in the underground economy and through forms of care work necessary to sustain themselves and their families; *Fruitvale Station* suggests that for Black workers, emergent possibilities of class alliance can be shattered by the unmitigated, gratuitous force of state-inflicted racial violence.

All three films take up the social reproduction of the working class and suggest that in the contemporary moment working-class culture and identity are profoundly unstable. For *Gran Torino*, this instability is a source of immense anxiety, but also possibility, as new relations between different fractions of the world's working population are initiated. For *Frozen River*, the precariousness of working-class women's lives is deeply unsettling for the women and those in their care. Yet the state of emergency in which Ray and Lila find themselves also generates a state of emergence, and the film suggests that it may be in the realm of reproduction rather than production where some alternatives, however provisional and tentative, to capitalism's vigorous assault on poor and laboring peoples might be found. In *Fruitvale Station*, Black and Latinx working-class reproduction is brutally interrupted by authoritarian racial violence that upends the emergence of an expansive interracial family and community. If *Gran Torino* and *Frozen River* underscore the tentative formation of new alliances in an era of labor precarity, *Fruitvale Station* stresses the profound biopolitical and economic vulnerability of working-class life, family, and reproduction and implies that Black labor exists under the sign of a radical precarity that Christina Sharpe calls the singularity of antiblackness.[5]

Similar to *Continental Drift*, discussed in chapter 1, *Gran Torino* and *Frozen River* suggest that stories of white working-class men and women in the post-Fordist era are also stories of transborder, interethnic relation. Indeed, these two films contribute to the constitution of a new, post-Fordist subgenre: what might be called the *narrative of transnational proletarian encounter*, which explores imaginative possibilities for working-class identification and solidarity across lines of race, nation, and ethnicity through stories of white, U.S.-born workers who are pushed by declining socioeconomic circumstances to form uneasy alliances with workers of color (and it is worth noting that while these films try to imagine alliances between white and nonwhite workers, they are both narrated largely—and in the case of *Gran Torino* almost exclusively—from the white characters' point of view). If the proletarian bildungsroman, which traced the emergence of the young artist as worker and revolutionary, constituted the canonical narrative form of the CIO working class during the era of the cultural front, stories of cross-cultural connection and conflict are emerging as the contemporary equivalent.

The production of racial identity, division, violence, and solidarity have been central preoccupations of U.S. working-class literature throughout its long history.[6] Within this tradition, writings by Black authors, from *The Narrative of the Life of Frederick Douglass, an American Slave* (1845), Harriet Wilson's *Our Nig* (1859), and Harriet Jacobs's *Incidents in the Life of a Slave Girl* (1861), up through Richard Wright's *Native Son* (1940), Ann Petry's *The Street* (1946), Toni Morrison's *The Bluest Eye* (1970), and Jesmyn Ward's *Sing, Unburied, Sing* (2017), have focused not only on possibilities provided by escape, migration, and border crossing, but also on barriers to racial justice and working-class solidarity, often crystallized in images of partition and confinement, such as the plantation, the garret, the slum, the prison. Working within this narrative tradition, *Fruitvale Station* challenges the tentative optimism that infuses *Gran Torino* and *Frozen River* by underscoring how institutionalized structures of racial violence can undercut burgeoning alliances and Black life itself. In this context, precarity comes to have another meaning, referring not only to economic contingency, but also to a much more fundamental biopolitical insecurity in which Black and other targeted populations are actively rendered surplus and disposable, their exploitation founded on and compounded by state-sanctioned exposure to premature death.[7]

Cinema and the Working Class

As *Gran Torino*, *Frozen River*, and *Fruitvale Station* respond to narratives of proletarian struggle from earlier eras, they also and more specifically take their place within the long tradition of U.S. (and global) films about working people, immigration, and race. Most Hollywood productions have a marked bias toward middle- and upper-class characters, settings, and perspectives, but working-class figures and concerns have in fact been a steady, if often minor, presence in American cinema. In fact, the early history of American film was rooted in working-class culture. Films first became mass entertainment in early-twentieth-century nickelodeons, with working-class moviegoers as the primary audience. As Steven Ross argues, movie theaters not only "took root in blue-collar and immigrant neighborhoods," but silent-era filmmakers were also deeply "concerned with portraying the hardships of working-class life."[8] This changed after the development and consolidation of the well-financed studio system, which established film as an increasingly middle-class form of entertainment housed in movie palaces rather than local storefront nickelodeons. As film became a middlebrow art, Ross explains, filmmakers "abandoned old themes of class conflict in favor of making films that promoted conservative visions of class harmony; films that shifted attention away from the problems of the workplace and toward the pleasures of the new consumer society."[9]

Yet even after the emergence of the Hollywood studio system, which has continued almost unswervingly to justify and normalize prevailing capitalist social relations, several landmark American films, including *The Grapes of Wrath* (1940), *On the Waterfront* (1954), *Norma Rae* (1979), and others, have featured working-class protagonists and addressed labor politics in a fairly direct, if not always politically progressive, fashion. Often, Hollywood stories of working-class life—such as the tales of working women in popular films like *Working Girl* (1988), *Pretty Woman* (1990), and *Maid in Manhattan* (2002)—provide the occasion for "rags to riches" narratives in which economic hardships and class divisions are overcome through pluck, a bit of luck, and by falling in love with a member of the wealthy classes. Emmett Winn has argued that in addition to tales of upward mobility, Hollywood films about working-class people frequently follow two other narrative threads: stories in which characters "cope with failed mobility without questioning the basic tenets of the American Dream," and narratives in which distressed upper-class characters are redeemed by contact with characters from a lower class.[10] Focusing on films from the 1980s and 1990s, an era of stagnating working-class wages and expanding economic disparities, Winn argues that Hollywood films about working people—from *Breaking Away* (1979) through *Good Will Hunting* (1997)—tend to reinforce the notion that structural, social inequalities can and should be addressed as personal, individual concerns.[11]

Other critics tend to agree. In a study of films from the 1930s through the 1970s, John Bodnar has argued that while depictions of working people are in fact diverse, Hollywood films about blue-collar life largely affirm a fundamentally liberal conception of society that frames social and political issues in essentially private terms.[12] More critically, Linda Dittmar contends that most American films about working-class people ironically obscure class as a category of thought: "It is not that films fail to depict characters from all walks of life, but that they discourage awareness of the fact that 'walks' translate into classes, and that classes are defined by incompatible interests responding to gross inequalities and injustices."[13]

There have been significant exceptions to this prevailing cinematic pattern, however. In particular, a range of relatively small-budget, independent, often expressly radical films—including *Salt of the Earth* (1953), *Killer of Sheep* (1977), *El Norte* (1983), *Matewan* (1987), *Bread and Roses* (2000), *Sorry to Bother You* (2017), and *Blindspotting* (2018)—have foregrounded the travails of working people, including poor and working-class immigrants, women, and people of color. These films not only feature working-class protagonists, but also make issues of labor conflict and injustice—poverty, exploitation, unionization, campaigns for economic and social dignity, racial and ethnic discrimination—central dramatic concerns. In various ways, and to different degrees, these films invite viewers to think about class as a stubborn, structural dimension of American life and about the intersections of economic conditions with race, gender, and immigration.

In turn, these American films are part of a larger international cinematic formation addressing working-class displacement and community that forms the intertextual context for the films I discuss in this chapter and the succeeding one. This global cinematic subgenre includes such films as *La Promesse* (1996), the Palme D'Or–winning film by Jean-Pierre and Luc Dardenne, which explores the unexpected alliance between seventeen-year-old Igor, a gas station attendant living in late-industrial Belgium, and Assita, an undocumented African immigrant whose husband is killed while working an illegal construction job for Igor's father, Roger; and *Amexicano* (2007), Matthew Bonifacio's intriguing, if uneven, film about the friendship between a down-on-his luck, blue-collar Italian-American, Bruno, and an undocumented Mexican immigrant, Ignacio, who work day labor jobs together in Queens, New York. The basic plot of these two films, which chart emerging solidarities between immigrant workers and white native-born workers, is echoed in Finnish director Aki Kaurismaki's wry film *Le Havre* (2011), about an impoverished shoeshine man, Marcel Marx, who, with assistance from his plebian neighbors in the French port city of Le Havre, helps a young refugee from Gabon, Idrissa, escape immigration enforcement authorities and make his way to London, where his mother is living. These films of transnational transit and relation are complemented by films about the travails of immigrant workers struggling in the new global economy, such as *Choking Man* (2006), a magical realist–inspired story about a pathologically shy Central American dishwasher and his coworkers in a diner in Flushing, Queens, and *Dirty Pretty Things* (2002), about the convergence of African and eastern European immigrants in an organ-smuggling operation in London. These films—and others in the same vein—explore the volatile spatial, cultural, economic, and affective intersections created by the flows of planetary migration in and across the major cities of the advanced capitalist world, and provide global cinematic context for *Gran Torino*, *Frozen River*, and *Fruitvale Station*.

"Get off my lawn": *Gran Torino*

Gran Torino centers on Walt Kowalski, a retired, recently widowed Ford autoworker and decorated Korean War veteran who lives in a crumbling Detroit neighborhood that was once an enclave of white-ethnic, blue-collar workers but is now home to a growing population of Hmong immigrants. A cranky, isolated man who spouts racist epithets in casual conversation, Kowalski begrudgingly befriends the Hmong family next door after meeting plucky young Sue Lor and her geeky brother Thao, whom Kowalski catches trying to steal his prized possession, a 1972 Gran Torino, as an initiation stunt for a Hmong gang that is trying to force Thao to join its ranks. Thao's family insists that he repay his transgression by volunteering his labor to Walt for a week. Kowalski takes a liking to Thao, whom he helps get a construction job, and he uses his rifle to ward off the gang members, who try to kidnap Thao and eventually rape Sue. In the film's climactic scene, Kowalski confronts (and taunts) the gang members, but rather than outshoot them, he sacrifices himself as they gun him down in the street, where he falls in a Christ-like pose as the police arrive.

Written by Nick Schenk, a former construction worker, truck driver, and liquor store clerk who had labored alongside several Hmong immigrants in a Minneapolis factory, *Gran Torino* contains a dynamic blend of what Fredric Jameson refers to, in a well-known formulation, as ideological and utopian elements. "[W]orks of mass culture," Jameson insists, "cannot be ideological without at one and the same time being implicitly or explicitly Utopian as well."[14] He continues: "[E]ven if their function lies in the legitimation of the existing order—or some worse one—[mass cultural texts] cannot do their job without deflecting in the latter's service the deepest and most fundamental hopes and fantasies of the collectivity, to which they can therefore, no matter in how distorted a fashion, be found to have given a voice."[15] From an ideological perspective, *Gran Torino* is indeed a highly problematic film which, I argue—counter to the claims of several reviewers and critics—largely affirms the patriarchal, racist, imperialist politics that on the surface it might be said to contest. Yet the film also possesses, I contend, buried within it and without itself being able to articulate it, a kernel of anticipatory hope for forms of collective being and belonging that constitute a potential, yet crucially unrealized counterpoint to such oppressive, reactionary politics.

In the film's own terms, the overarching narrative is a story of generational transition and of redemption: of Walt himself, who is haunted by the atrocities he committed during the Korean War; of Detroit, as a city that has been decimated by capital flight and abandoned by middle-class homeowners; and of the United States and its misguided foreign policies, which sent good men like Walt off to war, only to see them put in positions to commit violent atrocities. As the film opens, Kowalski is an embittered, racist man with a penchant for using a gun to resolve problems. In an early scene, the gang visits the Lors' house, and when they try to drag Thao into their car, a scuffle ensues as Sue, Thao, and their mother attempt to resist. When one of his garden gnomes is broken during the skirmish, Kowalski emerges from his house, brandishing the rifle he was issued during the Korean War. "Get off my lawn," he warns, and responds to a gang member's command to go back in his house by saying, "I shoot you in the face, and then I go back in the house, and sleep like a baby. You can count on that. We used to stack fucks like you five feet high in Korea, use you for sandbags." Muted snare drum taps play in the background. When Sue thanks Kowalski for chasing off the gang, he responds, "Get off my lawn."

Perhaps to its credit, the film posits that even as Walt ultimately rescues his Hmong neighbors from the predatory gang, it is they who save him, giving him a sense of peace, purpose, and even love that allows him to set his war-induced traumas behind him. The film casts Walt as a martyr who sacrifices himself for his immigrant friends in the climactic scene. The implication is that he is at peace because he has befriended and saved his Hmong neighbors, who have treated him with greater kindness and respect than his own sons have. As Walt says to himself at one point, "I have more in common with these gooks than with my own spoiled, rotten family." The reference to his sons and their children (his only remaining "family") as "spoiled" suggests, significantly I think, that Kowalski's identification with the Lors is in part economic: he realizes that they are the next generation of working people, and like him, they are making Detroit their home. Of course, the fact that Kowalski refers to the Hmong as "gooks"—not only to himself, but also openly to Thao and Sue—suggests his ambivalence about his emotional attachment to them, an attachment that contradicts the racist ideologies that have been so deeply ingrained in him. Kowalski's continual use of racial epithets, even in reference to individuals like Thao and Sue who become his friends, is played for humor in the film, most notably in the barbershop scenes, in which Kowalski trades ethnic slurs with his haircutter, and is at some measure undoubtedly designed to make audiences recognize and condemn Kowalski's racist attitudes. "The slurs," one critic contends, "are presented with candid matter-of-factness so that we can examine how racism operates. By exposing racism, the movie defuses its power."[16] At the same time, however, the repetition of the slurs also reinforces them. The derisive resonance of their original meanings may diminish as Kowalski becomes friends with the people he calls "zipperheads" who live next door, but his racist language is never directly challenged in the film. In fact, in the one comment he makes about Kowalski's language, Thao admits, "I don't care if you insult me or say racist things, 'cause you know what? I'll take it."

Some critics read the film as an anti-imperialist text, a "repudiation" of the extra-legal violence and muscular masculinity personified by Dirty Harry and other vigilante, cowboy figures that Eastwood has played. In an essay in *Jump Cut*, for instance, Robert Alpert argues that the film dismantles the narrative of empowerment through violent, "manly" action perpetuated by several other Eastwood films.[17] And it is true that the film's climactic confrontation between Kowalski and the Hmong gang members subverts our expectations: rather than perform the kind of violent revenge that we associate with Eastwood's wandering cowboy and hard-hearted rogue cop characters, Kowalski sacrifices himself, giving up his life so that the Hmong gangsters who shoot him, an unarmed man, will be arrested.

Yet the strongest evidence for *Gran Torino* as an anti-imperialist narrative that challenges the logic of violent intervention and retaliation that has underpinned so many previous Eastwood—and Hollywood action—films is not Kowalski's refusal to resolve the violent confrontation by using his gun, but rather the story of Kowalski's postwar traumatic stress. When asked by Father Janovich why he chased the gang off his lawn with a rifle rather than call the police ("What were you thinking? Someone could have been killed," the priest intones), Kowalski asserts, "When things go wrong, you gotta act quickly. When we were in Korea and a thousand screaming gooks came across our line, we didn't call the police; we reacted." Without missing a beat, Janovich responds, "We're not in Korea, Mr. Kowalski." Fifty years after his military service, Kowalski is still haunted by the atrocities he witnessed and committed in America's interventionist war in Korea. Indeed, he's still reliving them. Near the end of the film, when Kowalski locks Thao in his basement to prevent him from attending the final showdown with the gang, Kowalski reiterates that he's carrying a burden of guilt for killing other men in Korea. "You want to know what it's like to kill a man?" Kowalski asks. "Well, it's goddamn awful, that's what it is. The only thing worse is getting a medal of valor for killing some poor kid that wanted to just give up, that's all. Yeah, some scared little gook, just like you. I shot him right in the face with that rifle you were holding in there a little while ago. Not a day goes by that I don't think about it." Kowalski's openly racist attitudes and readiness for racist violence, the film suggests, are not merely products of his own mind, but flow from the larger structures of U.S. imperial violence that have historically deployed working-class men of all races as front-line actors for the assertion and extension of American military violence around the world.

As a meditation on labor, immigration, and contemporary America, *Gran Torino* is in certain ways noteworthy and innovative. First, the film underscores the value of physical work, which is rare for a major Hollywood production and significant in a society in which, as Mike Rose explains, "labor, as a political and social force, has diminished in power and has less immediate grab on the national imagination."[18] *Gran Torino* is not a class-conscious film, but within the contemporary cinematic landscape, it stands out for its blue-collar protagonist and its emphasis on manual labor. As a retired autoworker who installed the steering column in the very Gran Torino he owns while he was working on the automobile assembly line, Kowalski is, as critic Kim Nicolini puts it, "the living breathing symbol of Fordism."[19] His ownership of and meticulous care for the car represents a Fordist variation on the dream of unalienated labor, the fantasy that workers could close the circuit of production and consumption by acquiring the goods they themselves had a hand in making. Of course, the notion that Fordist manufacturing, organized around an assembly line that moved at the pace set by managers rather than by workers, whose labor was reduced largely to repetitive tasks, constituted a nonalienating system is a profoundly nostalgic misperception. Indeed, assembly line work represented the modern example par excellence of labor's proletarianization and alienation. Yet Fordism, as it took shape in the midcentury compact between labor and business, in which corporations pledged steadily rising wages and benefits in exchange for labor peace, raised living standards for workers, paying them enough to be able to purchase the products, like the Gran Torino, they were building. During the post-1945 "era of compression," autoworkers like Walt were often able to purchase a house and send children to college on a single, male wage. Facing a post-Fordist world, in which manufacturing jobs have been shipped overseas, unions have been broken, and cities like Detroit abandoned by capital and most middle-class residents, it is easy to understand the appeal that the Fordist era holds for white men like Kowalski, and for the Eastwood-directed film itself.

But Walt's working-classness—specifically, his identity as a working-class man—is linked not just to the factory, but to his ability to work with his hands. His capacity to fix and repair things, represented by his vast collection of tools, including not only his wrenches and pliers, but also his rifle and pistol, are a sign of his authentic, "old school" masculinity. Indeed, what separates Walt from the young gang members and almost all the other Hmong characters in the film, none of whom seem to have jobs, is his productive capacity, his blue-collar know-how and ability to get things done (the gang, after all, wants to *steal* what Walt *built*, the Gran Torino). At the same time, however, it is precisely this working-class knowledge that he seeks to pass on to Thao, who earns Kowalski's respect during the week he works for Walt, as he demonstrates competence and fortitude in completing a range of home repairs in the neighborhood that Kowalski assigns him. In contrast, Walt's biological sons live in large suburban houses, drive expensive Japanese cars, and have spoiled children and wives ("your wife's already gone through Mary's jewelry"). They have abandoned Walt, his neighborhood, and his way of life. Contending that "sales," the profession his wealthy son Mitch has chosen to pursue, is a "license to steal," Walt and the film offer a critique of commercial manipulation in favor of preservation, restoration, and repair—of cars, dryers, freezers, sinks, ceiling fans, gutters, even gardens—through manual work. Walt's working-classness is fairly stable and legible, embodied in the ability to perform physical labor, to earn a wage that can sustain a family, to wield a gun to "protect" his property. But for Thao, as I will suggest below, class is a much more uncertain question, and the movie suggests that the terms on which he will come to inhabit a working-class position are very much in the midst of formation.

A second putatively innovative feature of the film is its story of rapprochement between Kowalski and Thao, which offers an allegory of cross-ethnic, class-based, intergenerational solidarity. Scholar Adrienne Davis argues that in *Gran Torino*, interracial intimacy, embodied in the homosocial alliance between Walt and Thao, but also in the broader relations between Walt and the Lor family, redeems not only Walt, who sacrifices himself at the film's conclusion, but also by extension the political future of the United States. The film rejects racial nationalism, Davis asserts, in favor of "a multi-ethnic future."[20] And indeed, as the credits roll, Thao is driving the Gran Torino along the shores of Lake Michigan; he is literally in the driver's seat, having inherited the mantle of working-class masculinity, embodied in the car itself, which Walt conspicuously wills to Thao rather than to his biological family (I discuss the gender politics of this dynamic below).

The film's focus on working-class alliances and its critique of imperial wars, however, are cross-cut by several deeply conservative, indeed reactionary, ideological elements.[21] First, while the film gives notable mainstream cultural visibility to the Hmong community—a segment of the Asian/Asian American population whose historical entanglement with, and presence in, the United States is habitually effaced by prevailing civic discourses—it also trades in stereotypes. Other than Thao, the only young Hmong male characters in the film are savage, ruthless gang members. As Hmong Studies scholars Nancy Schein and Va-Megn Thoj point out, the film presents a community that is divided between the helpless and the hyperviolent.[22] In addition, Walt's alliance with his Hmong neighbors is predicated on and facilitated by the demonization of African Americans, who appear only briefly and stereotypically in the film, as gangsters. The most egregious example occurs in a scene that almost all the critics I have read gloss over, in which three Black men, cast as savage sexual predators, verbally abuse and threaten to violate Sue after dispatching the young, white man she was walking with. Walt literally rides his pick-up to her rescue, calling the Black men "spooks," and brandishing a pistol, Dirty Harry style. "Ever notice how you come across somebody every once in a while that you shouldn't have fucked with? That's me," he warns them, with a mixture of humor and hubris that recalls other Eastwood vigilante characters from earlier films. This is the *only* scene featuring Black characters in the film, a representational scandal that is amplified by the fact that the movie is shot in Detroit, a majority-Black city heavily identified with African American culture and a history of Black labor radicalism.[23]

As this scene suggests, white masculinity remains the normative, and dominant, gender discourse in the film. Sue says to Walt, "I wish our father would have been more like you," and Walt does become a surrogate patriarch to the Lor family, a source of male authority and competence that the film wants us to think they lack and need. Both Walt and the gang members continually call Thao a "pussy," and while the film may expect viewers to bristle (and laugh) at this language, it effectively endorses the claim that Thao needs to be, as Walt puts it, "manned up." After all, it is only under Walt's tutelage that Thao acquires what Sue calls "some direction," which in terms of the film means a job, a date, and the capacity to talk cars and tell crude racist and sexist jokes. Henry Ford, whose Highland Park plant in Detroit inaugurated assembly line production in 1913, famously sought to discipline and homogenize his workers, demanding that immigrants take English-language classes and establishing a sociology department to monitor Ford employees and ensure they were living "respectable" lives. In *Gran Torino*, Walt himself takes on the task of assimilation, using his gruff, stern demeanor to teach Thao the value of hard work (which Walt mistakenly presumes he doesn't already possess) and the cultural codes, behaviors, and language of traditional working-class manhood (of course, Walt himself, who often spends his days drinking in solitude on his porch, is not exactly the kind of model citizen–worker of whom Henry Ford would have approved).

To some extent, Walt is successful: Thao demonstrates his mastery of the good-ole-boy repartee Walt teaches him in his conversation with the construction manager, and he embraces the job he lands as a result. Yet the father-son, master-apprentice narrative, in which Walt takes Thao from wimp to manly man, is undercut by the fact that Thao's performance of manliness proves that Walt's masculine ideal is just that: a performance. The story Thao delivers to the construction manager, for instance, is pure fabrication; it's effective, but completely fictional. Tania Modleski argues that Thao represents "the model-minority, 'feminized' Asian male" who fails to live up to the "ideal of masculinity represented by Eastwood, who in the persona of Walt must constantly rescue the hapless young man."[24] As I explain below, Kowalski's position as the older, white authority figure does render Thao passive in several key scenes, but it's not accurate to say that Thao personifies the model minority, primarily because he seems to lack the upwardly mobile ambitions associated with the model minority stereotype. Rather, Thao troubles the very terms of masculinity in which the film seems to be framing gender and ethnic roles. His modest, blue-collar ambitions, his embrace of construction work, and his lack of interest in education as a pathway into the middle class distinguish him from the archetypal model minority figure. Yet he also refuses to fulfill Walt's image of the ideal blue-collar man: the heterosexual plot that Walt tries to establish for him is dropped (in the film's final scene, the figure on the seat of the Gran Torino next to him is not his ostensible love interest, Yueh, but Walt's dog, Daisy). Moreover, his almost comic performances of white-ethnic tough-guy behaviors suggest that rather than a model of gender and national assimilation, Thao complicates the very frameworks that the film establishes to make sense of—and indeed to discipline—him.

In the end, Walt becomes not only Thao's mentor, but also the Lors' savior, the figure of decisive action who rescues one (passive, feminized) segment of the Hmong community from another (the violent, savage gangs) because they cannot save themselves. In this way, the film allegorically replays and rewrites America's war in Vietnam, allowing, as Schein and Thoj suggest, "the central figure of the white US citizen to complete the project of saving Asians from themselves that was so humiliatingly aborted in Southeast Asia."[25] Walt's "heroism," it is important to underscore, infantilizes Thao, whom Walt locks in his basement (ostensibly for his "own good") as he strides off to the film's climactic scene. Thus, while Walt—and the film—offer a critique of America's military interventionism, the film's resolution nonetheless replicates a colonial dynamic, in which the white man acts assertively to save people of color from themselves. This dynamic has especially deep historical ironies for Hmong people, many of whom were enlisted to fight alongside U.S. troops in Vietnam and carry out America's secret war in Laos, only to be largely abandoned by the United States when it evacuated Southeast Asia in the mid-1970s. As Tania Modleski explains, "In reality then, Hmong people gave up their lives trying to save Americans, but in the film the old white man dies to save the *Hmong* and achieves absolution for the sins of American imperialism."[26] This redemptive narrative, in which the film's critique of war serves perversely to absolve imperial action, is the film's most forceful ideological implication.

Even more disturbing, Walt's actions to save the Lors are also predicated on, and justified by, one of the most unsettling plot turns: Sue's rape. Sue is an articulate, forceful character in the first two-thirds of the film. She facilitates Walt and Thao's friendship by inviting Walt to a barbecue at their house, translating for him so he can talk to other Hmong community members and insisting that Thao work for Walt to make up for the attempted theft of Kowalski's car. Even in the scene when she is accosted by the three Black men only to be rescued by Kowalski, she proves feisty, lambasting the racial and gender clichés her would-be attackers use in an effort to demean her. But once she is raped by the gang members, she falls into silence.[27] This retrograde narrative pattern, in which assertive, white male action is authorized by sexual assault on women (a pattern that in fact occurs twice in the film!), can be traced in cinema back to at least *Birth of a Nation*, and it has driven any number of Hollywood action films, including Eastwood's *The Outlaw Josey Wales* and *Unforgiven*. Thus, although the film appears to subvert the Dirty Harry model of masculine vigilantism (Walt notes in his conversation with his local priest, "The thing that haunts a man the most is what he isn't ordered to do [but does anyway]"), it nonetheless reproduces a deeply sexist trope in which female passivity and violation become the occasion for male action.

The film's contradictory cultural politics—its effort to imagine a progressive alliance between working peoples from different nations and traditions on the one hand, and its reproduction of a sexist, racist white male savior narrative on the other—are echoed in the movie's uneven aesthetic. Perhaps surprising for a major studio release featuring a world cinematic icon, *Gran Torino* features several first-time actors in the Hmong roles. Warner Brothers found its Hmong cast by working through Hmong community organizations in Fresno, Detroit, and St. Paul, where seven hundred people turned out to audition.[28] In addition, Eastwood's actor-centered directorial tendencies gave actors space to improvise and inhabit their roles, giving them a greater-than-usual degree of autonomy. The Hmong actors were allowed to create bits of dialogue and inserted Hmong language into the film. This was significant for several of the Hmong cast members, who were wary of being reduced to stereotypical figures, and who welcomed the opportunity to help develop the characters they played. The flexible, improvisational acting complemented other elements of realism in the film, such as its focus on a down-and-out setting and on-location shooting, its emphasis on some details of decay and poverty, such as abandoned and dilapidated houses as well as broken sinks, fans, and freezers. Yet the film's realist elements are overrun, in the end, by the film's Hollywood imperatives: its dramatic momentum, its fast pacing and narrative climax that builds to a decisive and violence-filled confrontation between "good" and "bad" guys. If the film is in many ways nostalgic for Fordism, it is itself very much a classic mass-production item, organized by (rather than challenging) easily recognizable, mass culture formulas.

My analysis of *Gran Torino* has a final twist that returns to the issues of class with which I began. As I noted earlier, Fredric Jameson has asserted that the power of a text's ideological pull depends on its capacity to evoke a utopian dimension. I think that this notion holds for Eastwood's film, which is in most ways politically and ideologically noxious. While the film charts the demise, even rupture, of collectivities (the traditional nuclear family, an older, unified working class, even the nation itself, as an imagined homogenous cultural-political unit), its emphasis on such collective forms, no matter how broken and flawed, and on the possibility (however compromised by the film's incapacity to think beyond white male privilege and authority) of affiliation between Walt and his Hmong neighbors, contains, I think, seeds of a utopian longing for collective belonging, albeit one that the film itself does not recognize and cannot formally acknowledge. More than just a metaphor for cross-ethnic working-class collaboration, or the symbol of an emergent multicultural future, the bond formed between Walt and Sue and Thao is also an allegorical figure, however faint and unrealized, for something more ambitious, which the film itself cannot actually name: collectivity per se, that is, a form of collective solidarity and unity that stands as the repudiation of and potential antidote to the deeply privatized, individualized, reified, violent, and stratified imperial-capitalist society that the characters inhabit. This, I submit, is the film's utopian element, and it is one that the film does not—indeed cannot—articulate. In other words, the tension or conflict between the film's deeply conservative aspects (its nostalgia for industrial modernity, imperial power, white patriarchy, and traditional gender roles) and its more progressive features (its effort to imagine cross-ethnic, intergeneration affiliations, its optimism about the future that Thao and Sue embody) can be, if not resolved, then at least understood as features of a more elemental/foundational longing for cooperative, collective being as the ultimate anodyne for the competitive and colonialist global society that has scarred (albeit in quite different ways) both Kowalski and the Lors. But in its own terms, the film—which professes to reject violence—can only imagine collectivity *through* violence, and can only imagine its projection of white-immigrant alliance through the expulsion, excision, and figurative, if not quite literal, death of Black figures.

"There's no border here": *Frozen River*

Set in the north country of upstate New York and on the Akwesasne (Mohawk) Reservation that straddles the U.S.-Canadian border, *Frozen River* narrates the encounter and eventual partnership of two impoverished women: Ray Eddy, a white mother of two boys (TJ, age fifteen, and Ricky, age eight) who works part-time as a retail clerk at a discount store, and Lila Littlewolf, a Mohawk bingo parlor employee who is trying to regain custody of her infant son from her former mother-in-law. Ray and Lila meet when Lila appropriates a car that had been abandoned by Ray's husband, a compulsive gambler who has abruptly left Ray and their sons, absconding with the money they had been saving to purchase a new double-wide mobile home. Desperate to make up the stolen money in time to purchase the new mobile home before Christmas, Ray teams up with Lila to transport undocumented immigrants from China and Pakistan into the United States by driving across the frozen St. Lawrence River through the Mohawk reservation. After a few successful runs, including one during which they accidentally abandon a baby in a duffle bag on the ice, only to the retrace their tracks and rescue her, Ray and Lila are finally followed by Canadian and New York State police, who wait on the edge of the reservation and demand that one of the traffickers turn herself in. Lila decides to give herself up, but then Ray, realizing that her racial privilege will ease her passage through the courts and prison, submits to arrest. Lila takes custody of her young son and moves in with Ray's two sons to care for them until Ray is released.

Produced with a $1 million budget and released in 2008, *Frozen River* is the first feature-length film written and directed by Courtney Hunt, who lived for several years in the area where the film is set, researching the story.

The film was lauded by many critics, including Roger Ebert, and was awarded several prizes, including the Grand Jury Prize at the Sundance Film Festival. It also received Academy Award nominations for best screenplay (Hunt) and best actress (Leo). Like *Gran Torino*, the film offers a meditation on interethnic, transnational working-class affiliation in the age of globalization. Yet *Frozen River* attends much more closely than Eastwood's film to the details of economic desperation, underscoring the harsh poverty its characters are laboring to escape. In addition, Hunt's film focuses on the particular challenges faced by working-class women in a capitalist system that is both patriarchal and settler colonialist. The film suggests that the economic, gender, and racial barriers to its protagonists' well-being are substantial, but it holds out hope that transcultural solidarity between women can produce unorthodox forms of social relation and belonging capable of countering, or at least mitigating, contemporary neoliberal capitalism's harsh logics of punitive abandonment and dispossession.

Thematically, *Frozen River* is a film about the possibilities of and trenchant obstacles to physical, social, and economic mobility in a globalizing world, especially for poor women and undocumented immigrants. It is a film about border crossing: about immigrants traveling across national boundaries, about Ray and Lila's efforts to work across the national and cultural boundaries that separate them, and about the larger economic and political barriers these two impoverished women face. These issues are raised in the film's opening sequence, which I want to examine closely as a way of grounding my analysis. The film commences with the following shots: a steady pan of a frozen river; a shot of birds flying overhead; a shot of a bridge, with a barbed wire fence in the foreground, and a large eighteen-wheel transport truck and cars coming off the span, approaching a U.S. customs toll ("Inspection required!"; "Be prepared to show identification"; "Declare all articles acquired outside USA"); a shot of cars lining up for the toll, with a slightly obscured sign "Welcome to the United States" visible in the distance; a shot of a lone pickup truck driving down a road; a full-frame shot of a sign, "Welcome to Massena. Gateway to the Fourth Coast"; a shot of a yard, covered in melting snow, with a white shed and a jerry-rigged merry-go-round in the foreground; a shot of the rear of a car parked in front of a light blue mobile home, the front passenger side door wide open; a shot of a woman's toe with a tattoo on it, and then a slow pan up the woman's body (she's wearing a pink bathrobe and holding a package of cigarettes and a lighter) to her heavily lined face. She takes a long drag on a cigarette, and a tear roles down her face; the camera cuts to the open, empty glove compartment of the car.

If Russell Banks's *Continental Drift*, discussed in chapter 1, takes as its core metaphor the shifting plates of the earth's crust, the symbolic centerpiece of Hunt's film, as indicated by its very first shot, is the frozen St. Lawrence River. At once beautiful and foreboding, the frozen river is a deeply ambivalent icon, embodying possibility and danger, motion and immobility, stability and impending collapse. On one hand, the ice provides a remarkably sturdy natural bridge ("I've seen semis cross it," Lila notes) which, for Lila, Ray, and the immigrants, constitutes a passageway to new lands and new opportunities and the possibility of circumventing governmental restrictions. In its location running through the Akwesasne Reservation, the frozen river is an alternative ecological and geopolitical zone where U.S. and Canadian sovereignty does not reign.[29] Although the river and reservation are sites where Ray feels much less comfortable than Lila, they stand as spaces in which the two women collectively possess agency they lack elsewhere, and can carve their own path. The ice-covered river, and the reservation more broadly, constitute a sovereign "third space" (or "fourth coast," as the sign in the opening shots tells us), outside the U.S. nation-state's jurisdiction.[30] When Ray pauses during the first smuggling run, insisting, "I'm not taking [these immigrants] across the border. It's a crime," Lila responds, "There's no border here. It's free trade between nations." The film largely endorses this view, which sees the reservation as a sovereign territory outside the parameters of the U.S. and Canadian nation-states. By crossing the border between the United States and Canada that cuts through the Akwesasne nation, Lila (and Ray with her) affirm Indigenous sovereignty.[31] The river and the reservation though which it flows thus constitute spaces largely outside the everyday structures of Western, capitalist governmentality that confine, demean, and exploit the film's two protagonists.

Yet if the frozen river supports fugitive lines of flight and Indigenous forms of sovereignty, it is also physically and metaphorically fragile, subject to cracking and collapse. The solidity of the ice is contingent on consistent cold temperatures and can be deceptively thin and slippery. For Ray and Lila, the fragility of the ice stands as a metaphor for the precarity of their lives. For those being smuggled, the ice offers passage to other nations and the potential for new economic possibilities and political freedoms, yet these grueling migrations take place under constant threat of interruption by border police, corrupt smugglers, and the various travails of illegal travel, including hunger, injury, and mistreatment. Moreover, these migrations come at a heavy price, as Lila explains to Ray: "The snakeheads pay to get them here, and then they gotta work off what they owe." "How much does it cost?" Ray asks. Lila responds, "Forty, fifty thousand. Depends on where they're coming from. Sometimes they've got to work for years to pay it off." "To get *here*?!" Ray exclaims. "No fucking way." Ray realizes that her economic opportunity entails delivering other people into exploitation, in fact into indentured labor. Moreover, the immigrants' desire to reach the United States, even "illegally," strikes Ray as an obscene joke, since for her America has been a place in which realities have never lived up to the much-advertised dream. Paradoxes abound here, embodied in the ice itself, which is a fluid material temporarily frozen solid.

The shots in the film's initial sequence that follow the pan of the frozen river—of birds flying overhead and of cars and trucks crossing the fenced, guarded U.S.-Canadian border—foreground spatial, geopolitical, and cultural boundaries, and the regulation of those boundaries, that are central to this film about unauthorized immigration. Throughout the film, images of failed linkages and faulty connections proliferate: ropes between cars snap; the makeshift swing set that TJ is building needs to be soldered; exchanges of immigrants threaten to go awry; the loss of the baby, hidden in a duffle bag, that Ray and Lila mistakenly abandon on the ice. And throughout, images of crossing and connection are countered by motifs of barriers, from the customs tolls and signs marking the boundaries of the reservation, to the woman at the bingo game who refuses to let Ray in to look for her husband unless she pays the admissions fee, to the car windows being rolled up and down. In other words, the film posits possibilities for mobility and spaces of autonomy from established regimes of control, but continually demonstrates the vulnerability and provisionality of those possibilities and spaces. Mohawk sovereignty is depicted as a powerful alternative to prevailing U.S. and Canadian ways of organizing and controlling bodies and space, yet the reservation is surrounded on all sides, its borders vigilantly policed, its authority limited to a tightly circumscribed area.

The opening sequence culminates in the slow pan of Ray Eddy from her tattooed foot to her face, which is captured in close detail, sharply framed by the camera. We see the roughened silver polish on her short nails, the tight lines that crisscross her face, and the dark shadows under her eyes. This intense close-up recalls Dorothea Lange's 1936 photograph "Migrant Mother," which foregrounds the pensive isolation of its central figure, whose deeply furrowed brow and gaze into the distance seem to express an ambiguous state of worry.[32] The woman Lange photographed, Florence Thompson, was living in a canvas tent in a muddy pea-pickers camp, feeding her children frozen vegetables pulled from the surrounding fields.[33] In evoking (intentionally or not) this iconic Depression-era documentary image, the film signals a realist focus on the hard facts of economic desperation for women and children. And throughout, the film, which Roger Ebert describes as "the story of two lives in economic emergency," places a sustained emphasis on the harsh economic demands and limitations that shape Ray's and Lila's lives. We see, for instance, the dirty, decaying state of Ray's mobile home, including the mold-laced tub, rusted showerhead, rotted board and ripped insulation underneath. We see the hardships and humiliations of poverty: Ray stuffing towels around the windows to protect against drafts; the menu of Tang and popcorn that sustains TJ and Ricky; Ray fishing for school lunch money in the couch cushions; the indifference of young men refusing to deliver a mobile home or preparing to repossess a Rent-to-Own television (a loss narrowly averted by Ray's first cash payment for smuggling); the tinfoil-wrapped ready-made dinners that TJ prepares for himself and Ricky on Christmas Eve; the scorched end of their trailer, stained gray from the smoke of the fire started when TJ tried to warm the water pipes. The family's aspirations are correspondingly modest: a trip to Price Chopper with cash to buy groceries, a mobile home with a bedroom for each member of the family, a Hot Wheels "Blast-N-Crash Track" set for Christmas, a rust-free bathtub in which Ray could use her soaking salts, and the leisure time to take a bath. On Lila's side, we see the cramped, drafty trailer in which she sleeps, in her clothes, under a pile of blankets; the label flaking off the plastic Pringles potato chip can in which she leaves money for her son. We see her walking along the side of the highway as a huge truck rumbles by, underscoring her vulnerability; her poor eyesight and lack of glasses, which prevent her from being able to count the money she and Ray are paid by smugglers. In a cinematic context in which so many major motion pictures take place in pristine middle-class homes, and in which corporations pay to place their shiny new products as not-so-subtle visible advertisements, *Frozen River* stands out for its grim images of economic deprivation, material decay, and quotidian struggles for basic needs.

Equally significant, Lila's and Ray's struggles are placed in the context of larger, global flows, not only of the immigrants, who enter into sizeable debt to reach the bottom rungs of the American economy, but also of commodity circulation. An exchange between Ray and her son Ricky suggests their awareness of capital's global reach and power. "Mommy," Ricky asks, "what's gonna happen to our old house when we get our new house?" She replies, "They're gonna flatten it and send it to China." "Then what?," he asks. "Then they're gonna melt it down and make it into little toys." "Then what?" "Then they're gonna send 'em back here so I can sell 'em at Yankee Dollar." "Can you give me some?" "That's right." This fable is designed to reassure Ricky, but in fact suggests global capital's unsettling powers of creative destruction. The house in which they are living, they acknowledge, is just so much raw metal for a hungry, transnational system of production.

While capital and commodities circulate across national borders with ease, the movement of working people is restricted. The immigrants Lila and Ray smuggle risk life and limb to reach the United States. The immigrants do not emerge as individually identifiable characters in the film, but stand as shadowy figures for the unofficial, underground circuits of human migration and sacrifice that keep the formal economy running. The chilling scene in which the immigrant baby is abandoned in the snow and then retrieved, somehow still alive, conveys the radical vulnerability of undocumented workers, whose passage across the icy border in the trunk of a car is a symbolic, and potentially all-too-real real, death. Driven to desperation by the global economy, living labor is at risk of becoming dead labor.

Ray and Lila are icons of what I am calling *labor-in-motion*, working people circulating and crossing boundaries in a desperate search for sustenance, whose motility suggests the uncertainty and instability of late capitalist working-class conditions. Yet they are also stuck in place, spatially and socially confined. Ray has been left behind by her husband, who departs just before the film starts, assuming that Ray, in her role as mother, will stay with TJ and Ricky. Ray has a car but has to forage in her pockets for coins and small bills to buy gas. For Lila, too, transportation poses a challenge: the local automobile dealer will not sell her a car because she's likely to use it for smuggling; as a result, she's forced to walk to work and back along a highway with no sidewalk. Ray is also stuck in her dead-end job. She has been waiting two years for a promised promotion to full-time work, but her young male boss brushes her off with disdain. At the end of a shift, Ray pulls him aside and asserts, "I need to come on full time." He replies, "I see you as a short-timer." "What is that?" "Not here for long, not really committed." "When I started working here you told me it would be six months before I could come on full-time," she replies. "That was almost two years ago." "That's my opinion," he finally responds, not even offering the pretense of logical justification. Ray insists to her sons that she can make ends meet and provide the new home the family wants, but viewers—and TJ—see the fragility of her claims. Early in the film, as Ray scrounges for lunch money, TJ insists, "I can get a job, you know." Ray replies, "You're going to finish school," to which TJ replies, "You think we can make a living on what you earn at Yankee Dollar?!" Ray's admission of this reality is what leads her to smuggling.

Significantly, especially when placed in dialogue with *Gran Torino*, *Frozen River* underscores the particular challenges faced by working-class and poor women. Economic struggle is, the film suggests, gendered; it has different textures for women, and for mothers, than for men and for those without primary responsibility for children. The opening images of Ray sitting in her car, having just realized that her husband has absconded with their savings, prefigures another shot of Ray crying as she prepares for work, tears ruining the mascara she is trying to apply. This shot exposes the discrepancy between dominant ideals of feminine beauty, which demand that women appear flawlessly composed, "made up," and sexually appealing at all times, and the realities of Ray's working-class life, which is dominated by struggles to secure basic needs such as food and safe shelter for her children, and which leave almost no time or surplus money for self-care and personal maintenance. Just after Ray's boss dismisses her request for full-time work, Ray encounters the cashier for the next shift, who is arriving (late) for work. Younger than Ray, she has blonde hair and a tattoo on her lower back, asking "How you doin'?" Ray offers a knowing nod at the tattoo, signaling her awareness that the manager's treatment of his employees is shaped by sexism. Ray's failure to progress at work, the film intimates, has nothing to do with her abilities or commitment and everything to do with sexism.

Frozen River is, I have suggested, a story of abandonment and dispossession, of two women left by their male partners and both devalued and actively disciplined by the dominant civil, social, and economic structures of U.S. and Canadian society. Yet it is important to underscore, as the film does, that the social conditions of these two women are different. Ray is adrift and alone, isolated from any community as far as we can see. Her boss disrespects her, and she doesn't appear to have any close friends, neighborly ties, or connections to family, other than her children. At night, when she is alone in her room, rather than call friends or relatives to seek support, Ray obsessively records and rerecords her cell phone voicemail message. She seems to be completely on her own. Lila, too, is isolated, but she is also embedded in the Mohawk community, although her relations with tribal leaders and neighbors are by no means seamless. In fact, members of the Mohawk tribe tend to treat her as problem to be tolerated or managed: the young car salesman refuses to sell her a car that he knows she will use to transport undocumented immigrants; the tribal police chief, Bernie, corrals her into taking a temporary job answering phones that she quits a few hours later; her former mother-in-law, who has care of Lila's son, views Lila as an interloper from whom the toddler must be shielded; Jimmy, who facilitates Lila's cross-border transportation runs, insists, "I shouldn't even be dealing with you." Finally, when the tribal council learns that Lila and Ray have been tracked by state troopers who are waiting at the edge of Mohawk territory to arrest one of them for smuggling, the chiefs vote to expel Lila. The film thus does not present a naïve or simplistic vision of the Mohawk community, which it suggests is riven by political differences, divided opinions, and power struggles. Nonetheless, Lila lives in a community of people who know her intimately and whose fates and feelings are deeply entangled with hers. And despite her often antagonistic stance toward the expectations that others in the tribe have of her, the tribe's worldview—especially its sense of Indigenous sovereignty—shapes Lila's own sense of the world and what is permissible, even possible. This becomes most evident when Ray and Lila are driving to their first trip ferrying undocumented immigrants through the Akwesasne nation and across the U.S.-Canadian border:

LILA: "Turn up there."
RAY: "There's no road"
  "There's a *path*."
  "I'm not crossing that."
  "Don't worry, there's no black ice."
  "That's Canada."
  "That's Mohawk land. The Res is on both sides of the river."
  "What about the border patrol?"
  "There's no border."

Here Lila demonstrates the alternative epistemology she possesses as a Mohawk, which allows her to see paths where there are not officially marked roads and to discern the continuity of an Indigenous nation where Ray can see only see a political boundary. Lila's understanding of the Mohawk conception of natural and geopolitical space opens up room for what Michael Shapiro calls "thinking beyond state sovereignty," that is, a form of thinking that challenges hegemonic models of inclusion and exclusion based on established state boundaries and cultures.[34] This alternative sense of space serves, finally, as a metaphor for the film's own efforts to chart an alternative to the dominant masculinist ethos of working-class narratives and Hollywood films.

In a short article written for a screenwriting magazine, Hunt explained that "In *Frozen River*, the question was: Can two women from different cultures stick by each other when their own survival is threatened?"[35] For Hunt, then, the film concerns the prospect of intercultural alliance in the face of hardship, fear, and desperation. Yet the film suggests that Ray's and Lila's lives are shaped not simply by "cultural difference," but also, and perhaps more fundamentally, by the social construction and policing of race and the legacies and still ongoing dynamics of settler colonialism, which are subtly visible in several elements of the film. For instance, the film suggests that the differential conditions of economic possibility for these two women echo the lines of colonial power. However poorly Ray and her two children may be faring, Lila's chances for economic well-being are structurally even more challenging. While Ray struggles to make ends meet by working at Yankee Dollar and to house her kids in an aging, single-wide mobile home, Lila's home is an equally old, even less well-insulated, and much smaller camper, and her only employment option seems to be even less lucrative and potentially more demeaning work as a waitress at the reservation's bingo parlor. In addition, the film quietly yet consistently draws attention to Ray's white privilege and to the way it conditions what is possible for her relative to Lila. As the two women leave the reservation with immigrants smuggled in the trunk of the car, Lila reminds Ray that once they cross into New York state, her whiteness affords her a freedom from scrutiny that Lila on her own lacks. "What if the troopers stop us?" Ray asks. Lila responds, "They're not going to stop you. You're white." Explicit talk about white privilege returns in the film's decisive moment, when Ray turns herself in to the troopers to protect Lila from having to do so. To explain her decision, Ray notes, "Just a couple of months, right? I've got no record, and I'm white." Ray has absorbed the lesson that Lila taught: she now understands the scope and social significance of white and Indigenous racial identities and the way those identities mold life possibilities in contemporary America. Lisa Hinrichsen argues that in the film the "myth of racial privilege fails to materialize" because Ray goes to jail.[36] Yet she surrenders to the police precisely because she understands that her white privilege will protect her in the courtroom and even in prison.

The bond that Lila and Ray develop is an unusual kind of solidarity. The two are both women and both poor, but they are separated by substantial cultural, national, and epistemological differences. Their alliance stems not directly from a shared identity, a common principle, or even a mutual vision of the social and political world. Indeed, their association begins in conflict, confrontation, and mistrust; it proceeds to a tussle in the car, which ends with Lila's ejection and a knock on the head for Ray. Theirs is a bond without a telos, based—at least initially—almost entirely on pragmatic concerns, namely, making enough money to support their respective children. The immediate, pragmatic, and economic basis for their collaboration is evident when Ray returns to Lila's trailer the day after their first smuggling run to ask for her share of the money. When Lila tells her the money is gone (she left it for her son), Ray responds, "Then I wanna get more of those Chinese.... I just want enough to buy my double-wide and them I'm out of this. I'm not a criminal." Lila responds, "It's not a crime." Ray replies, "You people can call it what you want. I just want my double." In response to Ray's condescension, Lila states with disdain, "I don't usually work with whites."

Yet the two women do work together, and the film suggests that their bond develops a degree of staying power, even as it remains in a state of flux. The climax of the film turns on an about-face, as Ray doubles back on her initial decision to leave Lila to confront the police. Her reversal suggests the unsettled quality of their mutual relations, roles, and obligations, and yet also the strength of their connection. Indeed, Ray's return to help Lila contradicts her own self-interest, indicating the sense of reciprocity that the two women have forged. Similarly, the very ending of the film, in which we see Lila and her son living with TJ and Ricky, suggests that however temporary or provisional their affiliation may be, it has generated a sturdy, if necessarily fluid, sense of commitment. Appropriately enough, the concluding scene is awkward. Ray, who is serving a jail sentence, is not present. Lila, we realize, is not that much older than TJ, and the four of them (Lila, her son, TJ, and Ricky) seem a bit disoriented or decentered as they exit the trailer and two youngest children get on the merry-go-round that TJ built. But to some extent this awkwardness is the point: this alternative domestic arrangement, in which Lila, an unmarried Mohawk woman with an infant of her own, is caring for Ray's sons (one of whom, TJ, is in fact a primary caretaker for his brother) in Ray's absence, cuts against convention. As a scene of family reunion, it confounds traditional expectations: this is a nonnuclear, interracial grouping, a mélange of two families headed by women living without male partners or support. (And the sense of institutional alternatives in this scene is enhanced by the arrival of the tribal police officer who, rather than formerly charging or arresting TJ for the credit card scam he used to steal money from an elderly woman earlier in the film, merely asks him to apologize.[37])

In sharp contrast to *Gran Torino*, which silences its primary female speaking character, *Frozen River* foregrounds the economic and social struggles of poor working (and underemployed and often nonworking) women, suggesting that their fates are intertwined and that their partnership can help them withstand (at least some of) the patriarchal, capitalist, white supremacist forces arrayed against them. Yet like *Gran Torino*, which concludes with the image of Thao driving into an uncertain future, *Frozen River* ends on a note of resonant ambiguity, which qualifies the sense of idealism with which the film positions us to regard the counternuclear family scene at the end. Will this relationship withstand the challenges ahead, including the pressures of making a living? When Ray is released will the women's partnership continue? Will Lila be able to return to Mohawk territory, and on what terms?

Wilfred Raussert argues that the film's conclusion echoes, by way of contrast, the opening sequence, which is dominated by images of boundary policing: fences, barbed wire, and federal customs signs. Yet the end of the film, especially the "shift from the representation of a static, lifeless merry-go-round to one in motion, filled with life by the young members of a newly emerging patchwork family," emphasizes mobility and transition.[38] Born in and symbolized by jagged, tension-filled, and unorthodox forms of motion, negotiation, and border crossing, the new transnational, transethnic community embodied by Ray, Lila, and their children is unsettled, "has no stable home."[39] The depiction of this grouping is affirmative, but not sentimentalized or idealized: the final shots zoom in on the faces of the characters, who look happy, yet still uneasy. The nonnuclear "family" they have (temporarily) formed does not represent an established, final collective, and it does not provide respite from the economic struggles that brought these women together in the first place, despite the shot of a new (single-, not double-wide) mobile home—a symbol of the family's transient location—coming down the road.

The film's thematic focus on hybrid spaces, mixed cultural formations, and labor-in-motion is echoed in its uneven aesthetic composition, which blends elements of neorealism with the outlines of a fairly conventional noir thriller. From the neorealist tradition, the film draws several impulses and techniques: it is shot on location, uses several local, nonprofessional actors, and at times has a deeply naturalistic, documentary look, with handheld camera work. At one point, for instance, balloons obscure our view of Ray as she works in the store, in what looks like (but obviously is not) a poorly framed shot (as A. O. Scott notes, neorealism may appear naturalistic, but is usually highly composed[40]). In the nighttime scenes, a lack of intensive lighting produces an abundance of black space, occasionally obscuring our sense of what is happening. The forms of obfuscation and lack of clarity generated by the camera work echo the sense of disorientation that Lila and Ray frequently feel as they stumble their way toward economic survival. The documentary resonance (evident not only in the naturalistic, choppy camera work and the low-level lighting, but also in the unorthodox sounds of automobile trunks squeaking, open car doors beeping, and other ambient noises) gives the film a realist tenor in line with its focus on poor people living in trying circumstances, hallmarks of what I am calling precarious realism.

At the same time, the film exhibits features of a relatively conventional Hollywood suspense film. In particular, the prevalence of nighttime shots, especially in the latter stages of the film, form a pattern of visual and thematic elements (such as the sense of isolation and desperation that marks the way the film depicts Lila and especially Ray), including a nighttime exchange of smuggled immigrants at seedy strip bar, that recall film noir, part of the long history of Hollywood cinema about the underside of the bright, shiny surface of American life. The noir dimensions of the film include its accelerating suspense-and-action-oriented finale, but these elements are used to underscore the structural challenges of gender, race, and economics that Ray and Lila face. As Ray and Lila leave the Quebec strip joint with two female immigrants in their trunk, the Canadian smuggler fires at Ray, who had wielded her gun to wrest the full payment from him after he had initially tried to give them only half. When Ray had pulled the gun, Lila had told her to put it away, that she would make up the difference in pay. "Let's go! I'll give you the rest of the money. You're going to get us all killed," she tells Ray. As they drive away, Ray explains, "I'm so tired of people stealing from me." Here, noir motifs—the nighttime gun play and the ensuing car chase, in which Ray and Lila abandon their vehicle on the warming ice when it starts to sink—serve to underscore the economic desperation these women are experiencing. Ray, in particular, is so frantic for money that she is willing to risk her life over a fairly modest sum. In addition, the high drama at the film's conclusion highlights the corrupt, institutional, and overwhelmingly masculine forces arrayed against them: the male smuggler who tried to cheat them, the state troopers (all of whom in the film are male) who watch them and eventually arrest Ray, and their husbands, who have abandoned them.

In the end, then, it is heterogeneity and flux—embodied in the fluid, female-led domestic arrangements forged by Ray, Lila, and their children; in the mixed stylistic elements that Hunt mashes together to give the film its unique texture; in the image of the handmade, one-of-a-kind carousel TJ has crafted from recycled parts; in the prospect of an uneasy, yet sustained alliance between women inhabiting different nationalities and racial positions—that *Frozen River* emphasizes. For *Frozen River*, as for *Gran Torino*, the globalizing world is a terrain of deep and expanding instability marked by declining wages and collapsing conventions, volatile cross-cultural encounters and amalgams, and pervasive violence and anxiety. These stories cognitively map uneven developments of contemporary capitalism, even if they cannot fully imagine or chart the totality of its structuring forces. Both films focus on economic degradation and dispossession, largely from the perspective of white workers, but neither traces connections between the financial and social upheavals the characters face and the governing forces—corporate outsourcing, in the case of Eastwood's film, and the regional underdevelopment of economic production in the case of *Frozen River*. Yet both films see possibilities for working-class alliance and solidarity in the unprecedented meetings brought about by globalization's human and capital flows. For *Gran Torino*, the primary drama concerns the effects of this newly tumultuous, transnational world on the fading, white industrial proletariat. Eastwood's film is in some large part an elegy for Fordism, and to the extent that it imagines a post-Fordist, indeed post-American future, it imagines one that follows in the male, proletarian mode. Yet the transition it imagines is unfinished and uncertain. Walt may have handed the mantle of blue-collar masculinity to Thao, who seems to have embraced the construction job that Walt helped him secure, but the film indicates that the cultural, linguistic, gender, and sexual terms on which Thao's working-class sense of self will develop are quite different from the white-ethnic, patriarchal, midcentury terms that defined Walt's life under Fordist capitalism in the United States. *Frozen River*, on the other hand, imagines a much more thoroughgoing and reciprocal transnational transformation, in which women whose options were severely restricted by Fordism's regimes of economic and gender hierarchy could, when facing personal financial crises and the absence of men in their lives, forge alternative modes of relation and being based on urgently pragmatic, yet also deeply felt needs and desires for which hegemonic cultural forms have afforded all too little space for articulation.

In sum, then, both *Gran Torino* and *Frozen River* register the crisis of older ways of imagining the American working class and foreground the increasingly unstable and precarious position of working people in the post-Fordist transnational economy. Both films suggest that contemporary conditions call into question singular, discrete identity categories, including the category of worker itself (insofar as Indigenous persons were ever figured in U.S. culture as members of the proletariat, it was primarily as skywalkers, not waitresses, peace officers, or office workers). In both films, stable work—whether in auto plants, barbershops, or retail stores—is disappearing or altogether gone, and along with it the classic image of the American working class as a white male industrial laborer. In confronting a social setting in which the absence of work is more prevalent than work itself, the films imply that class is not an underlying essence, a stable or normative identity, a uniform factor. Rather, class figures differently in the lives of different workers (some of whom may be unemployed, or underemployed, or informally employed), contingent on its interlocking relations to other axes of identity and sociality. In addition, these films suggest that in the contemporary moment, working-classness is a matter of borders: geopolitical boundaries between nations; cultural and linguistic borders between peoples and traditions; racial, gender, and economic divisions separating whites, immigrants, and Indigenous peoples.[41] Both films imagine the proliferation of borders, which throws into doubt narrative and symbolic conventions for framing class and working-class identity, as both a crisis and an opportunity. On the one hand, these conditions allow new stories to emerge: tales of transnational contact and translation in which class formation is cast through the problems and possibilities of cross-cultural connection, and in which previously occluded working-class figures—women, Hmong immigrants, citizens of the Mohawk nation—become protagonists in modernity's drama. At the same time, in their efforts to chart new narratives, these films fall back on reductive formulas from an earlier era, especially the action suspense dramas that have been Hollywood's stock-in-trade for so long. The plot of *Frozen River* uses the desperation of undocumented immigrants to forge a partnership between Ray and Lila; *Gran Torino* reproduces a binaristic moral logic of "good" and "evil" and relies on the demonization of Black figures to cement the alliance between Walt and the Lors. For this reason, especially, *Fruitvale Station* represents a potent counterpoint.

"I'm done with that shit": *Fruitvale Station*

Oscar Grant was executed three weeks before Barack Obama was inaugurated as the first Black president of the United States, and *Fruitvale Station* was released the week that a jury in Florida acquitted George Zimmerman of manslaughter and second-degree murder in the death of unarmed African American teenager Trayvon Martin. *Fruitvale Station* was the first major feature film by writer and director Ryan Coogler, an Oakland native who was twenty-seven years old when the film was released, the same age Grant would have been at that time. *Fruitvale* won the Grand Jury Prize and Audience Award at the Sundance Film Festival and the Prix de l'Avenir at the Cannes Film Festival, among other awards. Coogler would eventually direct *Black Panther* (2018), among other films. *Fruitvale* was distributed by the Weinstein Company, renowned for its support and promotion of independent cinema.

Perhaps not surprising for a film that achieved substantial commercial success and critical acclaim, *Fruitvale* is undergirded in part by a liberal politics of recognition rather than a more radical political vision. The primary focus of the film is to make audiences feel for Oscar Grant rather than provide a structural critique of the root, interlocking systems that produce Black vulnerability to state, economic, and social violence. As Coogler declared, his aim was to "humanize" Grant, to make him empathetic to a broad audience. Clearly, Grant was less than fully human to Johannes Mehserle, who executed Grant as he lay face down on the train platform, and the other BART officers at the scene; encouraging audiences to see Grant as a complex, sympathetic individual could challenge the dehumanizing gaze that made it possible for Mehserle to shoot Grant. "What I felt was lost was the fact that this guy was a normal person," Coogler stated in an interview in *The Atlantic*. "I hope that people will watch the film regardless of where they are from, regardless of what their political views are, and regardless of what their ethnicity is, see the film and see a little bit of themselves in the human being in the film."[42] As this quotation implies, Coogler did not envision the film as a politically pointed project; rather, he hoped a focus on Grant as a "normal guy" would touch audiences from all social and political persuasions. Coogler aspired to make audiences see Grant as an individual rather than a stereotype, to make him a figure viewers could identify with. Coogler explained that in media accounts of the trial that followed his murder, Grant "became this saint or this idol that people held up. He became a rallying cry and a symbol for whatever kind of impressions you wanted to make him a symbol for. And the other side has demonized him. He's a criminal. He's a thug. He got what he deserved. Personally, he's not either one of those things."[43]

In *Fruitvale*, "humanizing" Grant is a complex and artful cinematic operation, entailing at least three primary strategies. First, the film focuses on mundane, everyday events and struggles to underscore the nonsensational, "unexceptional" nature of his life. This is a "day-in-the-life" film, with jittery camera work and a neorealist, documentary feel. Like *Gran Torino* and *Frozen River*, *Fruitvale* culminates in dramatic action, but the lead-up to the climax underscores the "ordinary" aspects of Grant's day-to-day existence: dropping his daughter off at preschool, chatting with a former coworker, selecting a card for his mother's birthday, picking his girlfriend up from work, eating dinner with his extended family. The stress on the quotidian is part of Coogler's effort to make Grant "relatable," something of an everyman.

A second tactic is the film's focus on Grant's relationships, which demonstrate the way he is connected to other people, part of larger web of relations, and therefore someone whose life and death reverberate widely and deeply. We see Oscar chatting happily with relatives at his mother's birthday party; we see Oscar's close relationships with his gang of friends on New Year's Eve; we see his openness to the people—many of them white—he encounters throughout the day. The message: Oscar is not a misanthrope, loner, pariah, or problem. Rather, he is embedded in a multifaceted community of rich, if fluid and varied, relationships. His relationships with the three key female figures in his life—his mother, Sophina, and his daughter Tatiana—are complex and multifaceted. In the film his relationship with his mother is punctuated by the prison flashback, where she informs Oscar, after he engages in verbal sparring with a fellow inmate during her visit, that she won't be coming to visit him anymore. Her decision, followed by her refusal to give him a hug as she leaves the visiting room, is devastating for Grant, who is restrained by officers as he tries to follow her, pleading and apologizing. Yet later, in the film's present, we see the mutual sweetness and thoughtfulness they have for one another: Oscar refuses reimbursement for the crabs (including one more than she had requested) he buys for her birthday stew; she embraces and chats fondly with Sophina during her birthday party, and, in a moment that replies to the prison flashback, gives Oscar a warm embrace when he leaves, insisting that she'll finish washing the dishes.

Third, *Fruitvale* highlights the contradictory aspects of Grant's character, to counter any one-dimensional image of him as either a "saint" or a "thug." And yet the film also wants to suggest that Grant is on a morally upward trajectory, turning away from infidelities and drug dealing in an effort to "make good." The film's liberalism is invested in showing that despite Oscar's checkered past, he's now trying to improve himself.[44] He may have made mistakes, but he's trying now to "play by the rules": he dumps his stash of marijuana in the bay rather than sell it, and he finally confesses to Sophina that he has lost his job two weeks earlier. "I dumped [the weed]. I'm done with that shit. I'm tired. That's what I'm trying to tell you." Further, he clearly loves his daughter, and the film depicts him as a dedicated father. We see Oscar sneaking Tatiana an extra packet of fruit snacks, or pretending to bite her toes when putting her to bed at a sleepover; Oscar and Tatiana racing one another as they exit her preschool; Oscar wrestling playfully with Tatiana and her cousins at Sophina's sister's house. And despite previous infidelities, the film suggests he is fully committed to Sophina. Yes, he has dealt dope, but the film implies his dealing was a response to economic hardship and insists that he is a devoted father, loving son, committed boyfriend, and caring community member.

The focus on the mundane activities and intimate aspects of one day in Oscar's life, and the insistence that Oscar is "morally upstanding," opens the film to criticism that it downplays the structural, historical forces, including racism and white supremacy, that shape his existence. By focusing tightly on the personal and interpersonal dynamics of his final day, and by implying that the tragedy of Oscar's death is in part connected to his upward moral trajectory—as if to say "what a shame he was killed just as he was turning his life around"—the film, as one commentator put it, could be said to lose sight of "the fact that we live in a society of deeply entrenched, systematic racism, in which an event like this, no matter the circumstances of the victim, could happen at all."[45] Rather than underscoring the racism woven into the fabric of Oscar's life, the film presents the Bay Area as a diverse community defined by racial tolerance and interracial fellow-feeling: Oscar extends himself generously to the young white woman at the grocery store by placing her on the phone with his grandmother, who shares a family recipe; the young woman in turn miraculously appears on the train when he is killed as a concerned witness. Oscar has a heartfelt and honest conversation about marriage with a white man he bumps into on New Year's Eve, and the train ride to San Francisco turns into a feel-good multiracial party, as Black and white travelers share smiles and furtive drinks and dance together. Beyond these scenes of interracial generosity, the film doesn't seem to offer much evidence that racial tensions pervade the Bay Area or Oscar's life.

Additionally, *Fruitvale* does not depict the public unrest and protests that followed Grant's murder in Oakland, especially the mass actions of January 7, 14, and 30, 2009. The uprisings and direct action helped lay the groundwork for Occupy Wall Street, which had an especially strong presence in Oakland, and set a precedent for the Black Lives Matter movement.[46] The film's final shots are documentary footage of a commemorative event held on January 1, 2013. This scene depicts community mourning and remembrance, but not the collective resistance, organizing, and outrage that erupted immediately after Grant's death and continued for years.[47] Although BART Officer Johannes Mehserle was sentenced to only two years in prison for involuntary manslaughter, the fact that he was the first police officer in the history of California to be charged and convicted with murder for an on-duty shooting was testament to the power and force of the coalition that came together to press the authorities and demand justice. This crucial aspect of the story is left unexamined by the film.

But the liberal humanist impulses that drive the film—the effort to make Oscar sympathetic to a broad audience and the focus on Oscar as an individual at the expense of a robust focus on institutional racism or the mass unrest that occurred in the wake of his death—sit alongside a latent, but still palpable and politically ambitious emphasis on the convergence of state-sanctioned racial violence and economic struggle. Specifically, *Fruitvale Station* offers a potent critical commentary on the conditions of Black labor under racial capitalism in the United States, in at least three ways.

First, the film highlights labor contingency, working-class hardship, and the imbrication of racism and economics. Indeed, the film presents a powerful narrative of economic precarity as well as racial vulnerability. Oscar himself is unemployed, having just lost his job working at the deli counter of an upscale supermarket, Farmer Joe's. Early in the film, Oscar visits the store, in part to purchase crabs for his mother's birthday dinner, but also to request his job back. His former boss reminds Oscar that he was fired for repeated tardiness, but also mentions that if he were to rehire Oscar, he would "have to let someone else go. Someone with no felonies." Here the film connects Oscar's economic precarity to the mass incarceration system; his status as an ex-prisoner compounds the challenges he faces in an already saturated low-wage labor market and suggests the way state and corporate policies converge to punish the working class.

When Oscar returns home from the supermarket, the camera zooms in on the calendar posted on the refrigerator, with the words "RENT DUE!" written in red and circled on the following day, January 1, suggesting the seriousness—and uncertainty—of whether Sophina and Oscar can generate the necessary funds. The theme continues as Oscar speaks on the phone to his sister Chantay from her job in a restaurant kitchen, which the script identifies as a Kentucky Fried Chicken. Chantay informs Oscar that she cannot attend their mother's birthday party that evening because she has to work an extra shift, and then she asks Oscar if he can lend her $300 to help pay *her* rent. Housing insecurity, the film suggests, is common in Oscar's community. Sophina, too, works a low-wage job at a big box store identified in the original script as Walmart. "I'd rather die than come here on my day off," she tells Oscar when he drops her off for work in the morning. Oscar's mother, Wanda, seems to have a modest, lower middle-class lifestyle, and in the one scene we see of her at work, she appears to be a manager. Notes in the script indicate that she works at UPS, so while she is earning more and may have some job stability, she, too, works in the service-retail sector where wages have been stagnating and labor is increasingly precarious.[48]

A second way that *Fruitvale* contradicts the liberal individualism that otherwise frames its narrative is by underscoring—albeit in subtle ways—the structural, institutional factors governing Grant's life and death. The film's flashback of Wanda visiting Oscar in prison reminds us that the story's present must be understood in the context of Grant's time in the mass incarceration system, which was expanded dramatically in late twentieth-century California and disproportionately caged Black and Latinx residents.[49] The repeated motif of BART trains zooming in the background of various scenes, or in establishing shots, suggests the enduring, structural presence of a broader infrastructure of violence. As film critic Wesley Morris noted, "your pulse goes up every time Coogler furnishes a shot of a bulleting BART train and the accompanying whooshing scream produced by metal, velocity, and air. It's an alarming sound that, under these circumstances, portends death."[50] If *Gran Torino* and *Frozen River* recount tales of capitalist disinvestment, *Fruitvale Station* is set in a context of capital investment in a gentrifying region that is also a vast infrastructure of social control. The violence visible in the opening cell phone footage, and again in the climactic scenes, hovers at the edges throughout the film, palpable in the sight of passing police cars and zooming BART trains, which imply that Oscar's everyday life is in fact subject to a pervasive machinery of racial power and policing.

Third, the film suggests that Black workers (and Black workers without work) are always vulnerable to arbitrary, gratuitous violence and death. The film's liberalism establishes a narrative of choice and freedom and underscores the agency Oscar has, emphasizing that he is trying to "better" himself, that he's not a "thug." Yet, crucially, Oscar's moral rectitude is beside the point. Regardless of Oscar's moral trajectory, his murder by police is an inexcusable, avoidable, unnecessary, malicious crime. And the film makes this clear, ultimately indicating the false logic of making "smart choices." The film does not underplay the irrationality and cruelty of the violence that takes Oscar's life. Oscar's death is utterly unnecessary; he is shot in the back while lying face down on the train platform beneath two officers. The officer who drags him off the train accosts Oscar and his friends with impunity, exhibiting unapologetically racist, malicious behavior, taunting and physically abusing them. These scenes demonstrate the tautological way that Oscar and his friends are actively criminalized by the very forces charged ostensibly with maintaining "public safety." The police officers treat Oscar and his companions as criminals, which in turn provokes (and in the officers' eyes justifies) the use of extreme, prejudicial, violent force. The film shows that the discriminatory exercise of such violence is at once arbitrary (it makes no sense why Oscar and his friends are targeted for violent treatment), and yet calculated and intentional (the officers act with conviction and without hesitation). Here we get a clear view of how the machinery of social death operates as a form of racialization and social discipline over laboring people. In the hospital, we hear the voice of Oscar's mother praying for his recovery as we see the medical staff pulling tubes out of his body, signaling that he is already dead, and that her prayers are in vain. Ironically, given that she had refused to hug Oscar in the prison flashback, she begs the medical staff to let her hug him. "He didn't like to be alone," she tells them. This scene, and the scenes of Oscar's friends and relatives gathered at the hospital in a prayerful vigil, defy the notion that his body and life are expendable and ungrievable.

In narrating a labor story that is simultaneously a tale of state-executed Black death, the film as a work of precarious realism suggests that capital accumulation, racialization, and the political and administrative management of individuals and populations are interrelated. As I have argued, the film shows, in a range of subtle but palpable ways, the conditions of economic insecurity under which Grant, his girlfriend, and his friends struggle.

Fruitvale underscores their status as workers, and in Grant's case, as a member of what Marx calls the floating reserve army of labor, a worker who crosses in and out of employment, in and out of the formal wage economy, subject to hyperexploitation and to being rendered disposable.[51] The film also underscores the racialized nature of the violence to which Grant is subject; it is inseparable from Grant's vulnerable social and political status as a young Black, working-class man. In *Fruitvale*, then, Black racialization is marked by the combination of economic insecurity *and* exposure to state violence. In the film's account of Grant's life, economics and violence, labor and racial precarity, exploitation and disposability are intertwined.[52] Charisse Burden-Stelly argues that under global capitalism, race serves critical economic *and* civic functions: "Blackness is a capacious category of surplus value extraction essential to an array of political-economic functions, including accumulation, disaccumulation, debt, planned obsolescence, and absorption of the burdens of economic crises. At the same time, Blackness is the quintessential condition of disposability, expendability, and devalorization."[53] *Fruitvale* provides grounds for grasping this duality: economic value production through the maintenance of Black poverty and precarity *and* the evacuation of human value through the subjection of Black lives to violent death at the hands of the state.

A key story behind *Fruitvale* is that the post-1970 industrial decline and transformation of the U.S. economy—the essential backdrop to *Gran Torino* and *Frozen River*—was accompanied by an intensified demonization of Black Americans in the wake of, and as a backlash to, the civil rights movement. The dismantling of the welfare state and the massive expansion of the prison industrial system were both facilitated by a right-wing campaign to associate Black working-class and poor people with moral failure, deserving of punishment rather than assistance.[54] Writing in the early 1980s, Manning Marable argued that anti-Blackness and capitalist exploitation go hand-in-hand, that racial violence is crucial to profit accumulation in the United States. "It is the interests of capital," he contended, "that permits the climate of racist terrorism to continue"; "acts of brutality which take place across the face of Black America every day, in relative isolation and in broad daylight ... form the bars which imprison every individual member of the Black working class, every poor and unemployed person, every Black woman."[55] Yet, writing as the Reagan era's increasingly punitive racial logic was being put into place and the mass incarceration system was expanding dramatically, Marable noted a shift: "What is qualitatively new about the current period is that the racist/capitalist state under Reagan has proceeded down a public policy road which could inevitably involve the complete obliteration of the entire Black reserve army of labor and sections of the Black working class."[56] Violent, arbitrary death has always been a tool to manage Black workers and citizens; in the post-1970s era, Marable warned, it threatened to become even more widely enforced as public policy.

Written in response to an economic system that promotes the exploitation as well as the potential "obliteration" of Black workers, many narratives of African American labor are not only stories of internal migration, informal labor, and transnational contact, like many of the other narratives examined in this book, but also tales of labor under the sign of death and confinement. One potent emblem of this tradition appears near the end Jesmyn Ward's 2017 novel *Sing, Unburied, Sing*. The image emerges as the novel's protagonist, JoJo, follows the ghost of a young man killed on Parchman Farm, the Mississippi state penitentiary, to a stand of trees behind JoJo's house. JoJo sees that the branches are filled with other ghosts who "speak with their eyes," articulating their stories of abuse and violent death: suffocations, hangings, shootings, beatings, gougings, and more. JoJo stands there looking up "until the forest is a Black-knuckled multitude."[57] This striking figure of "the Black-knuckled multitude" crystallizes the novel's braiding together of work and death. The ghosts JoJo sees are unable to rest easy because they met violent ends; the reference to the hand ("knuckle") and the use of the word "multitude," a term associated in critical theory and to some extent in popular discourse with Michael Hardt and Antonio Negri's revisionist theory of the global working class, suggest that these restless ghosts are also in some important measure figures of labor.[58] Here and elsewhere, Ward's novel, and the harrowing story of carceral labor and violent death at its heart, suggests that Black workers are constituted *through* violence, through the exposure to the threat or reality of premature death. That threat of death, and its corresponding violent realities, have been used to render Black life precarious and disposable, and also to extract energy, labor power, and life itself to propel capital accumulation.

Similarly, as a narrative of Black labor, *Fruitvale* is not only a story of living labor-in-motion; it is also a story of *dead labor*, that is, labor under the persistent threat of premature death.[59] In this context, *precarity* is not only a term of political economy, but also of biopolitical subjectivity, referring not just to the uncertainty of labor, but also to the insecurity of life, civic identity, and physical and emotional well-being. *Fruitvale*, and other narratives of Black labor such as Ward's novel, or Wright's *Native Son*, or Toni Morrison's *The Bluest Eye*, are tales not only of exploitation, but also of exclusion, of civic and physical vulnerability, stories of being outside the state's protections or subject to its sovereign violence, marked by what Lisa Cacho, adapting a term from the work of Orlando Patterson and others, calls social death.[60] An analysis that sees precarity only or primarily as a product of the contemporary neoliberal, postindustrial era fails to see that African Americans have lived under the sign of hyperprecarity since arriving in the United States.[61]

The concept of living labor speaks to the categories of work and worker, while also foregrounding their limits. Living labor refers to life within, but also *beyond* political economy. It is a Marxist category that gestures to the shortcomings of political economy as a conceptual framework to render and analyze the lives and narratives of working and nonworking peoples. It suggests that workers are always *more than workers*, that the category of work is insufficient to explain the full scope of a person or a class or group. It also indicates that workers are positioned and conditioned *differently*, that capitalism both demands uniformity and order (abstract labor) and also relies on, produces, and exploits difference, and that lines of difference are generated inside and outside the realm of the economic.

Fruitvale suggests that Black labor is rendered surplus and that Black life itself is rendered disposable, targeted for destruction and premature death, yet also that Black labor and life have been crucial to capitalist development. We might say that Black labor represents a *precarity of another kind*, a precarity beyond precarity, what Saidiya Hartman describes as "the precarious life of the ex-slave, a condition defined by the vulnerability to premature death and to gratuitous acts of violence."[62] Black labor has been essential, but Black persons, especially Black workers, have also been marked for death, considered fungible as flesh that can be violated, discarded, destroyed whenever it is deemed less than useful, resistant, or expendable. Racial capitalism is also necrocapitalism, which actively produces the social, civic, and physical death of targeted populations who are "consigned to zones of abandonment, containment, surveillance, and incarceration."[63]

As a story of Black labor and disposability, *Fruitvale Station* challenges the fundamental narrative structures of Eastwood's *Gran Torino* and Hunt's *Frozen River*. Both of the latter films are organized as narratives of suspense, in which time unfolds in a linear, progressive fashion, with outcomes that are unknown and not determined in advance. That is, those films are animated by *a logic of possibility*, in which what happens is open to change and fundamentally unsettled (suspense is made possible by the fact that different outcomes are possible, that we don't know how things will end). This lack of determinacy is echoed by the themes of border crossing, migration, and movement, all of which suggest that the characters in those films are capable of altering their fates, able to make decisions that will mold their futures, even if those futures are still shaped by larger forces. In contrast,

Fruitvale Station has a recursive structure, in which the end is already determined at the start. The film opens with grainy cell phone footage of Grant's execution by Mehserle on the BART platform, and then backs up to tell the story of the twenty-four hours leading to Grant's death. The structure here is circular, and the outcome set from the film's opening moments. The film is thus predicated on a *logic of inevitability* and closure that contradicts and denies the sense of open-ended possibility that drives the films by Eastwood and Hunt. In the film's terms, Grant's death is inevitable (nothing in the film will allow him to avoid it) *and* utterly gratuitous (there is absolutely no justification for it).

Gran Torino and *Frozen River* both gesture toward emergent working-class connections and solidarities across national, ethnic, and linguistic boundaries, yet the visions of cooperation they project are speculative and provisional, restricted not only by the force of the divisions being crossed, but also, especially in the case of *Gran Torino*, by the imaginary limitations of the films themselves, as Eastwood's film in fact reinforces at the level of form the racial hierarchies that it proposes on its face to contest. Like Eastwood's and Hunt's films, *Fruitvale Station* is a story of labor-in-motion, rife with motifs of transit and encounter, notably the car, the train, even the BART platform. But its tale of police murder and its recursive narrative structure underscore the determinative power of necrocapitalism's racialized violence to truncate not only movement and social solidarities, but life itself. Racialized violence is not just an intrusion into economic and social production, but is the *foundation* of economic accumulation under capitalism, which has been since its inception a machine of both exploitation and annihilation, of living labor and of dead labor, too.

4 • "The Uprooted Worker at the Center of the World"

Labor, Migration, and Precarity on the Urban Underside of Independent Cinema

Turning from the three widely distributed feature films discussed in the previous chapter, this chapter examines three independent films about the low-wage labors of racialized workers in New York City: *Man Push Cart* (2005) and *Chop Shop* (2007), both directed by Ramin Bahrani, and *La Ciudad/The City* (1998), directed by David Riker. Although these films were released before *Gran Torino*, *Frozen River*, and *Fruitvale Station*, I position this chapter after the one on Eastwood's, Hunt's, and Coogler's films because, as low-budget, indie productions, *Man Push Cart*, *Chop Shop*, and *La Ciudad* occupy a much less visible place in the cultural landscape, and because they depict the plight of racially marked precarious workers without filtering them through the stories of white workers, as do *Gran Torino* and *Frozen River*. Collectively, all six films contribute to what I am identifying as a burgeoning international line of films about labor, race, and precarity in the context of neoliberal globalization, part of the larger literary and cinematic tradition of precarious realism. All six films draw to some extent on neorealism, although they represent different modes of cinematic production, and those differences both shape and reflect their political imaginaries. *Gran Torino* features several nonprofessional actors and focuses on an immigrant community that is acutely underrepresented in mainstream American culture, but the film is a major studio (Warner Brothers) production, stars a global Hollywood icon (Eastwood), and grossed $270 million worldwide. *Frozen River* was director and screenwriter Courtney Hunt's first feature film; it was made on a fairly modest ($1 million) budget and shot on location, but it starred a well-known actress (Melissa Leo), was purchased for distribution by

Sony Pictures Classics, and grossed $6 million. *Fruitvale Station* was Ryan Coogler's first major feature film and featured actors who at the time were not especially prominent, but it was distributed by the Weinstein Company and grossed $17 million world-wide. The three films discussed in this chapter were made on frugal budgets, starred nonprofessional and novice actors almost exclusively, and generated very modest box office earnings (*Man Push Cart* grossed $55,000, *Chop Shop* $221,000, and *La Ciudad* $240,000).[1]

To a significant extent, the proximity of these films to the heart of the Hollywood system is reflected in their cinematic perspective and aesthetics.[2] Of the six films, *Gran Torino* has the most tightly wound, violent, action- and suspense-oriented plot, and tells its story of transnational encounter and intergenerational alliance almost exclusively through the eyes of its native-born, white-ethnic, gun-toting protagonist. *Frozen River* and *Fruitvale Station*, independent films with substantial distribution, feature more well-known actors and slightly slicker production values than the three lesser-grossing films discussed in this chapter, but they still offer more critical political perspectives than Eastwood's film. In contrast, *Chop Shop*, *Man Push Cart*, and *La Ciudad* were produced at a significant distance from the Hollywood studio nexus and are grounded in a naturalistic (if also, in the case of Bahrani's films, carefully plotted and rehearsed) aesthetic that critic A. O. Scott calls neo-neorealism.[3] These films have slower pacing than *Gran Torino*, *Frozen River*, or *Fruitvale Station* and a documentary-like style of handheld shots focused on quotidian life. Although *Man Push Cart*, *Chop Shop*, and *La Ciudad* feature transnational and transcultural relations, the focus of all three films lies squarely on impoverished, racially marked immigrant figures rather than on the white or native-born characters with whom they intersect.

Centered on migrant workers who bear the brunt of contemporary global capitalism's harsh, tumultuous dynamics of displacement, dispossession, and low- or no-wage uncertainty, the three films discussed in this chapter contribute to what Lauren Berlant terms an emergent "cinema of precarity" that addresses the crises of economies, institutions, and fantasies of the good life under neoliberalism.[4] Precarity has manifold meanings: it can refer to economic and political insecurity when contingent, flexible, low-wage labor is increasingly normative; its reference can also extend, in the words of Brett Neilson and Ned Rossiter, "beyond the world of work to encompass other aspects of intersubjective life, including housing, debt, and the ability to build affective social relations"; and it can refer, at a more existential level, to the bodily, psychic, and emotional uncertainty and vulnerability that characterize life for many in the contemporary world of global social flux and turmoil.[5] Berlant uses the term to connote a spreading social, economic, and political condition of pervasive instability: "the dominant structure and experience of the present moment, cutting across class and localities."[6] In this chapter, the term refers more discretely to the working and living conditions of migrant workers whose precariousness in the neoliberal economy is a function of laboring in hyperexploitative, un- or underregulated jobs, and by the resonant uncertainty of their citizenship status, which, along with their racial status, makes them vulnerable to various forms of economic, social, and physical violence. In these films, precarity describes the radical vulnerability of workers hovering on the boundary between work and no work, between formal and informal labor, between citizenship and civic "illegality."

As fables of globalization, then, these films foreground not the knowledge workers that Richard Florida calls the creative class, but migrants, women, and young people scrambling to find a foothold at the bottom of the economy and on the fringes of civil society. In the face of claims that the new global economy is built on "immaterial" labor, these films direct our attention to the informal and semiformal manual and service work—unlicensed construction, sweatshop sewing, food cart vending, and sex work—that continues to be essential to late capitalist cities like New York. These films stress the economic, physical, psychic, and political peril experienced by contemporary low-wage workers on the cusp of wageless life and their ceaseless, often desperate, hustle to stay afloat.[7] Emblems of what I have been calling labor-in-motion, the central characters in these films inhabit what Berlant terms "survival time, the time of struggling, drowning, holding onto the ledge, treading water—the time of *not-stopping*."[8] These are stories of desperate vulnerability, focused on the plight of figures rendered minuscule against the backdrop of the corporate city's imposing architectural infrastructure, who face the threat of being crushed beneath the gears of the capitalist machine. And yet these films insist that to understand contemporary New York City, and by extension the world economic system, we must attend to these very figures and their stories.

While *Frozen River* and *Gran Torino* are set in locations—upstate New York and inner-city Detroit, respectively—that capital has selected for strategic disinvestment, Bahrani's and Riker's films take place on the underside of contemporary New York City, an exemplar of what Saskia Sassen has called a "global city." (In this way, Bahrani's and Riker's films resemble *Fruitvale Station*, which is set on the fringes of another global gentrifying city, San Francisco.) Global cities are highly contradictory sites, structured by intense economic and cultural discrepancies; they are home to concentrations of immense corporate power and financial wealth, but also acute poverty. In global cities, uneven development's geographies of capitalist contradiction are inscribed in stone and concrete, visible in patterns of residential and educational segregation, political power, and everyday life. For the migrants in the films discussed in this chapter, New York represents at once the promise of social possibility—a place where migrants fleeing war and colonial economic deprivation can find community and make their way—and a harsh realm of consolidated capitalist power and relentless exploitation.

Shortly after the release of *Chop Shop*, geographer David Harvey published an essay, "The Right to the City," which argued that urban development has historically served to absorb excess capital and to contain and resolve social unrest. Harvey and other radical geographers contend that if urban spatial and architectural forms reflect prevailing relations of economic and social power, then the contemporary shape and fabric of New York City embodies the financialized, hypercommodified culture of global corporate capitalism. "The quality of urban life," Harvey argued, "has become a commodity, as has the city itself, in a world where consumerism, tourism, cultural and knowledge-based industries have become major aspects of the urban political economy.... This is a world in which the neoliberal ethic of intense possessive individualism, and its cognate of political withdrawal from collective forms of action, becomes the template for human socialization."[9]

The contemporary global city, however, is home not only to corporate and financial elites who have colonized urban space with a culture of privatized consumption; it is also is a site where, in part because of the density and diversity of the city's populations, counterhegemonic social movements and subjectivities can develop. More specifically, in New York City, the last decades of the twentieth century—the period leading up to the production of Bahrani's and Riker's films—witnessed the emergence of a new, transnational urban labor force. "By the 1990s," labor historian Immanuel Ness reports, "substandard jobs employing transnational workers had become crucial to key sectors of the economy of New York City. [In 2005], immigrants have gained a major presence as bricklayers, demolition workers, and hazardous waste workers on construction and building rehabilitation sites; as cooks, dishwashers, and busboys in restaurants; and as taxi drivers, domestic workers, and delivery people."[10] By 2000, immigrants made up 47 percent of the city's workforce and 62 percent of the low-wage workforce. The status of these workers is particularly precarious. Like the immigrant working class that developed at the turn of the last century in the United States, these laborers are being pulled by the demand for work that, however low in wages, often represents opportunities superior to the ones in their home countries.

Yet unlike the predominantly European immigrant workers in 1900, whose immigration was legally sanctioned, these new transnationals are often here without documented immigrant status and the right to citizenship.[11] The jobs accessible to these workers, especially in service and low-wage manufacturing work, are frequently contingent and informal, without union protections or job security. As a result, these workers are especially vulnerable to hyper-exploitation. "On the one hand," Ness notes, "low-wage immigrant labor is readily available. On the other, immigrant workers' illegal status increases employers' leverage in all aspects of the employment relation."[12]

Yet despite the insecure positions they typically occupy, these new immigrant workers have become crucial to the contemporary economy, which runs on their labor. And they have created new forms of solidarity and collective resistance, visible in a range of strikes by retail, fast-food, and other low-wage workers, under the auspices of the Fight for Fifteen, the New York Taxi Workers Alliance, the immigrant rights movements, and other coalitions. There are, Harvey notes, "urban social movements seeking to overcome isolation and reshape the city in a different image from that put forward by the developers, who are backed by finance, corporate capital and an increasingly entrepreneurially minded local state apparatus."[13] Echoing this, Sassen argues that global cities are not only sites of elite economic consolidation, but also spaces for the formation of what she calls "new claims" by "economically disadvantaged sectors of the urban population, which in large cities are frequently as internationalized as is capital."[14] As nodes of congregation and intersection, Sassen asserts, where an increasingly internationalized workforce is brought into being, the global city "is a strategic site for disempowered actors because it enables them to gain presence, to emerge as subjects, even when they do not gain direct power."[15] This process of developing new forms of social and political agency starts with what Sassen describes as the "unmooring" of identities, as the cultural traditions and expectations that originated elsewhere are reterritorialized in the context of the global city's diverse, transnational conditions of encounter and conflict.[16] As traditional sources of identity are transformed in the global city's crossroads, unprecedented notions of subjectivity, community, and belonging emerge, including the possibility, in Sassen's words, of "going *beyond* the politics of culture and identity, though at least partly likely to be embedded in it."[17]

The prospect of moving beyond established or discrete cultural identities without abandoning them is at the heart of Bahrani's and Riker's films, but it remains elusive. Indeed, both filmmakers are adept at narrating the unmooring of identities, and the forms of displacement, anomie, and isolation that such unmaking can engender. But Bahrani and Riker have a much harder time envisioning the remaking and reconstellation of alternative political identities, especially through collective means. More specifically, Bahrani's delicately composed neorealist films narrate the precariousness of low-wage, semiformal labor, the tenuousness of life for immigrant workers in the neoliberal city, and the uneven spaces that structure their existence. And, appropriately enough, the films themselves are uneven, in both thematic and aesthetic terms. Thematically, the films focus on precarious labor, but they are almost entirely stripped of a larger vision of working-class unity. The films recount stories of individual struggles by laboring people with almost no sign of collective belonging or resistance, at least at the manifest level of the narrative. Indeed, as Polina Kroik argues, the films' emphasis on personal economic travails, even when placing stress on the impediments to upward mobility, threatens to affirm the neoliberal ideology of entrepreneurial selfhood, which demands that individuals disavow collective rights and affiliations and make their own way in the economy as singular, supposedly self-activating agents.[18] What's more, Bahrani's films also enact a willful erasure of history and historical context: we never hear the longer story of how and why the protagonists of the two films—Ahmed and Ale—find themselves in their current circumstances. Questions that would seem to be central to the films—Why did Ahmed abandon a successful career as a rock musician in Pakistan? When and why was Ale orphaned?—are willfully disregarded. And yet, I contend, even as they fail to provide a vision of collective possibility and historical depth, Bahrani's films blend materialist and metaphorical modes of representation that challenge us to see both the singularity of the characters depicted and the commonality of their circumstances.

Riker's film is even more acutely engaged with the dialectic between isolation and collectivity. Indeed, the two narratives that bookend his four-story film turn on questions of solidarity, asking if migrant workers from disparate locations in the Latinx diaspora, caught within the exploitative web of the late capitalist low-wage labor system, can find common cause to advance shared aims. While *La Cuidad* does not offer a portrait of collective resistance, it raises the dynamics of solidarity directly and forcefully, both in the stories it tells and the manner in which it tells them. The working class has always been heterogeneous, and working-class collectivity is always a matter of forging solidarities across social, geographical, and political divisions. Bahrani and Riker both foreground the tensions embodied in the possibility of working-class solidarity, which historian Richard Hyman describes as the dialectic "between unifying and fragmenting tendencies," between what Marx and Engels call "competition" and "association."[19] Neither Riker nor Bahrani provides an explicit image of collective action, but each film in its own way suggests the immanent potentiality of common identification and affiliation, even when conditions prevent them from being realized in everyday struggles.

The tension between unification and fragmentation takes on spatial dynamics, as the three films depict cities as urban border sites of division and contact. On one hand, the films underscore the radical gaps between wealth and poverty, the forms of deep, asymmetrical division that structure the global city, keeping workers from being able to realize the commonality and collective power that might connect them. In Riker's portrait of the Bronx and Queens, and Bahrani's image of Willet's Point, Queens, we see visions of the city that seemingly bear no relation to the iconic images of midtown Manhattan; they could be *another country*. Yet in several moments the films indicate the proximity of these seemingly distant spaces to the core of corporate power, visually underscoring the way the urban capitalist structures condition the lives of these figures who are so far removed from the city's center, and also how integrated these workers in fact are into the heart of capitalist production. If these films thus direct our attention to the vital importance of low-paid migrant workers of color to the contemporary global city, they struggle—and in Bahrani's case essentially fail—to imagine a politics of solidarity that could bring these workers together, in however fluid or provisional a manner. In the end, this narrative ambiguity reflects the uncertain, transitional nature of the material spaces, contradictory forces, and historical moments these films engage, when the composition, contours, and political fate of the emerging, post-Fordist American working class was far from clear. Grappling with these circumstances, cinematic form itself constitutes what I call precarious realism—an uneven, experimental, amalgamated brand of neorealist film that is as formally dense and unstable as the narrative contents and cultural politics of the stories themselves.

"Check to check, month to month, day to day": *Man Push Cart*

Ramin Bahrani's *Man Push Cart* centers on Ahmad, a Pakistani immigrant who runs a bagel and coffee cart in midtown Manhattan. The plot of the film is loosely structured, more a constellation of scenes and encounters than a tightly formed dramatic arc. The opening scenes depict Ahmad pulling his cart through the Manhattan streets in the early morning hours and serving customers. One of his customers is Mohammad, a young, wealthy businessman and fellow Pakistani who hires Ahmad to paint his apartment and later recognizes him as a former rock star from Lahore.

Using money Mohammad advances him for his painting work, Ahmad makes the last payment on his cart. Ahmad also befriends Noe, a young woman from Barcelona who works in a nearby newsstand and also knows Mohammad. The three of them go away for the weekend to Mohammad's country house, and when they return, Noe and Ahmad kiss, but he quickly pushes her away without explanation. Details of Ahmad's past are never fully revealed, but we learn that his wife died a year before the film opens and that his five-year-old son is now living in Brooklyn with his in-laws, who eventually cut their ties with Ahmad. Mohammad uses his business connections to get Ahmad a job selling admission tickets at a local nightclub, but Ahmad quits the first night after seeing Mohammad enter with Noe. Noe returns to Barcelona and, soon after, Ahmad's cart is stolen when he leaves it briefly unattended one day. Ahmad asks Mohammad for a loan to purchase another cart, but Mohammad is upset that Ahmad quit the club job, and he refuses. Distraught, Ahmad pushes Mohammad, who yells at him to leave his apartment. In the film's final sequence, Ahmad aids a fellow cart operator whose van breaks down while he is driving to his corner. In the concluding scene, Ahmad sets up and opens his friend's cart for business, while the glittering lights wrapped around the trees in a nearby plaza go dark as dawn approaches.

Man Push Cart is a quiet, contemplative film, without a strong, linear narrative drive. Although the film is anchored by repeated scenes of Ahmad pulling, cleaning, and setting up his cart and serving customers, its psychic tension revolves largely around his relationships with Mohammad, Noe, and his son, who appears only once in the film but whom he references in conversations with others. The film's seemingly divided focus—between a realist emphasis on the details of precarious pushcart labor on the one hand, and on the dramatic effects of Ahmad's mysterious backstory and present relationships on the other—raises questions. Does the film's somber tone and dissipated sense of narrative progress reflect the emotional trauma of Ahmad's life (the death of his wife, estrangement from his son), and are the matters of immigration and labor secondary or incidental, or at least nondeterminative, features of his existence? Or is economic and social struggle a central and shaping force in the protagonist's life and in the film as a whole? In fact, I think, the film exposes this putative opposition between existential despair and political economy as a false opposition.

One can argue persuasively that the film privileges its emotional, psychological story—and its own aesthetic prerogatives—over its social, political story and over a realist interest in the hard facts of working-class, immigrant life. The film offers no exposition or backstory to explain Ahmad's current state and struggle. Rather, the film centers on the poetics of the present moment, largely decontextualized. Even as it foregrounds the ubiquity of service workers in the shadows of midtown and the grinding, exhausting nature of their labor, the camera lingers on the aesthetic quality of the sights and sounds that mark the city and Ahmad's work: a constellation of early morning taillights as taxis rush down a midtown avenue; the steam billowing off the warm, wet cloth Ahmad uses to wash his cart; the glistening pavement, wet after being hosed down; colorful candy wrappers and magazines in a newsstand alongside the bulky shadow of a sanitation truck caught in profile. The demanding labor that Ahmad and other early morning service workers perform becomes, in the hands of cinematographer Michael Simmonds, an object of beauty. More than one critic has argued that Bahrani's focus on visual poetics displaces the historical or political dimensions of his setting and story lines.[20]

Similarly, *Man Push Cart* can be said to situate Ahmad's problems and his muted demeanor, as well as the film's dark tone, not in social and political concerns but in psychological issues that remain only vaguely represented. This is an atmospheric film that seems as interested in establishing an emotional tone as in exploring social issues. As a narrative, *Man Push Cart* lacks pace, linear momentum, and clear ends. It culminates in a dramatic moment, when Ahmad's cart is stolen, but it concludes on a note of profound ambiguity, in media res. It is a patchwork of scenes, many of which look and feel like set pieces, stitched together, often without clear connections. Ahmad has few spoken lines, and many of the scenes feature him poised in isolated silence, alone or drifting through the city and his routines: pulling his cart through the streets; stacking pastries and cups in preparation for business; standing and smoking in the early morning light; lying in Mohammad's apartment in the middle of the night, unable to sleep; sitting in a nightclub, exhausted and disengaged, while friends talk, joke, and sing karaoke; washing his cart after a shift; petting and feeding the stray kitten he rescues while drinking a bottle of beer in his apartment; tossing crumbs to the pigeons behind his cart; sitting in his cart in the early morning darkness, watching a group of car service drivers joking across the street; smoking at night in the parking lot of "Toys R' Us," waiting for his father-in-law to bring his son. A spare, plaintive refrain, performed on oboe, piano, and muted trumpet, lingers over many of these scenes, heightening the sense of solitude and the emotional poignancy. Much of the film takes place at night and was shot on location outdoors; the lighting is low, the atmosphere dark. In many of the daytime scenes, it is raining, which augments the dreary, somber tone.

As the description of these scenes suggests, Ahmad cuts a profoundly isolated figure. In addition, he is reticent, exhibiting what reviewers describe as an "extreme passivity," a "frustrating inertia."[21] He refuses to fight for custody of his son and allows his mother-in-law to insist without rebuttal, "He is not your son anymore," and he watches silently as his son turns his back on him. Likewise, he refuses, or fails, to tell Noe how he (apparently) feels about her, or to articulate clearly to any of the other characters details about his past or his hopes for the future. Ahmad's reticence, and the film's tendency to render him in isolation, prompts one reviewer to describe his tale as a "quiet tragedy."[22] This reading foregrounds the film's existential rather than political dimension, tracing Ahmad's isolation and anomie to vaguely sketched issues of exile and personal pain. Seen in this light, Ahmad's working-class condition and immigrant status are largely metaphorical, signs of a more generalized psychosocial marginalization that stems from his emotional rather than material life.

Yet this interpretation of *Man Push Cart* as an allegory of existential angst and struggle stands in tension with aspects of the film that foreground the concrete political and social dynamics shaping Ahmad's life in New York and his response to those dynamics. Consider the film's opening sequence, which foregrounds the material details of Ahmad's work as a pushcart vendor. The first shot is a blurred red light, obscured behind translucent plastic, which we come to see is composed of plastic strips hanging in the doorway to a garage. Inside, men move about quietly but quickly, opening pushcarts and loading them with shallow cardboard boxes (presumably of pastries), as the sounds of tools, engines, and mechanical instruments beep, whirr, and whine. The camera focuses on one man in particular, who opens and loads his cart. The scene is so dark that it disorients us, fading to almost complete blackness at points; we cannot always tell exactly what is happening or see the man clearly. The man, who we later come to know is Ahmad, wheels his cart out of the garage, and we see him struggle to pull it down the street in the early morning darkness as taxis, sanitation trucks, and commercial vans speed past, lending a foreboding sense of vulnerability and danger to his endeavor. At one point, a large truck, lights blazing, drives up directly behind Ahmad and his cart before veering to the side to avoid him. Ahmad stops at a traffic light and bends over to rest, breathing hard; a man driving a van with a pushcart in tow passes, and asks in Urdu if Ahmad is okay or needs help. Ahmad waves him on, and proceeds as the light changes, eventually pulling his cart up onto the sidewalk in front of a large fashion display window on Avenue of the Americas. Ahmad lights the burner in his cart, prepares the coffee, and stacks the pastry, as the film cuts to other nocturnal and early morning workers—garbage collectors, sidewalk cleaners—and then to customers buying breakfast from Ahmad's cart later in the morning. The sequence proceeds, as Ahmad eventually closes his cart and pulls it back through the streets, crowded with zooming taxis, and then begins what is apparently his "second shift" of labor—selling bootleg DVDs to newsstand cashiers, other cart vendors, and an array of service workers. Darkness falls again, and we see Ahmad sleeping on the subway, the Chrysler building visible in the distance out the window, as he heads to Brooklyn.

The scenes of Ahmad pulling (not pushing) his cart down Manhattan avenues are repeated, and they punctuate the film. These moments are typically shot either from across the street, so that cars, trucks, and buses whiz between the viewer and Ahmad, temporarily blocking him from sight, or from a distance in front of him, so that, given the collapsed perspective such shots create, the vehicles surround and bear down on him, as if they are about to run over him. Such shots have a documentary feel, yet are also loaded with symbolic resonance. As a result, they take on a double function: they convey the literal, material dangers and travails of Ahmad's work, which is physically demanding and perilous, yet they also have a metaphorical quality, casting Ahmad as a Sisyphean figure, caught in an absurd, existential cycle of what Camus refers to as "futile and hopeless labor" in the underworld.

To its credit, I contend, the film refuses to sacrifice one side of the dialectic, between the metaphoric and the metonymic, to the other. Even as it lends Ahmad's life a mythic valence and hints that emotional and psychological traumas—the premature death of his wife, his estrangement from his young son, the loss of his apparently successful singing career in Pakistan—may be responsible for his abject condition and dismal stance toward the world, it *also* grounds the hardship of his life in a consistent, carefully, and neorealistically rendered set of economic and social forces that have placed him in an immensely demanding and vulnerable position. His subjective ennui thus mirrors his economic precarity, and his dire economic circumstances are echoed and amplified by the deep-seated emotional stress that simmers below his outwardly calm disposition.

I am suggesting, then, that in *Man Push Cart* the harsh, grinding demands of immigrant service labor represent both a metaphor for the more generalized social anomie of a globalizing world *and* also a metonymic representation of the concrete system of exploitation that underpins the lifestyles of global city elites. Critic Sukhdev Sandhu argues that Bahrani's films are "anatomies of isolation that shine troubling revelatory spotlights on the kind of male figures—hawkers, pedlars [sic], busboys, street sweepers, flower sellers—who represent exactly the kind of subaltern labourers [sic] rarely seen on television screens or in multiplex cinemas."[23] His films, Sandhu contends, are "less about migration as [they are] exercises in migratory aesthetics, using men and women new to cities, or operating almost unnoticed in its corners and at its fringes, to offer fresh takes on contemporary life."[24] These are compelling claims, but what must be added is the filmmaker's focus on the economic structures of such migratory lives, the way in which relations and conditions of work shape Ahmad's daily life, his sense of possibility, and the aesthetic quality of the film itself. *Man Push Cart* is a film about the existential solitude of migration, but also about contemporary migrant labor, about the reliance of global capitalism on the energy and labor of a vast population of underpaid, precarious, fugitive workers, whose lack of secure citizenship status and social power makes them vulnerable to economic desperation and hardship.

The question of whether psychological-emotional or political-economic issues are the driving, or determinative, factors in Ahmad's story is ultimately left unresolved. The film's unique contribution is that it links the character's affective life and symbolic potential to detailed material conditions, connecting the fate of this rootless exile to the state of contemporary late capitalism, in which the well-being of well-to-do Manhattanites—signified by their ability to purchase a muffin and cappuccino on any given corner of Midtown—is made possible by the labors, low pay, and social and economic insecurity of an almost invisible population of service workers like Ahmad. And indeed, while the film underscores Ahmad's social and emotional isolation, it also insists that he is part of a larger community of nocturnal workers. Shots of him cleaning, pulling, and setting up his cart are intercut with shots of other laborers—sanitation workers, delivery personnel, store and newsstand clerks—who clean and prepare Manhattan to serve the masses of largely well-off white-collar workers like Mohammad and the other mostly polished persons who purchase breakfast from Ahmad. The relations of disparity and service that define the invisible army of service workers—most of whom in the film are people of color—to the wealthier, whiter segments of the city's population are suggested in one brief scene about two-thirds of the way through film. As Ahmad stands inside his cart in the dark, early morning hours before his customers arrive, a limousine drives by, pumping rock music into the air. Two young, blonde women, standing up through the car's sunroof, scream and raise their shirts, exposing their breasts in a gesture that seems especially hedonistic in the context of the sober, exhausted routine in which Ahmad and other low-wage service workers in the area are engaged.

Here the film suggests that the self-indulgent pleasure of these women, and other men and women like them, depend on the steady, often hidden, labors of poorly paid, struggling workers.

The film's director, Ramin Bahrani, has asserted in interviews that his focus on the world's proletarian workforce—not as marginal figures but as representative of global majorities—is intentional. "I'm focusing on how half the population of the world lives, at least half, probably far more," he asserted. "While I think Woody Allen is an amazing filmmaker, that's one percent of the population. And I think that 99 percent of Hollywood films and American independent films are about 'marginalized' people who are privileged and white."[25] Striking a similar note in an interview published in *Filmmaker* magazine, Bahrani states, "I bring you to these places that no one wants to accept that they exist. These movies aren't about marginal characters, despite what people say. These movies are about how most people in the world live: check to check, month to month, day to day."[26] The immigration status of the characters in *Man Push Cart* and *Chop Shop* is left deliberately ambiguous; Bahrani refers to them in one interview as "immigrant-type characters," stating that immigration is not the essential issue of the films.[27] Ahmad is obviously a recent immigrant, but the terms of his residency in the United States are not addressed in the film; whether or not the two protagonists in *Chop Shop* are immigrants never becomes clear. But both films certainly foreground the work the protagonists do, more so than most films about working-class people, which rarely include detailed or lengthy scenes of people working, as Bahrani does.

This is, then, a film about low-wage labor and the psychic stress of economic precarity, about the uncertainty of living hand-to-mouth, with no social safety net. After Ahmad's cart is stolen, he asks the man who sold it to him to search for it (the man had told Ahmad to insure the cart, but Ahmad couldn't afford to do so). When the man replies that a search for the cart will take two weeks, Ahmad replies, "Two weeks! I can't wait that long." With little savings and with all of his modest capital invested in the cart that has been stolen and which he could not afford to insure, Ahmad cannot afford to take two weeks off from work. If the film thus suggests that Ahmad, as a former rock star and widower, has unusual circumstances that shape his emotional life, it also insists that economic hardship generates immense psychic stress. Halfway through the film, a car service driver who knows Ahmad stops by his cart. When Ahmad asks how he is doing, he replies, "Not good, man. The city is driving me nuts. Company got me working the late nights, I can't get any sleep. I gotta get out of this place." He then refers to a mutual friend, saying, "I hear he's got it sweet. He's up in Albany, he's working in

Dunkin Donuts. That's the life, man." From the perspective of this taxi driver, who like Ahmad is a service worker operating as an independent contractor, circulating constantly in search of customers in competition with other desperate drivers, even the most low-paying commercial food service labor appears inviting for its regularity.

Work is also important in the film because acts of labor, however small and informal, facilitate and structure relationships among the film's characters. Ahmad's friendship with Noe begins in earnest when she asks him to help her load bottles of iced tea into the cooler at her newsstand; Mohammad recognizes Ahmad as a well-known singer after he has hired Ahmad to paint his apartment; Ahmad's social network with other midtown service workers is clearly a product of their similar labors or the various forms of exchange and barter they practice (Ahmad trades DVDs for cigarettes, and tea for music magazines). Moreover, economic disparities also shape Ahmad's relationships, most significantly his friendship with Mohammad. When Mohammad realizes that Ahmad is a well-known musician whom he listened to as a young person in Lahore, he expresses amazement that Ahmad is now operating a pushcart, and he confesses, "I never would have hired you to paint my apartment [if I had known who you are]." Mohammad says he's going to try to revive Ahmad's career by organizing a concert for him in the United States, and he introduces him to an acquaintance, Maneesh, who coordinates private parties in nightclubs. Yet throughout, even as Mohammad uses a language of informality and conviviality ("Take a break [from painting], have a beer"), he continues to treat Ahmad as a hired hand. Speaking on the phone in earshot of Ahmad, Mohammad admits he's exploiting his compatriot, telling the person on the other end of the line, "He's done a pretty good job, and he's barely charging me anything."

Through Ahmad, the film offers an emblematic figure of work in a neoliberal age in which the social safety net has been stripped away, and in order to secure even the most meager living, individuals are driven to desperation. Ahmad inhabits a world of people hustling and scraping to get by, working for small handfuls of cash, without any job security, never mind benefits such as health care or paid sick and vacation days. It is true that the film's engagement with the larger political context is limited, in large part because the frame is focused so tightly on a single figure and the draining daily routines in which he is so deeply immersed. Broader, contextualizing issues, such as the politics of immigration and the treatment of South Asian immigrants in the wake of 9/11, and background information, such as why and how Ahmad's wife died and why his son is living with his in-laws, remain vague. (In the lone scene in which prejudicial violence against Pakistani immigrants is addressed, the story of a young man who was knifed by men claiming he was a "terrorist" gets told by a character the film depicts unsympathetically.) What's more, the film is unable to imagine a collective response to these conditions by the workers and immigrants themselves. Yet the film's focus on the everyday does acquire a politically charged valence. This is a story about precarious labor, focused on the unforgiving dynamics of work, debt, poverty, and stress faced by immigrant workers struggling to survive in the shadows of American capitalist abundance, signified by the imposing towers of midtown Manhattan that serve as the film's primary setting. Ahmad's former wealth and fame have virtually no bearing on his present condition, which is governed by the overwhelming demands of menial labor and economic and social insecurity. The relentless, fatigue-inducing nature of his daily grind is reflected in the film's refusal to demarcate time clearly, to distinguish day from night, or one round of hard work from the next.

The precariousness of Ahmad's situation is underscored in the film's culminating plot turn, when Ahmad's cart is stolen as he leaves it momentarily to follow two street vendors around a corner to buy a bright blue plastic recorder from them. Satisfied with his purchase, he walks casually back to his corner, only to find that his cart is not there. As he dashes through the crowded streets, anxiety swelling on his face, cars honk, jackhammers pound, and sirens blare, amplifying the sense of stress and confusion. An unmistakable reference to *The Bicycle Thief* (De Sica, 1948), which ends on a note of ambiguity like *Man Push Cart*, this sequence links Bahrani's film to the neorealist tradition. Several other crucial elements of the film—its use of several first-time and nonprofessional actors, its documentary-like look and camera work, its emphasis on quotidian hardship and struggle, and that it was filmed outdoors on location—confirm its link to this cinematic line.

The film's neorealism is evident not only in its focus on the materiality of labor, but also in the resolutely anticathartic quality of its plot. Notably, the film raises, but subsequently undermines, sentimental and romantic motifs. For instance, rather than have Ahmad reconcile with his wife's family and reclaim his relationship with his son, the film ends that narrative thread when his son Sajjad turns his back on his father. Ahmad finds a symbolic surrogate for his son in an abandoned kitten that he takes home. The possibility of caring for the cat raises the prospect of redemption, but Ahmad actually overfeeds the animal and it dies. Noe comes to Ahmad's cart to let him know she is returning to Barcelona, but he never visits her to say good-bye or explain his apparently conflicted feelings toward her, which remain opaque throughout the film, surfacing ambivalently in the scene in his apartment in which he embraces her, then pushes her away.

The anticathartic, unresolved quality of the film reflects its naturalism. As Ahmad pulls his cart through the dark, early morning streets near the end of the film, he trips, and the cart, already in motion, almost runs him over. He recovers, and as he continues down the street, straight into the camera, his cart careening behind him, we can hear him panting and see the stress and concentration on his face. This moment, at once material and metaphorical, both conveys the literal, physical hazards of his job and signals the film's downward narrative arc. Even more, this awkward instant—a halting lurch in which danger emerges in the midst of everyday struggle—stands as an allegory for the film as a work of precarious realism, which is organized not by a clear, clean linear thread, but rather by moments of acute unease, uncertainty, liminality. At the level of aesthetics, too, I have been arguing, the film is betwixt and between, unsettled and uneven.

Echoing this, the film is permeated by forms of spatial, cognitive, and political unevenness that gesture to the contradictory systems that structure Ahmad's daily struggles. Perhaps most apparent, the constant presence of midtown Manhattan's towering glass skyscrapers, looming over Ahmad and the other characters, literally placing their lives in shadow, signals the presence of consolidated wealth and capital, which the film subtly yet persistently insists constitutes the essential context for Ahmad's story. The parallels between and juxtaposition of other spaces in the film, perhaps most notably the contrast between Mohammad's clean, clinically white, upscale apartment, high above the street where Ahmad works, and his own grimy, poorly lit apartment, which we only see in fragmented glimpses in brief scenes, likewise suggests the radical spatial and economic asymmetries that cut across Ahmad's life, the film, and late capitalist New York. The unevenness here is not only at the international scale, between Pakistan (where Ahmad was wealthy and well-known) and the United States (where he toils in obscurity and near-pauperism), but within the United States and New York itself, where extremes reside side-by-side, giving meaning to one another through perverse contradiction. The contradictory, or uneven, nature of immigrant labor in New York is crystallized in the cart itself, which is at once an opportunity and an albatross, an emblem of (upward) mobility and an aluminum prison, an icon of economic investment and a four-wheeled debt machine. The cart, which is at once individual (it's Ahmad's cart and embodies quite literally his own economic struggles and aspirations) and collective (a version of his cart sits on the street corners throughout midtown, all of them identical at a distance), also stands as an emblem of class itself. Contradictions, the film suggests, not only shape the relations between nations or regions of economic development, they reside at the heart of New York City, where the consolidation of wealth is intertwined with the production of surplus populations in what Marx referred to as the "absolute general law of capitalist accumulation."[28]

At the end of the film, Ahmad is even more isolated than he was at the beginning. Indeed, the film charts the failure and dissolution of his relationships with Mohammad, with Noe, with his in-laws, with his son, with the man from whom he purchased his cart. At the film's conclusion, he has lost not only his cart, and thus his chief investment and hope of economic stability, but also his primary emotional connections. What remains are his relations with his customers, who keep coming, and with the scattered community of vendors and other workers who inhabit the underside of Manhattan's corporate-consumer complex, performing the basic service labor needed to make the system run. If there is any glimmer of optimism, or even hope—and it is hard to argue that there is—it stems from the fact that in the final scene, Ahmad is temporarily operating his friend's cart, while the other vendor retrieves his broken-down van. The arrangement gives Ahmad an interim job and allows his friend to undertake a task he normally wouldn't have had time for. Such small gestures of mutual support between immigrant workers, the film may be hinting, might provide a starting point for Ahmad and other such workers to develop the collective power to begin to counteract the forms of deceit, exploitation, and hardship that the film insists so clearly dominate their lives. This small-scale act of solidarity is vital, but it does not lead to a larger sense of collectivity or coalition. In this way, it is akin to the form of cinematic seeing the film invites us to undertake: to observe and follow closely one individual story, with persistent gestures to larger dynamics that are never fully fleshed out. It is a form of attention that models commitment, but where it might lead, and the larger stakes of such commitment, are left open.

"I'm working. You should be working, too": *Chop Shop*

Bahrani's second feature-length film, *Chop Shop*, focuses on two Latinx orphans: Alejandro, or Ale (Alejandro Polanco), a twelve-year-old who works various jobs in and around the auto body shops in Willets Point, Queens, and his older sister, Isamar, or Izzy (Isamar Gonzalez), who comes to stay with him in the makeshift quarters above a repair shop where he lives. Ale survives by constantly hustling: selling candy on the subway and bootleg DVDs to local residents, finding (in some cases stealing) car parts for the repair shops, coaxing drivers who need repairs into the shop that belongs to his benefactor, and helping strip stolen cars for another shop owner, Ahmad (played by Ahmad Mavzi, the star of *Man Push Cart*). Ale is known by many of the vendors in the area, and he gets Izzy a job working in a local food truck. One night, when Ale and his best friend Carlos are watching prostitutes and their clients at a local truck stop, Ale sees Izzy and realizes that she has been performing sex work too (although he doesn't tell her he has seen her). Ale has been saving money to purchase a used food truck in the hopes that he and Izzy can start their own business. After learning that Izzy is performing sex work, he steals money from her and buys the truck. Soon after, however, he learns that the truck's cooking equipment is not in good enough shape to use. Devastated, he punches Carlos, whose uncle sold him the truck, and snatches a purse and cell phone from a patron at the U.S. Open tennis tournament at Flushing Meadows, adjacent to Willets Point. When Izzy asks Ale where he got the cell phone she sees him trying to sell, he shouts, "I'm working. You should be working, too," suggesting that he knows Izzy has been laboring as a sex worker and should continue. Ale decides to sell the truck to Ahmad for parts, accepting a huge loss on his investment. In the film's final sequence, Ale goes to the truck stop, where he finds Izzy giving a blowjob to a customer in a car. Ale attacks the man, and he and Izzy run back to the auto shop, where Izzy refuses to talk to him. The next morning, when he sees Izzy sitting outside the body shop, Ale tosses birdseed on the ground to attract the local pigeons. Brother and sister smile ever so slightly at one another, and Izzy stamps her feet and shouts, scattering the pigeons into the air as the camera rolls toward the sky.

Like *Man Push Cart*, *Chop Shop* has a documentary feel, due largely to several cinematic features typically identified as hallmarks of neorealism, including handheld camera work, the use of nonprofessional actors, on-location filming, and a gritty setting (in this case, the greasy auto repair shops and junkyards in the shadow of Shea Stadium, home of the New York Mets at the time the film was made). Yet the seemingly raw, spontaneous look and feel of the film is in fact the product of deliberate planning, coordination, and rehearsal. "Of course there are scenes in the film that are just documentary," Bahrani explained in an interview, "when Alejandro's calling these cars in, he's really calling these cars in to make money—but the bigger scenes that are involving him and his sister, him and other characters, they were all scripted, incredibly blocked out, with the goal that it would feel like an accident, that you would never feel the *mise en scene*." Indeed, Bahrani notes that the scenes were assiduously rehearsed.[29] As film critic A. O. Scott explains,

Bahrani and his cast and crew spent months in the area of Willets Point, known as the Iron Triangle. . . . He also spent a long time rehearsing with Alejandro Polanco and Isamar Gonzales, the amateur actors who play Ale and Izzy, and when it came time to shoot, he pushed them through 20 or 30 takes of each scene. Every camera movement, nearly every bit of incidental business—a plastic bag blowing along a dark, empty street like a tumbleweed; a pigeon fluttering into the frame—was blocked out, controlled, adjusted, repeated.

In other words, although the film has an unaffected, raw, documentary feel, it was in fact carefully plotted and rehearsed.[30]

As with *Man Push Cart*, one can argue that the film's diligently crafted, documentary-style realism is overly poetic and privileges aesthetic interest over social critique.[31] In refusing to provide much contextual exposition or backstory, and in focusing so tightly on visual details, Bahrani might be said to downplay or occlude the possibility of a social or materialist understanding of the story he narrates. *Chop Shop* can be read as a universalistic tale of striving against the odds, a timeless narrative of survival and perseverance in the face of disappointment and the cruelty of fate, which have left Ale alone, drifting through a largely indifferent adult world. Yet *Chop Shop*'s focus on the quotidian details of Ale's life attends closely and consistently to material and economic concerns, returning again and again to the manner in which the young boy's varied labors and his efforts to economize and accumulate some small measure of surplus cash shape his most intimate relations and seemingly innocuous actions. Much as *Man Push Cart* blends a focus on the aesthetic and psychological elements of Ahmad's narrative with attention to the concrete demands of his work routine, so *Chop Shop* mixes a tendency to lend this ostensibly "minor" story a transcendental significance with a markedly realist emphasis on the particularities of Ale's quotidian struggles to cobble together a living in a harsh world of low-paid, informal physical work. If this story has an allegorical dimension, then, it might best be understood as an allegory of survival in neoliberal times, in which every citizen, no matter how young or socially marginal, is called to meet the relentless demands of an economic system that provides only the barest sliver of remuneration for the reproduction of self and subjective life. Indeed, from capital's point of view, Ale is a worker ideally suited to the contemporary flexible, low-wage economy: scurrying from one task to the next—selling candy on the subway or pirated DVDs to his fellow junkyard workers, finding or stealing car parts to feed the auto body industry in which he scratches out (barely) a pauper's living, working shift after shift in multiple chop shops—Ale is a model of commitment and consistency in an informal labor market that runs from dawn to midnight. Living in a cramped, poorly constructed room above a shop where he works and sustaining himself on popcorn and soda purchased with the modest handfuls of cash he is paid by his various employers, he requires almost nothing from the system to keep going. If neoliberal capitalism increases its profit margins in part by lowering to the barest minimum the cost of reproducing its labor force, then Ale's existence is exemplary: it's hard to imagine a more productive, active worker who could survive on less.

Chop Shop is structured by what David Bordwell calls "threads of routine," ordinary events that establish a baseline against which especially dramatic actions can be measured. In Ale's case, most of these events are acts of labor. Consider, for instance, the opening sequence of the film, which establishes the setting and main characters by following Ale through a typical day. The film opens abruptly with a shot of Ale waiting alongside several Latinx day laborers. A truck pulls up and the driver announces that he needs three men, telling Ale he has no work for him today. As the truck slips back into traffic, however, Ale hops in the back, only to be pulled out moments later by the employer, who, as he sends him off, hands him a bill and tells him to get breakfast ("I know you need me for the crawl spaces," Ale insists. "I don't have any crawl spaces," the contractor replies). As Ale trudges away from the departing truck, the Manhattan skyline looms hazily in the distance, punctuated by the Empire State Building. Ale walks off the edge of the screen, but the camera holds its view for an instant, and we are left gazing across the industrial landscape of Queens to Manhattan. In doing so, the film establishes a relation of proximity—and by extension of dramatic asymmetry—between Ale's labors and the wealth embodied by Midtown's corporate towers (and perhaps the scene recalls the early 1930s, when the Empire State Building was constructed). The struggles and strivings of this young Latinx orphan, the film suggests, have implications beyond the outer boroughs where his story plays out. This is, *Chop Shop* seems to be saying, a story not only of a boy, but also of capital and labor, not only of a neglected neighborhood, but also of a global city.

The opening sequence continues, as the camera cuts to bold letters announcing the film's title, and then to Ale talking on a payphone, trying to reach his sister, Izzy ("Did she go to the safe home?" he asks). Apparently stymied in his efforts to find out where she is staying, Ale trades insults with the person on the other end of the phone ("*You* fuck off," he says, slamming down the receiver). The film then cuts to Ale and his friend Carlos as they sell candy on the subways ("We are not gonna lie to you," they announce to the train passengers, "We are not selling candy for no school basketball team. In fact, I don't even go to school"). After Ale and Carlos divide their earnings ($15 each), the camera follows Ale to the auto repair yard, where he steers a customer into the shop where he works. We see Ale scamper into the back of the shop to find a new mirror, and then we see him learning how to apply wax to the hood of a car. Finally, we see the shop's owner, Rob, leaving at the end of the day, as Ale sweeps up debris. "Make sure you lock everything here up good," Rob says. "And go to Stella's and get yourself something to eat before ten o'clock, okay?"

In this ten-minute opening sequence, the film presents Ale largely through his diverse and exhausting labors. He is a hustler and a scavenger, living on the edge of wagelessness, who survives by guile and immense effort. Indeed, what's striking about Ale is his constant motion. Unlike *Man Push Cart*'s protagonist Ahmad, who is a noticeably still, even placid character, Ale's demeanor is frenetic. He's perpetually moving: rushing down the street pushing a spare tire, riding his bike with spare car parts on the back, dashing to drop his money in the hiding spot where he keeps it, running off to a Mets game in a rare moment of leisure. In addition, although he's younger than Izzy, he plays the older sibling in many ways. He's the one with the plan to buy a truck and start a business, and it's he, rather than Izzy, who finds them a place to live and starts saving money. Yet Ale is still a young person, and it's his youth and inexperience (and his inability to read the fine print on the title transfer documents) that Carlos's uncle takes advantage of in selling him a junked truck. Insofar as the film is about Ale's relationship with Izzy, it's about the difficulty they have understanding and supporting each other, about what they hide from one another as much as what they share. Their story, in an important sense, is an allegory of isolation, about the lack of family and connection. Ale and Izzy are what Lauren Berlant calls "survivalists, scavengers bargaining to maintain the paradox of entrepreneurial optimism against defeat by the capitalist destruction of life."[32] As young people of color without adult guardians, they are exposed to capitalism's brutal logic in a way most American children are not. This impoverished, abandoned, young racially marked person, the film suggests, personifies the predicament in which neoliberalism has placed almost all working people.

As a child laborer, Ale recalls the newspaper sellers, messenger boys, garbage pickers, and other young male service and industrial workers documented by Lewis Hine in his early twentieth-century photographic campaign against child labor. Employed by the National Child Labor Committee, which sought to build support for the abolition of child labor through federal legislation, Hine traveled the country photographing young people at work in canneries, mills, mines, factories, farms, and on city streets. Although Hine's straight, black-and-white photographs may seem artless, they were in fact carefully composed and structured to deliver a message (Hine himself referred to his own practice as "interpretive" photography). Specifically, Hine aimed to underscore the precarity and vulnerability of the young people he photographed, and thereby to demonstrate the horrors of child labor. As a result, he often captured isolated figures juxtaposed with imposing industrial machinery: a lone spinner, standing between two massive looms; a young newspaper seller, hanging perilously off the end of a large black trolley car while a conductor looks the other way; two young doffers, perched uncertainly on a loom in a southern mill; a young boy, standing among debris and protruding pipes in a glass factory. These images, and others like them, clearly and powerfully emphasize the physical dangers to which child laborers are subjected. The young people are often dwarfed by the machinery, which seems ready to overpower or devour them, like a huge industrial beast. What's more, in Hine's images children are frequently figuratively or literally isolated, captured alone, without adults in the frame.[33]

Yet Hine's approach, which often captures his subjects as they gaze directly into the lens, refuses to cast young people as objects of pity or as abject victims. Rather, his images endow these children with integrity, even as Hine suggests the dangerous, often degraded conditions under which they live and labor. These young people need help, but they are not helpless; they may be exploited, but they are not deficient.[34] They are working when they should be playing or learning, Hine's images imply, but they are performing valiantly and they deserve our attention not simply because they lack agency, but precisely because they are full of verve, intelligence, and energy. Hine's appeal to his viewers, then, is not designed to create a relation of condescension or paternalism. In fact, it is precisely such relations that his camera work aims to challenge. In their place, Hine proposes relations of compassion, understanding, and respect. In positioning his subjects squarely in the center of his shots, and often giving them space to look directly toward viewers, Hine aspires to establish an aesthetic of equality and solidarity rather than power and pity.

While there is no reason to think that Bahrani is consciously indebted to Hine's oeuvre, his depiction of Ale in *Chop Shop* has much in common with the early twentieth-century photographer's portraits of child laborers. Most significant, the film balances an emphasis on Ale's vulnerability with a corresponding stress on his agency. The result is an appeal to viewers that asks us to grasp what Ale needs and what is wrong with the situation in which he finds himself, but that stops short of suggesting that we know better than Ale how to address his problems. When we see the decrepit food truck he longs to purchase in the garage, viewers recognize that his decision is not likely to end well. It doesn't, and we realize that this young boy has been taken advantage of by adults who understand more than he does. Yet even as we see that Ale needs help, it's hard to regard him as "an object of paternalistic sympathy or ethnographic fascination," in Polina Kroik's words, because the film has spent so much time detailing his resourcefulness, energy, and skill.[35] If the film makes us aware of his youth and inexperience, and his vulnerability to particularly severe and insidious forms of exploitation, even violence, it also underscores his precocious competence: his ability to earn a (meager) living, to feed himself and find a place to live, to subsist in a competitive underground economy with very little adult assistance or advisement.

Certainly, however, as a work of precarious realism, the film stresses Ale's vulnerability, his youth, the lack of guidance and protection, the instability of his low-wage existence, and the very insecurity of his body. His exposure to exploitation and harm is crystallized in one particular scene at Ahmad's garage. Ale is helping serve beer at a party when all of a sudden, Ahmad shoves him roughly into a group of men playing dominoes. Ahmad laughs, and an altercation follows between him and one of the men. Ale watches the scuffle, stunned—as are we—by the fact and force of the push he received. Because Ahmad is one of the few adults to whom Ale occasionally turns for help, and because he tends to treat Ale with kindness, the shove is a sobering demonstration of the raw power relations governing Ale's life in the chop shops, in which he is perpetually susceptible to mistreatment or abuse by the adults around him (that Ahmad hands Ale a beer to drink during the party also suggests the limits of his willingness to do what is best for his young employee).

Perhaps surprisingly, the film's focus on the struggles of young workers caught at the cusp of pauperism, its episodic rather than linear shape, and its emphasis on the dilapidated landscape of crisis capitalism recall several Depression-era narratives, such as Jack Conroy's *The Disinherited*, Meridel Le Sueur's *The Girl*, and Nelson Algren's *Somebody in Boots*. These 1930s novels are class-conscious narratives that lead their young protagonists to a sense of shared economic and political injustice, which Ale does not achieve. But the stories of young, desperate workers hustling, scraping, and scrapping, trying to survive amidst "the cruel competition for bare existence," as Conroy puts it in his 1933 novel, nonetheless serve as narrative antecedents for Ale's tale.[36]

In narrating the failure, rather than the fulfillment, of Ale's efforts to work his way up, the film defies the uplifting logic that often organizes young people's coming-of-age stories. Rather than a linear tale of *bildung*, of movement from estrangement to assimilation, from innocence to experience, from youth to maturity, *Chop Shop* offers ambiguity and uncertainty, laced with a sense of dread. At the end of the film, Ale has lost three thousand dollars and seems to be without a concrete plan moving forward. Yet rather than encourage Izzy's sex work, as he had when he had been desperate to raise money for the truck, he decides to interrupt his sister's labors, suggesting that he is rethinking the priorities that were driving him earlier in the film. But any sense of transformation or change, and certainly of "progress," is left undetermined, and as the film closes, uncertainty looms, even if the final shot—of Ale and Izzy, in a moment of quiet and calm, watching the pigeons take flight—represents an affirmative symbolic gesture. *Chop Shop* is a film with a foreclosed sense of time, without a past or a future. There is only the present, the effort to scrape through today's round of work and self-maintenance. Not only does the film refuse to gesture forward, to provide a hint of where Ale and Izzy go from there, and how they will end up, but the absence of a backstory is palpable. The absence of a path forward or a view into the past leaves viewers in an uneasy position. In this way, the film's episodic rather than progressive form, which defies the expectations of growth and development that organize conventional coming-of-age narratives, echoes its content.

The film's lack of resolution suggests that rather than trying to teach viewers a lesson or convey a moral, the film is encouraging us to take up a stance, to adopt a mode of looking that is also a form of relating. How does the film position us to feel and think about Ale and Izzy, to *see* them? While *Chop Shop* underscores the hard facts of their lives, it steers us away from feelings of pity or simple sympathy. Rather, it urges what its patient camera work models: a form of attention that manifests a desire to know, learn, and understand, but that holds back from judgment, and also underscores the *limits* of what we can see and know. What the film encourages, then, is a kind of approach to others that is marked by open-eyed, yet self-knowing understanding, akin to what Lauren Berlant describes fleetingly as "the arts of awkward, generous, investigative patience."[37] The film wants us to grasp the youth, poverty, and orphanhood that make Ale especially vulnerable in a competitive, capitalist world, as well as the energetic intelligence and sense of attachment to his sister that sustains him. *Chop Shop* presents him as a worker and as much more than a worker—as a brother, friend, creative young person. He is at once an allegory of labor's condition under neoliberal capitalism—which demands adherence to the brutal logic of an unmitigated market that recalls the turn of the century, pre–New Deal era of Lewis Hine—and an irreducibly complex individual. We are urged to confront the deep material and existential precarity of his existence while also noting the limits of our own knowledge and perspective, and of his as well. This manner of respectful, engaged looking might be given several names—solidarity and witness come to mind. It entails seeing the harm of the world and looking beyond it as well to the possibilities of another world in which such harms would be less likely to occur and more quickly remedied. It is a form of concerned but nonpresumptuous attention that holds out hope for social attachments that are not founded on the basis of an underlying sameness, but ongoing and open-ended explorations along and across social divisions.

The composite form of looking the film tries to embody might also be seen as a dialogic combination of the individual and the structural, the particular and the systemic, the detail and the panorama. Like *Man Push Cart*, *Chop Shop* balances a tightly woven focus on a single figure—Ale—over a short period of time. The camera focuses silently, persistently on Ale, who is often alone in the frame, following him and giving us an intimate portrait of his world. Yet repeatedly, the camera pans out to contextualize Ale's struggles. If the film is fascinated by Ale's face, his movements, his isolation, it is also focused on the material and social *landscape* in which he persists. In particular, this landscape is structured by the tension between the scale and glamour of Shea Stadium, which Ale peers into through a crack in the outfield fence, and the U.S. Open Tennis complex, which Ale enters to steal a cell phone from a well-dressed blond woman, and the muddy, rutted avenue running between the run-down autobody shops. The high-profile, gleaming sports venues, packed with fans at leisure spending money, strike a stark contrast to the harsh, crumbling world of Willets Point. Ale, mired in the economic struggles of the auto body world and only able to catch a glimpse into the palaces of sports entertainment, is physically and metaphorically caught in the fissures of capitalism's antinomies.

"We need to work together": *La Ciudad/The City*

La Ciudad tells four stories about immigrant workers from Latin America in New York City. In the first, "Ladrillos (Bricks)," a group of day laborers is hired to collect and clean bricks on the lot of an abandoned, crumbling building; while they work, one of the laborers is crushed by a collapsing wall and dies. In the second story, "Casa (Home)," two young people from the same town in Mexico meet by chance at a quinceañera and start to fall in love, only to lose contact as the man, who had arrived in New York the day before, gets lost in the unfamiliar housing development where the woman lives. In the third, "El Titeretero (The Puppeteer)," an unhoused, tubercular puppeteer tries to enroll his young daughter in public school, but is denied because he does not have rent or utility receipts to prove their residency. In the fourth, "Costurera (Seamstress)," a woman working in a sweatshop where she has not been paid in four weeks tries to raise $400 to send back home to Mexico for her ill daughter. The stories are intercut by brief scenes in a storefront photography studio where several of the film's characters come to have passport and other portrait photographs taken. Created in the neorealist tradition, the film was shot in black and white, filmed on location, and features nonprofessional actors, in this case, migrant workers who helped Riker develop the stories during five years of research and filming, from 1992 to 1997. The film played at more than twenty-five film festivals, won numerous awards, and grossed more than $200,000 in the year of its release.

Riker came to filmmaking from documentary photography, which he practiced until he realized that he wanted his subjects to be able to speak. Moving to New York to attend film school at NYU, Riker learned Spanish and worked with community theater groups in the Latinx section of Brooklyn where he was living. He made a short film about a homeless puppeteer and his daughter that eventually became the third section of *La Ciudad*, and when he screened it in the South Bronx, where it had been filmed, thousands of community residents turned out to see it and offered to help him expand the story. "People started opening up to me," he recalls in an interview, "inviting me to their homes, meeting me after work.... I tape recorded interviews, asking them about their experiences coming to this country.... From this, the core emotional thread of the film emerged."[38] Riker wrote the script, but the dialogue and the acting were products of collaboration between Riker and the immigrant workers who formed the majority of the cast. After conversations and interviews, Riker led dramatic workshops in which the workers and director got to know each other, shared their personal stories of immigration and labor, and prepared to act.[39]

In its focus on the persistence of popular ethnic and national traditions (the quinceañera and puppet theater, for instance) and on the social networks linking the film's characters to their countries of origin and also to their fellow migrants, the film underscores what Robert Smith calls the "transnational life" of Latinx immigrants.[40] Yet the film is not only about hemispheric migration and the way national, ethnic, and personal identities are reshaped under diasporic conditions; it is also a film about global labor. Riker made the film during a period when the number of Latin Americans, and especially Mexicans, in New York was rising rapidly, forming a key segment of what Ness describes as the city's "new, transnational labor force." The Mexican population in New York increased from approximately 40,000 in 1980 to almost 300,000 by 2000, making it the fastest growing ethnic group in the city.[41] Riker understood the crucial role that immigrant workers were playing in New York City's economy, and made the politics of labor central to the film. "I wanted to make a film about . . . the experience of being an immigrant in today's globe," he explained in an interview, "[because] in the last 25 or 30 years the immigrant has become the central subject of our time. That is, the uprooted worker is now at . . . the center of the global economic system . . . a key to understanding what is happening today on the planet."[42] For Riker, then, this film about Latinxs in New York is a planetary labor narrative told from the point of view of its central subjects: migratory workers.

From the beginning, as a work of precarious realism, *La Cuidad* locates those stories in a larger frame. The film opens and closes with a bleak, hazy view of the New York City skyline, as an elevated train moves slowly across the gritty, gray urban landscape. These shots are echoed by other shots of large-scale apartment houses, skyscrapers, and factories that punctuate the film. Together, these images underscore the context of the city itself as something that shapes the lives of characters who, like the snaking train, work their way laboriously through the landscape. In commencing and closing the film this way, Riker emphasizes the necessity of thinking about the materiality of migrant life and putting individual stories in a larger field of forces, flows, and structures. This tension—between individual predicaments and structural conditions—is echoed by another uneasy dialectic at the heart of the film: the friction between isolation and collectivity, the paradoxical manner in which capitalism brings workers together, thus making possible new forms of combination and collectivity, but at the same time positions wage laborers against one another as competitors in the labor market.[43] These tensions pervade the film's content, but are also extended to the form of the film itself; a collection of four separate stories, featuring singular characters and situations, the film asks viewers to search for threads of commonality that stretch across the stories, weaving together the otherwise independent tales.

The film's opening narrative, "Bricks," foregrounds the possibilities of and barriers to collectivity that are at the heart of working-class formation, as well as the dynamics of distance and proximity, longing and loss, that are central to migrant life. As the story commences, the camera rolls along the street outside the photography studio at car level while day laborers approach the lens, gesturing and asking to be hired ("Take me!" "I go!" "Mister, how many?"). The viewer is positioned as a prospective employer, and we see among the workers a range of skin tones, ages, and body shapes (if not genders), a heterogeneous collection of male laborers. They converge en masse, but each one appeals individually for employment. The scene then cuts to a shot of Luis, the man who is eventually killed by the collapsing building, standing on the street, reading a letter from his wife, which is delivered in a voiceover. As she reads the letter, which recounts a severe rainstorm and news of the man's young son, the camera cuts to several of the day laborers, sitting or standing alone on the sidewalk, looking forlorn, isolated. Shortly after, a van pulls up and a cluster of men rush to the passenger side, vying to be hired. We hear the voice of the driver—"One guy. Who wants to come? $40"—and see a man slip into the van, smiling slyly as it drives away. The shots of men competing for work are intercut with a scene in which an organizer visits the corner, inviting the men to a meeting to discuss efforts by police and shopkeepers to keep the laborers off the corner. Together, these scenes raise the prospect of collectivity, asking us to consider whether and how these migrant workers—of varying hues, hailing from different nations, thinking about the family members they have left behind in their countries of origin—might find common ground in the midst of a brutally competitive labor market.

The tension between isolation and collectivity pervades the story. As the men ride in the contractor's windowless truck to the job site, the camera surveys them individually as they sit silently, absorbed in their thoughts. They are traveling together, but locked in solitude. When they reach the job site—an abandoned ruin of a brick building on the water—the boss tells them he'll pay not the $50 rate he offered when he picked up the men, but fifteen cents per brick. The men object, but once one of them agrees to work, the others slowly resign themselves to the job, although one remains visibly upset, kicking the bricks and bickering with another worker.

The collapse of the wall brings the issues of isolation and collectivity to a head. As they gather around the injured man's body, the scavengers confront the horror of what has happened and try to understand its meaning. One of them laments, "The pain you go through in this country to start a life and look what happens." In response, another man asserts, "The problem is we're working separately. We need to work together." "For fifteen cents a brick?," another man asks. "Even more so," the first responds. "We need to unite." A third wonders, skeptically, "When we fight like dogs on the corner for work?" What sense does collectivity make, the men seem to be asking, in the context of the meager wages at stake? Is unity even possible when the men are positioned in such a sharply competitive struggle to earn a living? Despair and agony spill into the open. "All bosses are the same!," one worker shouts, while another pleads, "Don't fight." "They treat us like animals," one of the workers exclaims. "What did you expect?," responds another, and the two men start to scuffle, only to be separated by their coworkers. "Look what happened because we're not together," shouts the man who had urged unity. "Who will be next?" Some workers stumble back to the bricks while others remain squatting around the now dead worker. The camera pans out, showing the men among the stacks of brick, with the city skyline at dusk in the distance. The man who had urged unity emits a harrowing wail, and collapses on the chest of the dead man. Catastrophe brings the laborers together briefly, and all too tentatively. They remain separate, and fairly abject, isolated like the bricks scattered around the job site.

The second story, "Home," takes up these issues from a slightly different angle, exploring the ways in which migration can open up new social relations, yet also confine and constrict human possibilities. This story examines both the continuity of what Smith calls the "transnational life" of Mexicans in New York, and also the sense of disorientation and discouragement that the displacements of migration can produce. Walking down the street, Francisco (Cipriano Garcia) hears music emanating from a building and wanders into a quinceañera celebration, where he meets Maria (Leticia Herrera). The two dance, and then retreat out the rear of the building into a small, leafy yard. "Listen," he tells her. "The city has disappeared. You know, I feel like I'm back home. The music, the dancing, the people . . . maybe we're in Mexico." "Mexico is far away," Maria replies somberly, undercutting his nostalgic reading of the scene. After a beat, he says, "I don't know why I'm here. I really don't know." On a surface level, he's referring to the party, but on a deeper level, he's alluding to his status in the United States. "Nor do I," she responds. He continues, "I don't know anyone here. I heard the music [and entered the party]. I just arrived in the city. You see this bag. My entire life is here."

On the one hand, then, this story about two young people from the same town in Mexico who meet in New York foregrounds the persistence of local connections in a global setting. Yet, as in the image of life in a bag, the vignette returns again and again to motifs of exile and anomie. At her uncle's apartment, Maria asks Francisco what he plans to do in New York. "Look for a job. Save money and make my home. Have fun." "Do you really think it's like that?," she asks, puncturing his naïve hopes and alluding to the obligations and hardships that have marked her time in New York. Later, when Francisco asks if she looks more like her mother or her father, she responds,

"I miss them, Francisco. I haven't seen them in more than four years." He asks why she doesn't visit them, and she explains, "It's not that easy. They depend on me.... They need me to be here. I feel trapped."

Amplifying this sense of entrapment, the story culminates by underscoring the spatial and psychic confusion migration can generate. When, in a spirit of generosity, Francisco goes out and purchases some groceries for breakfast, he is unable to find his way back to Maria's apartment, which is in a massive housing development in which all the buildings look alike to him. The film ends by intercutting shots of him, looking lost and forlorn, and then pans up over the sea of apartment buildings and across the cityscape, emphasizing the massive scale and indifference of the built environment. The story thus suggests migration's double-edged dimensions of social possibility and displacement. Migration has the potential to bring together people who might not otherwise meet, even if they hail from the same town. Migration opens the door to new life possibilities, new experiences, new relations. Yet the film also underscores the disciplinary aspects of South to North economic migration, the way it regulates and constricts, the sense of angst and loss it engenders, the demands it places on workers like Maria. Her freedom is curtailed by the financial imperatives that drove her to leave her home country in the first place, imperatives that are products of hemispheric and global uneven development.

The isolation and disempowerment of migrants that dominates "Home" is magnified in "The Puppeteer." The protagonist, Luis (Jose Rabelo), is a talented performer, whose outdoor puppet theater, which he sets up in abandoned lots in the Bronx, attracts appreciative audiences. He has friends; in one scene, he and his daughter Dulce (Stephanie Viruet) share a meal with a couple in a restaurant who help him read a medical form about tuberculosis that he was given by a health worker at one of his shows. Yet the story is dominated by foreboding images of separation, loss, and failure: the puppeteer's inability to register his daughter for school; his cough, combined with their precarious, outdoor living arrangement, which suggest that he may not be able to care for Dulce much longer; her separation from other children and her absorption in a fairly tale book she cannot read, which indicate her social seclusion; the unexplained absence of Dulce's mother, alongside the elegiac story that Luis tells her about a wandering, crying mother (perhaps La Llorona), which conveys a deep sense of grief. In the face of despair and hardship, the puppeteer and his daughter turn to fantasy: his puppet shows, the story he tells Dulce, and the fairy tales she reads. The stories propel and sustain them, but they clearly have limitations as narratives for confronting daily life. The tragedy of the vignette is that the puppeteer lets his sense of aggrievement cloud his judgment: he storms out of the school just as the registrar seems to offer to help him find a way around needing a rent receipt to enroll Dulce in a class. The story ends without a sense of progress or resolution, leaving viewers to wonder about the fate of both the father, whose health is clearly failing, and the daughter, whose seclusion has left her vulnerable.

The tensions between separation and proximity, and competition and association, are revisited in the film's final story, "Seamstress." The vignette opens with exterior shots of an imposing brick loft building, emanating steam. The windows are obscured, but we can sense the labor within. The camera then moves inside to a roomful of sweating sewers and pressers at their machines. Shots of hands ironing and running sewing machines are intercut with shots of individual workers' faces. A white woman with a British accent, apparently a fashion designer, expresses her dissatisfaction with the stitching in the shirts she is shown by the sweatshop's Korean American manager (Taek Limb Hyoung), and she pledges to return the following day to collect her order. When she leaves, the manager then circulates among the workers, shouting at them to work faster, physically prodding one woman. After inspecting the work of one sewer and announcing, "This is no good," he fires her on the spot. The other workers look up, but do nothing to protest. When they file out of the building after work, a man—possibly a labor organizer—approaches a group of the women and asks if they were paid. "Not yet," one says, but seems unconcerned, insisting, "I'm sure they'll pay us." Another woman stresses that the shop managers have been repeating this line for four weeks, and she wonders if the workers will arrive one day to find the factory closed. "They're not that bad," asserts the first woman. Viewers, who have seen the harsh conditions of the shop and the draconian manner in which the workers are treated, are positioned to be skeptical of this reasoning, yet the workers at this point seem surprisingly indifferent to the warning signs and certainly unwilling to stand up for one of their number when she is fired. The workers here express rival opinions, and their differences prevent them from acting collectively to protect one another or challenge the sweatshop managers over their back pay.

While the story opens by foregrounding the status of the characters as workers, its dramatic turn emerges from circumstances outside the shop. One of the seamstresses, Ana (Silvia Goiz), gets a message to call her family in Mexico, from whom she learns that her six-year-old daughter is ill and needs $400 for medical care. She talks to her family from an isolated booth in a bodega, vacant except for the proprietor, who pretends not to hear her sobs. Here the technology of communication, which is designed to connect the migrant and her family, enforces a sense of separation, as she cries unconsoled. Ana's friends respond to her predicament with generosity. Her neighbor Consuela tries to sell several dresses she has made to a local store to raise the money Ana needs. But the store's manager refuses, asserting condescendingly that "we don't buy from the streets." When her fellow sewers hear about her predicament, they offer cash to her, but the offerings are modest, and when she tracks down her cousin, who owes her money, she finds him drunk, with only a few dollars in his pocket.

In a dynamic that recalls the 1953 film *Salt of the Earth*, in which women take over a picket line during a Chicanx miner's strike, Riker framed *La Ciudad* as a call-and-response format in which the women who work in the sweatshop answer the lamentable lack of unity displayed by the men in the film's opening segment, "Bricks." As Riker explained in an interview, "the seamstresses represent the strength people have when they stand together for what they believe is right, for justice." In the final scene, Ana stops sewing, a tear rolling down her cheek. When the manager approaches, she says she needs to be paid to help her daughter. He yells at her to work and tells her to leave, pushing and then yanking her, but she refuses and wraps her arms around her machine. Slowly, the other workers halt their labors, and the shop falls still. The manager and his wife survey the room, as the camera cuts to individual shots of the sewers and pressers, whose expressions seems to capture a mix of emotions: fatigue, despair, sadness, anger, resolve.

This is a scene of multiple languages—Korean, Spanish, accented English—as the conflict plays out across linguistic as well as economic and social divisions. In casting a Korean American couple as the managers and highlighting the varied, uncertain responses of Ana's fellow workers, the film places stress on the differences *within* the immigrant community, none of whom are native-born or proficient English speakers and are also not united by their status as linguistic—and cultural and economic—outsiders. Thus at the level of language, the film reinforces its thematic concern for how well key issues translate among and between differentially positioned immigrant workers who hail from opposite sides of the globe.

Ana's work stoppage originates in her life outside the shop, from her identity as mother and migrant. If her daughter had not been thousands of miles away and had not fallen ill, she likely would not have refused to work. "Seamstress" is thus about migrants as workers and also about the lives of workers beyond the work they do. Work is primary and also only partial, a point that Riker makes in an interview: "With the story of the garment workers, I had as . . . a starting point the desire to make a film that was a denunciation of sweatshop labor . . . but most of those sweatshop workers . . . wanted to talk about something else. I went with them."[44] Labor and class, the film suggests, are not discrete, autonomous categories, but are shaped by factors, feelings, and relations outside the realm of production, in Ana's case in the realm of social reproduction. This is living labor: workers' lives are shaped by the work they do, as their relation to work is shaped by their lives outside the shop, in their families, communities, and the larger world.

If the story's final scene constitutes a moment of class consciousness and class struggle, it is a decidedly open-ended one. Riker reads it as an instance of the women "standing together," but critic Laura Hapke contends that the scene captures "the silence of despair, not of a concerted job action."[45] And indeed, the narrative ends without indicating whether the momentary pause by workers translates into a collective act of resistance and protest. The scene ends abruptly, in media res, and the camera scales back, panning to the outside of the warehouse building containing the sweatshop, and then to the larger city skyline. Can the urgency of the scene unfolding in the life of this one worker, and this one sweatshop, translate to a broader horizon? While the silence that prevails as the camera recedes from shop to building to city suggests that such a possibility is doubtful, the film's final shots ask us to consider what it might take or what it might look like if these workers, and all the others in similar circumstances, were to stand together.

The lack of closure that marks the end of "Seamstress" is woven into all of the film's stories, which end on notes of uncertainty. The unfinished quality of the film's narratives—another sign of the director's debts to Italian neo-realist films like *The Bicycle Thief*—might be said to reflect the open-ended nature of migrant imaginaries and the contingency of class. Class, and the forms of struggle and solidarity through which classes are made, are processes, matters of social relation, shaped but never wholly determined by conditions and relations of production. If the film's narratives refuse to provide a realized model of solidarity, we might perhaps turn to the filmmaking process itself, which entailed years of collaborative, reciprocal listening, learning, and making. What remains latent in the content of the film's stories—the power of collectivity—may in fact be manifest in its very form.

The film's final sequence returns to the photography studio, as twenty-seven people—some in small groupings, but many as individuals—pose before the camera. The sequence emphasizes the multiplicity of the migrants, young and old, a range of skin colors (some very dark, others apparently white), individuals and families, "from every part of the Americas," as the closing title card explains. The sequence also touches on the difference between still photography and film. Motion pictures allow us to see the figures posing for photographs, and as they do, smiles, tics, expressions flit across their faces. They are posed, and composed, but not frozen, still fluid. Photography freezes and fixes the figures, while cinema suggests the infinity of existence beyond such moments. The final shot is of the man who died in "Bricks," thus brought back to life. Film here functions as an instrument of resurrection, overcoming death to put a figure in motion. This reminds us of the fictional nature of the film (only the character died, not the person playing him), which has a documentary-style look (including the use of black-and-white film), and also suggests film's power to bring together disparate stories and characters. Seen together, all of them photographed in the same manner, the figures compose a serial collective: immigrant workers. But the sequence underscores their heterogeneity.[46] They are both a class and more than a class, a group and still individuals, actors and also actual migrant laborers.

It is precisely the nascent, provisional, indeed proleptic nature of collectivity that *La Ciudad* as a work of precarious realism underscores. Much like *Man Push Cart* and *Chop Shop*, Riker's film is punctuated by moments of silence, disorientation, and isolation that convey the solitary, anomic dimension of migrant life. Yet all three films highlight migrants as workers, stressing the precarious, often informal and largely invisible labor performed by racially marked migrants on the underside of the global city, and the networks and connections—and divisions and conflicts—*between* workers. These narratives ask us to abandon an image of the working class as a homogeneous political or economic subject, and, through attention to living labor, grasp the constant, contested process of formation, deformation, and reformation through which classes come into being through daily struggle. Whether and how the new working class will achieve the kinds of coherence and stability that marked the midcentury industrial working class remains very much an open question. But what is clear, these narratives imply, is that our frame for viewing class and workers needs to change, from a static notion of industrialized, institutionalized, formal labor to a more capacious understanding that can account for the multiplicity of contemporary labor regimes and experiences. These films suggest that the violence of capitalist dispossession, accumulation, and inequality endures in the contemporary world, that, as Marx noted in *Capital*, "[f]orce . . . is itself an economic power," that "capital comes dripping from head to toe, from every pore, with blood and dirt."[47] Like the other narratives examined in this project, these films also suggest that the world's proletarianized peoples bear the brunt of those crushing forces, as they are set in motion, pushed and pulled around the globe and across borders, in an effort to make a living and forge forms of collective power in the face of a foundational precarity. The novels and films in this study suggest that class is not a fixed, stable, or readymade expression of economic conditions, and the proletariat is not a synonym for wage labor but that the working class is an expansive, heterogenous formation, and that working-class connection, belonging, and identity are matters of continuous negotiation and translation across social and cultural boundaries. To understand these dynamics, and to find new ways to narrate the violent, tumultuous impacts of contemporary capitalism on the world's working peoples as well as possibilities for anticapitalist solidarity, we need to read tales of living labor.

Coda

Forms of Solidarity in Precarious Times

I want to conclude this book by returning to what the narrator of *Continental Drift*, discussed in chapter 1, describes as the "intricate interdependencies" linking the planet's laboring peoples.[1] Banks's novel, which juxtaposes stories of a downwardly mobile white worker from New Hampshire and migratory Black workers traveling from Haiti to the United States, and recounts the fateful coming together of those workers off the coast of Florida, is interested in these interdependencies and the connective power they might have in the absence of more traditional, robust forms of class consciousness and in the face of potent racial, linguistic, and national divisions. When an established, shared sense of class—of "the working class" as a relatively discrete, coherent entity—no longer obtains, what relations of collective belonging and struggle among the laboring peoples of the world might be imagined? As my work on this book proceeded, solidarity emerged as a key word to describe the uneasy, unfinished dynamics of working-class connection across social and cultural boundaries that are at the heart of the narratives of living labor. What follows is a brief reflection on the precarious forms of solidarity these novels and films seem to offer us, and how they might help us think about class formation in the present.

The literary and cinematic texts discussed in this project chronicle the unmaking of the twentieth-century industrial proletariat as a social and economic formation and the uncertain emergence of a new, not-yet-organized or consolidated working class. These narratives trace not a stable or organic sense of class consciousness or identity, but the lineaments of fluctuating, uneven, often quite tentative forms of solidarity among working people who occupy different positions in relation to capital and to structures of racial, ethnic, gender, civic, and sexual power. In the narratives examined here, solidarity often appears as a fleeting or even impossible prospect. Indeed, in these works, solidarity figures as what we might call a precarious form—a tentative, fragile process, frequently a matter of speculation or a relation visible largely through the contours of its absence. Rather than durable forms of collective belonging, these stories envision unstable, emergent solidarities.[2]

The term solidarity has a long history.[3] Its modern usage emerged in the context of the French Revolution, drawn from the Latin adjective *in solidum*, for the whole. It evolved in the work of nineteenth-century European sociologists such as Auguste Comte and Émile Durkheim in their attempts to define the patterns that facilitated social cohesion among members of increasingly industrialized societies. These fairly conservative notions of solidarity, concerned with communal and national norms, obligations, and unity, were taken up by early French socialists, who used the concept to advocate for social protections based on the idea of equality. From there, solidarity became central to nineteenth-century social movements, particularly the Paris Commune, the First International, founded in 1864, and the emergence of an international workers movement, including the IWW, founded in 1905, which advocated (and still does) for one big union and which established locals not only in the United States, but also Canada, Chile, and Mexico. In this context, solidarity emerged not as a name for national cohesiveness, but as a quality of relationships, often global in scope, among working and other exploited people, with shared interests, engaged in common or interrelated struggles across varied boundaries and divisions. Forging solidarity has been crucial to a wide range of social movements across the late twentieth and twenty-first centuries that have sought to make connections between disparate locations, peoples, and political concerns, from the struggle against apartheid in South Africa, to the Black Lives Matter movement, to the movement for justice in Palestine, and many others.

Contemporary capitalism has altered the context for thinking about labor-based solidarity and how we might theorize it. Specifically, as the relatively stable forms of working-class consciousness and composition that prevailed under Fordism in the industrial North have unraveled under contemporary regimes of flexible accumulation, "relations of social solidarity," Sandro Mezzadra and Brett Neilson argue, have "become more fluid."[4] "Rather than assuming that society is a whole that labor divides," Mezzadra and Neilson write, "it is necessary to track the differences, inconsistencies, and multiplicities that invest the field of labor and in turn fragment the organic notion of society."[5] Along similar lines, historian Richard Hyman, in a 2009 address to the Alberta Federation of Labor, asked, "How do we understand the idea of solidarity if the old notion of an undifferentiated working class is abandoned?" Because "the labor market circumstance of different groups of workers are not only varied but often highly differentiated," he insisted, solidarities "must be multifaceted [and] flexible, not uniform."[6] Can solidarity, conceived as "multifaceted and flexible," help us to think about class beyond older notions of class as a stable function of one's economic position? Can solidarity help us theorize and understand relations among working and nonworking people from divergent social, political, and national locations? More broadly, might solidarity help us to think between and across the categorical and the concrete, the abstract and the living, the common and the singular, to imagine the production of social connections and collectivities that resist closure?

In *On Revolution*, Hannah Arendt distinguishes solidarity from both compassion and pity. Solidarity, for Arendt, is dispassionate, a matter of principle rather than sentiment. "Because it partakes of reason, and hence of generality," she writes, solidarity "is able to comprehend a multitude conceptually, not only the multitude of a class or a nation or a people, but eventually all [hu]mankind."[7] Solidarity, she notes, not only looks toward those who suffer, but can extend in all social directions, constructing relations with and between the powerful and the dispossessed, and between relative equals as well. Arendt's emphasis on solidarity's capacity for generalization and abstraction is helpful. As Michael Hardt and Antonio Negri have contended, the "concept of abstract labor—representing what is common to labor in different occupations—is what makes it possible to think the working class."[8]

Yet solidarity is not only an abstract, dispassionate principle, but also a visceral relation, a feeling experienced in the body, in specific moments and dynamics of engagement or action. "How do we ever find, or make, a sense of solidarity with others?" Richard Dienst asks. "What explains the feeling that, sometimes, a connection with one person enables us to make a connection with two, three, ten, many others?"[9] To understand solidarity, we need to think beyond the instrumental register and categorical abstractions, although those are often crucial to solidarity's emergence and durability. What's more, we need to move our conception of solidarity beyond its roots in a conservative Euro-American tradition of social and political thought that saw the term as a normative form of civic cohesion grounded in social similarity. If solidarity is to be of use to us in theory or practice, it should refuse what Mezzadra and Neilson term the "fantasy of common being."[10] Our notion of solidarity should focus on what Rubén Gaztambide-Fernández calls "the particularities of human interdependency rather than the generalities of human universality."[11]

One promise of solidarity is that it can connote a non-identity-based form of affiliation: solidarity not as a matter of being, but, to echo Jean-Luc

Nancy, of *being with*. This "being with" is something the narratives of living labor explore (how workers from disparate social locations and histories come into relation with one another) and also what fiction and film, as cultural forms that project us into the psychic and social lives of imagined others, practice. Solidarity is thus a question not only of theme, but also of aesthetic form. Distinct from witness, sympathy, and charity, solidarity names a horizontal and reciprocal relation, achieved without complete consensus or unanimity yet capable of supporting common struggle. Solidarity is the construction of a form of relationality that cannot be taken for granted, that does not exist before it is practiced. We often presume that class is already there, waiting to be joined, a foundational category that, once recognized, generates a sense of belonging and identity. By contrast, solidarity suggests something more active and more fragile—a relation that always needs to be created and recreated, that cannot rely on an established sense of shared values or culture to establish bonds of commonality. In practice, solidarity often fails, snagged or undercut by lines of uninterrogated and unprocessed power. Chandra Mohanty notes that solidarity is "always an achievement"; David Roediger reminds us that solidarity is always uneasy.[12] It can also be achieved through forms of social and political exclusion, as white working-class solidarity has often been poised against immigrants and racialized others.[13]

In *Cultures of Solidarity*, Rick Fantasia argues that solidarity implies a "fluidity not easily available in the traditional conception of class consciousness."[14] Class often sounds solid and singular: "*the* working class." By contrast, solidarity is more partial and provisional, frictive and fraught, reflecting tensions and ambiguities, forged through "relationships of incommensurable interdependency," according to Gaztambide-Fernández. As a term, solidarity places stress on the active nature of its creation, on the fact that it does not pre-exist the actions and the imaginings through which it is established. For that reason, it is a compelling frame for stories of living labor, which are in some ways precisely *about* the absence of a secure sense of working-class identity and belonging.

Sociologist Marcel Paret describes what he calls "precarious class formation," not only "the process by which insecurely employed and unemployed, low-income, and nonunionized individuals constitute themselves as collective actors," but also the precarity and continency of such forms of togetherness.[15] Narratives of living labor depict workers who move toward one another, and at times establish tentative or provisional bonds of mutual connection, but who are largely unable to envision collective working-class action. In the end, these texts—from *Continental Drift* to *Tropic of Orange* to *La Ciudad*—suggest that in the absence of a discrete or stable sense of working-class consciousness or belonging, solidarity is vital, but still hard to imagine. The impulse to collectivity pervades the narratives examined in this book; these films and novels explore possibilities for labor-based alliance and shared struggle, however faint. Yet it is the faintness or the fragility of, and the barriers to, solidarity that these stories underscore. Unlike so much contemporary U.S. fiction and film, these texts insist on the centrality to our world of work, workers, and the unemployed, of exploitation, of living and dead labor. But rather than an established working class that can be joined, these narratives imagine instead tenuous relations of labor-based solidarity that are in the early stages of being formed and tested. Solidarity is thus not a solution, but a challenge, a frame for thinking about the ongoing and unfinished project of creating a sense of collectivity in an expanding era of precarious work, transnational labor migration, and flexible accumulation. As an older working class unravels, and another one comes into being, narratives of living labor can help us discern the terms on which new, emergent forms of collective consciousness and relation might become, and are becoming, possible.

Notes

Introduction

1. Michael Denning, *The Cultural Front: The Laboring of American Culture in the Twentieth Century* (New York: Verso, 2011). While my emphasis in this book on the transformation of the U.S. working class focuses primarily on the impact of neoliberal globalization and post-Fordist production, it is important to note the crucial role of politics, especially McCarthyism and midcentury anticommunism. These reactionary campaigns destroyed many key institutions of the multiethnic, working-class cultural front, such as the left-led unions that were hobbled after the passage of the Taft-Hartley Act, and civil rights and related political organizations such as the Civil Rights Congress, American Committee for the Protection of the Foreign Born, the American Labor Party, and the International Workers' Order. What replaced these progressive, multiethnic, and at times multiracial organizations was often a far narrower, "more reactionary idea of class, . . . protecting the privileges of white workers as against both immigrants [and workers of color] below, and global firms above." For this formulation, I am indebted to Benjamin Balthaser (correspondence with the author). On the impact of Taft-Hartley and the Cold War on the U.S. working class, see, among other sources, George Lipsitz, *Rainbow at Midnight: Labor and Culture in the 1940s* (Champaign: University of Illinois Press, 1994); on midcentury anticommunism, see Ellen Schrecker, *Many Are the Crimes: McCarthyism in America* (Princeton, NJ: Princeton University Press, 1998).

2. Nate Cohn, "Why Trump Won: Working-Class Whites," *New York Times*, November 9, 2016, https://www.nytimes.com/2016/11/10/upshot/why-trump-won-working-class-whites.html.

3. Grace Kyungwon Hong argues that "for the white working class to become a legible and coherent category, it had to be defined through the pathologization and exclusion of a variety of non-normative formations: racialized, gendered, immigrant, rural, and colonized." Hong, *The Ruptures of American Capital: Women of Color Feminism and the Culture of Immigrant Labor* (Minneapolis: University of Minnesota Press, 2006), 92. Ira Katznelson argues that from 1935 through 1965, major federal and state policies and programs designed to aid working people disproportionately benefited whites and excluded and disadvantaged Blacks and other communities of color. Katznelson, *When Affirmative Action Was White: An Untold History of Racial Inequality in Twentieth-Century America* (New York: W. W. Norton, 2005).

4. On these uprisings, see, among other sources, Dawson Barrett, *The Defiant: Protest Movements in Post-Liberal America* (New York: New York University Press, 2018);

Alexander Cockburn, Jeffrey St. Clair, and Alan Sekula, *5 Days that Shook the World* (New York: Verso, 2000); Tamara Draut, *Sleeping Giant: How the New Working Class Will Transform America* (New York: Doubleday, 2016); Annelise Orleck, *"We Are All Fast-Food Workers Now": The Global Uprising Against Poverty Wages* (Boston: Beacon Press, 2018); Joshua Clover, *Riot. Strike. Riot* (New York: Verso, 2016); Lizzie Widdicombe, "The Year in Labor Strife," *The New Yorker*, December 21, 2021, https://www.newyorker.com/news/2021-in-review/the-year-in-labor-strife; Jacob Bogage, "Thousands of U.S. Workers Walk Out in 'Strike for Black Lives,'" *Washington Post*, July 20, 2020, https://www.washingtonpost.com/business/2020/07/20/strike-for-black-lives/.

5. Michael Hardt and Antonio Negri, *Multitude: War and Democracy in the Age of Empire* (New York: Penguin Press, 2004); Guy Standing, *The Precariat: The New Dangerous Class* (London: Bloomsbury, 2011). Standing's book makes the case for the precariat as a new class-in-formation, but it offers a less-than-affirmative portrait of this group, whose members he contends experience anger, anomie, anxiety, and alienation (33).

6. Draut, *Sleeping Giant*, and Orleck, *"We Are All Fast-Food Workers Now."*

7. Aashna Malpani, Deena Sabry, and Stephanie Penn, "Portraits of Essential California Workers," *New York Times*, July 14, 2020, https://www.nytimes.com/2020/07/02/us/essential-workers-in-ca.html; Campbell Robertson and Robert Gebeloff, "How Millions of Women Became the Most Essential Workers in America," *New York Times*, April 18, 2020, https://www.nytimes.com/2020/04/18/us/coronavirus-women-essential-workers.html.

8. On labor in contemporary art, see the Mass MOCA exhibit "The Workers: Precarity, Invisibility, Mobility," which was on view from May 28, 2011, to March 31, 2012, and which "examine[d] how contemporary artists have represented labor conditions over the past decade while engaging many of the traditions that have come before them." "The Workers" exhibition pamphlet, 2011, no page number. On art and poetry in the context of the postindustrial restructuring of labor, see Jesper Bernes, *The Work of Art in the Age of Deindustrialization* (Redwood City, CA: Stanford University Press, 2017); on art in the context of rising precarity and the diminishment of wages, see Leigh Claire La Berge, *Wages against Artwork: Decommodified Labor and the Claims of Socially Engaged Art* (Durham, NC: Duke University Press, 2019); on contemporary labor in photography, see Joseph Entin, "Working Photography: Labor Documentary and Documentary Labor in the Neoliberal Age," in *Remaking Reality: U.S. Documentary after 1945*, ed. Sara Blair, Joseph Entin, and Franny Nudelman (Chapel Hill: University of North Carolina Press, 2018).

9. Gabriel Winant, "We Live in a Society," *N+1*, December 12, 2020, https://nplusonemag.com/online-only/online-only/we-live-in-a-society/. See also Gabriel Winant, *The Next Shift: The Fall of Industry and the Rise of Health Care in Rust Belt America* (Cambridge, MA: Harvard University Press, 2021).

10. Sociologist Beverly Silver argues that there is a "constant transformation of the working class and the form of labor-capital conflict. Revolutions in the organization of production and social relations may disorganize some elements of the working class, even turning some into 'endangered species'—as the transformations associated with contemporary globalization have done. . . . But new agencies and sites of conflict emerge along with new demands and forms of struggle, reflecting the shifting terrain on which labor-capital relations develop." "The insight that labor and labor movements are continually

made and remade provides an important antidote against the common tendency to be overly rigid in specifying who the working class is (be it the nineteenth-century craftworkers or the twentieth-century mass production workers)." Beverly Silver, *Forces of Labor: Workers Movements and Globalization Since 1970* (Cambridge: Cambridge University Press, 2003), 19.

11. William Robinson and Xuan Santos, "Global Capitalism, Immigrant Labor, and the Struggle for Justice," *Class, Race and Corporate Power* 2, no. 3 (November 2014), 8, italics in original.

12. Karl Marx argued that as production accelerates and intensifies, capital can produce more with less labor, and the population of surplus labor continually grows. "The greater the social wealth," Marx asserts, "the greater is the industrial reserve army . . . [and] the greater is the mass of a consolidated surplus population." Karl Marx, *Capital, Volume 1* (London: Penguin, 1990), 798. On the generation of surplus populations as capital's response to the prolonged post-1970s crisis of accumulation, see Clover, *Riot. Strike. Riot*, esp. chaps. 7 and 8. "In this context, class might be rethought in ways that exceed the traditional model . . . with its relatively static and sociologically positivistic 'working class' and accompanying forms of struggle [i.e. the strike]" (159). See also Aaron Benanav and John Clegg, "Misery and Debt: On the Logic and History of Surplus Populations and Surplus Capital," in *Contemporary Marxist Theory: A Reader*, ed. Andrew Pendakis, et. al. (New York: Bloomsbury Academic, 2014), 585–608.

13. On this etymology of proletarian, see Timothy Kreiner: "At its root, proletarian is a Roman legal term. It refers to those with nothing to lose but their children, or *proles*. . . . Historically, moreover, *proletariat* gathered together—however rudely, and with no shortage of internal divisions too numerous to enumerate here—all those *both shackled by and excluded from* the wage relation. A proletarian is not a wage-laborer per se. The proletariat encompasses all those for whom the fate of more or less miserable and immiserated wage-labor is the only available dream" (my emphasis). "The Fate of the Fast against the Slow," *Viewpoint Magazine*, July 15, 2017, https://www.viewpointmag.com/2017/06/01/the-fate-of-the-fast-against-the-slow/; see also Michael Denning, "Wageless Life," *New Left Review* 66 (November–December 2010), which argues, "Unemployment preceded employment, and the informal economy precedes the formal, both historically and conceptually. We must insist that 'proletarian' is not a synonym for 'wage laborer' but for dispossession, expropriation, and radical dependence on the market. You don't need a job to be proletarian: wageless life, not wage labor, is the starting point in understanding the free market." https://newleftreview.org/issues/ii66/articles/michael-denning-wageless-life. Geoff Eley notes that we need to expand our notion of the working class beyond the "classic wage-earning proletariat" to include diverse forms of unfree labor. He writes that "the search for a 'pure' working-class formation, from which forms of enslavement, servitude, indenturing, impressment, conscription, and coercion have been purged, remains a chimera." Eley, "No Need to Choose: History from Above, History from Below," *Viewpoint Magazine*, June 27, 2014, https://viewpointmag.com/2014/06/27/no-need-to-choose-history-from-above-history-from-below/.

14. Keith Newlin: "Scholarship has long wrestled with the problems of definition. Is realism a genre, with a particular form, content, technique? Is it a style, with a distinctive artistic arrangement of words, characters, description? Or is it a period, usually placed as occurring after the Civil War and concluding somewhere around the onset of World War I?" Newlin, "Introduction," in *Oxford Handbook to American Literary Realism* (Oxford:

Oxford University Press, 2019), 3. Underscoring the instability of realism, Fredric Jameson describes it as "a hybrid concept, in which an epistemological claim (for knowledge or truth) masquerades as an aesthetic idea, with fatal consequences for both of these incommensurable dimensions." Jameson, *The Antinomies of Realism* (New York: Verso, 2013), 5.

15. As I argue below, precarity has a long history under capitalism, and precarious realism does as well, but it develops into a robust tradition of particularly self-conscious representation as Fordism unravels, and that is the primary focus of this book. I inserted the word "empire" into my description of precarious realism to signal that the narratives of transnational, global transit, encounter, translation, and struggle these narratives depict invariably engage the long histories and ongoing patterns of U.S. imperial conquest and racialized, colonial domination. These are labor texts, but that is not all they are. Or rather, these texts insist we can only think and understand labor with and through race, gender, nation, and empire—and vice versa.

16. Laura Hapke, "American Proletarian Fiction," in *Encyclopedia of Literature and Politics*, ed. M. Keith Booker (Westport, CT: Greenwood Press, 2005), 586.

17. I'm thus *not* suggesting that contemporary narratives of living labor complicate a putatively one-dimensional or simplistic tradition of working-class literature; to the contrary, reading back through labor narratives from previous periods, as the novels and films I discuss in this book encourage us to do, allows us to see the foundational instability of class politics and aesthetic forms in earlier texts with renewed clarity. On 1930s proletarian fiction as a literary genre focused on precarity, see Joseph Entin, "The Working Class," in *American Literature in Transition: The 1930s*, ed. Ichiro Takayoshi (Cambridge: Cambridge University Press, 2019), 56–74.

18. Likewise, the term "post-Fordism," which refuses to name a fully realized system that replaces Fordism, is an admittedly incomplete placeholder for naming the wide range of contemporary—and still ongoing—economic, political, and social transformations that have reshaped and are reshaping the twentieth- and twenty-first- century capitalist economy. More on these transformations later in the introduction.

19. Bourdieu, "The Essence of Neoliberalism," *Le Monde Diplomatique*, December 1998, https://mondediplo.com/1998/12/08bourdieu; Mitchum Huehls and Rachel Greenwald Smith, eds., *Neoliberalism and Contemporary Literary Culture* (Baltimore: Johns Hopkins University Press, 2017), 8.

20. On the limitations of neoliberalism as a universalizing cultural force, see Bruce Robbins, "Everything Is Not Neoliberalism," *American Literary History* 31, no. 4 (Winter 2019): 840–49.

21. In an interview, Vuong explained, "I wanted to have a much more diverse look at New England life, which is dependent on these brown and yellow folks to clean for them, to cook for them." Lakshmi Gandhi, "In Debut Novel, Ocean Vuong Pens Love Letter to His Mom and Working-Class Asian Americans," *NBC News*, June 4, 2019, https://www.nbcnews.com/news/asian-america/debut-novel-ocean-vuong-pens-love-letter-his-mom-working-n1013126.

22. Ocean Vuong, *On Earth We're Briefly Gorgeous* (New York: Farrar, Straus & Giroux, 2019), 90–91.

23. Anna Tsing, "Supply Chains and the Human Condition," *Rethinking Marxism* 21, no. 2 (April 2009): 154.

24. Tsing, "Supply Chains and the Human Condition," 154.

25. The literature on these economic, social, and political transformations is immense. For starters, see writings by David Harvey, Judith Stein, Saskia Sassen, Ellen Meskins Wood, Giovanni Arrighi, Michael Hardt, and Antonio Negri, among others. For the impact of these transformations on the U.S. working class during the 1970s, see Jefferson Cowie's magisterial *Stayin' Alive: The 1970s and the Last Days of the Working Class* (New York: The New Press, 2010). The outline that I offer of the broad impacts of these transformations is especially indebted to the discussion of globalization in Silvia Federici, "The Reproduction of Labour-Power in the Global Economy, Marxist Theory and the Unfinished Feminist Revolution," *Caring Labor: An Archive*, October 25, 2010, https://caringlabor.wordpress.com/2010/10/25/silvia-federici-the-reproduction-of-labour-power-in-the-global-economy-marxist-theory-and-the-unfinished-feminist-revolution/.

26. On deindustrialization as a complex, multifaceted process that is "uneven in its causes, timing, and consequences," see Jefferson Cowie and Jeff Heathcoat, eds., *Beyond the Ruins: The Meanings of Deindustrialization* (Ithaca, NY: Cornell University Press, 2003); Winant, *The Next Shift*; Sherry Linkon, *The Half-Life of Deindustrialization: Working-Class Writing about Economic Restructuring* (Ann Arbor: University of Michigan Press, 2018).

27. Joshua Freeman, "Labor in the American Century," in *A Companion to Post-1945 America*, ed. Jean-Christophe Agnew and Roy Rosenzweig (Malden, MA: Blackwell Publishers, 2002), 203.

28. Dan LaBotz, "What Happened to the American Working Class?," *New Politics* 12, no. 4 (2010), http://newpol.org/content/what-happened-american-working-class. "The historic and ongoing transfer of the manufacturing process to cheap labor areas overseas has resulted in a shift in the U.S. labor force structure from manufacturing to the service sector where wages are much lower." Walda Katz-Fishman, Jerome Scott, and Ife Modupe, "Global Capitalism, Class Struggle, and Social Transformation," in *Labor and Capital in the Age of Globalization: The Labor Process and the Changing Nature of Work in the Global Economy*, ed. Berch Berberoglu (Lanham, MD: Rowman & Littlefield Publishers, Inc., 2002), 181.

29. Steve Fraser, "The Archeology of Decline: Debtpocalypse and the Hollowing Out of America," *Tom's Dispatch*, December 2, 2012, http://www.tomdispatch.com/blog/175623/tomgram%3A_steve_fraser,_the_national_museum_of_industrial_homicide/.

30. Andrew Ross, *Nice Work If You Can Get It: Life and Labor in Precarious Times* (New York: New York University Press, 2009), 4, 9.

31. Sandro Mezzadra and Brett Neilson, *Border as Method, or, The Multiplication of Labor* (Durham, NC: Duke University Press, 2013). Mezzadra and Neilson's thesis echoes and draws from Marx's axiomatic assertion that "Accumulation of capital is therefore multiplication of the proletariat." Marx, *Capital, Volume 1*, 764. Likewise, in *The Grundrisse*, Marx contends that even as labor is consolidated, it becomes "more diverse, more internally differentiated." Capital's growth is thus "the development of a constantly expanding and more comprehensive system of *different kinds of labor, different kinds of production*" (my emphasis). Marx, *The Grundrisse* (London: Penguin, 1993), 408, 409.

32. Freeman, "Labor in the American Century," 204.

33. Mezzadra and Neilson, *Border as Method*, 100, 91.

34. Ross, *Nice Work*, 9. See also Brett Neilson and Ned Rossiter, "Precarity as a Political Concept, Or, Fordism as Exception," *Theory, Culture & Society* 25, no. 7–8 (December

2008): 51–72. For Berlant's take on precarity, see *Cruel Optimism* (Durham, NC: Duke University Press, 2011), esp. 191–94. In his history of deindustrialization and the rise of care work in Pittsburgh, PA, Gabriel Winant contends that the New Deal state in fact laid the groundwork for neoliberalism's social and political exclusions and labor precarity. See Winant, *The Next Shift*.

35. On precarious work, the production of surplus populations, and implications for class formation, see, among others, Benanav and Clegg, "Misery and Debt," and Jonathan White, "Precarious Work and Contemporary Capitalism," in *Monthly Review Online*, March 30, 2018, https://mronline.org/2018/03/30/precarious-work-and-contemporary-capitalism/.

36. According to the ILO, the number of global migrants increased from 5 million in 1975 to 191 million in 2005. *International Labour Migration: A Rights Based Approach* (Geneva: International Labor Office, 2010), 21.

37. David Harvey, *Spaces of Hope* (Berkeley: University of California Press, 2000), 42.

38. Harvey, *Spaces of Hope*, 64.

39. Saskia Sassen, *Globalization and its Discontents* (New York: New Press, 1998), 35.

40. Harvey, *Spaces of Hope*, 64.

41. Robin D. G. Kelley, *Yo' Mama's Disfunktional!: Fighting the Culture Wars in Urban America* (Boston: Beacon Press, 1998), 128.

42. LaBotz, "What Happened to the American Working Class?"

43. Kim Moody, "The State of American Labor," *Jacobin*, June 20, 2016, https://www.jacobinmag.com/2016/06/precariat-labor-us-workers-uber-walmart-gig-economy/?setAuth=d75decce57605811cc94414840b5beea.

44. Federici, "The Reproduction of Labour-Power in the Global Economy, Marxist Theory and the Unfinished Feminist Revolution."

45. Harold Meyerson, "If Labor Dies, What's Next?" *The American Prospect*, September 13, 2012, https://prospect.org/economy/labor-dies-next/; in addition, see Steven Greenhouse, *Beaten Down, Worked Up: The Past, Present, and Future of American Labor* (New York: Knopf, 2019).

46. Meyerson, "If Labor Dies, What's Next?" Marx argued that labor is the source of capital's value and yet also excluded from the very value it produces; it is capital's essential agent of valorization, yet also continually in the process of being displaced. Marx writes, "It is clear, therefore, that the worker cannot become *rich* in this exchange [with capital], since, in exchange for his [*sic*] labour capacity as a fixed, available magnitude, he surrenders its *creative power*, like Esau his birthright for a mess of pottage. Rather, he necessarily impoverishes himself . . . because the creative power of his labour establishes itself as the power of capital, as an *alien power* confronting him." Marx, *Grundrisse*, 307, original italics. And in one of his well-known axioms, Marx insisted, "The greater the social wealth, the greater is the industrial reserve army. . . . *This is the absolute general law of capitalist accumulation.*" Marx, *Capital, Volume 1*, 798.

47. Black unemployment increased from 8.1 percent to 14.7 percent in 1975; in 1992, when the official employment rate for all workers was 7 percent, the rate for African American workers was (still) 14 percent. See Manning Marable, *How Capitalism Underdeveloped Black America: Problems in Race, Political Economy, and Society* (Chicago: Haymarket Books, 2015 [1983]), 43. Walda Katz-Fishman et al., "Global Capitalism," 186. "Capitalist development has occurred not in spite of the exclusion of Blacks," Marable

contends, "but because of the brutal exploitation of Blacks as workers and consumers." Marable, *How Capitalism Underdeveloped Black America*, 2.

48. "Disparities in Wealth by Race and Ethnicity in the 2019 Survey of Consumer Finances," September 20, 2020, https://www.federalreserve.gov/econres/notes/feds-notes/disparities-in-wealth-by-race-and-ethnicity-in-the-2019-survey-of-consumer-finances-20200928.htm.

49. "Although the U.S. economy has traditionally been fueled by immigrant labor, the current dependence on undocumented labor is unprecedented." Richard D. Vogel, "Harder Times: Undocumented Workers and the U.S. Formal Economy," in *More Unequal: Aspects of Class in the United States*, ed. Michael Yates (New York: Monthly Review Press, 2007), 65.

50. "This creates the best of both worlds for employers. On the one hand, low-wage immigrant labor is readily available. On the other, immigrant workers' illegal status increases employers' leverage in all aspects of the employment relation." Immanuel Ness, *Immigrants, Unions and the New US Labor Market* (Philadelphia: Temple University Press, 2005), 15.

51. On mass incarceration as "partial geographic solutions to political economic crises," see Ruth Wilson Gilmore, *Golden Gulag: Prisons, Surplus, Crisis, and Opposition in Globalizing California* (Berkeley: University of California Press, 2006), 26.

52. Writing in the 1980s, just as the massive neoliberal expansion of the racially unequal system of mass incarceration was starting, Manning Marable notes, "Almost half of all prisoners in the U.S., at any given time, are Black.... The great majority of prisoners are from the working class ... Almost one-third of these men and women (31 percent) were unemployed during the four weeks prior to their arrest." Marable, *How Capitalism Underdeveloped Black America*, 112.

53. See Kathleen Arnold, *America's New Working Class: Race, Gender, Ethnicity in a Biopolitical Age* (University Park: Penn State University Press, 2007).

54. Freeman, "Labor in the American Century," 205.

55. Jason Read, "Work and Precarity," in *A Companion to Critical and Cultural Theory*, ed. Sarah Blacker, Sut Jhally, and Imre Szeman (London: Blackwell, 2017), 269–81.

56. Marx, *Capital, Volume 1*, 342.

57. Marx, *Grundrisse*, 298.

58. Marx, *Grundrisse*, 361. See also Bruno Gulli, *The Labor of Fire: The Ontology of Labor between Economy and Culture* (Philadelphia: Temple University Press, 2005).

59. On the distinction between "productive labor," which is labor that is made productive for and objectified in capital, and living labor, see Gulli, *Labor of Fire*, esp. chap. 2.

60. Engels, writing about industrial capitalism in Manchester, England, cited in Emma Laurie and Ian Shaw, "Violent Conditions: The Injustices of Being," *Political Geography* 65 (2018): 8.

61. Gilmore, *Golden Gulag*, 28.

62. Marable, *How Capitalism Underdeveloped Black America*, 115, italics in original.

63. Achille Mbembe, "Necropolitics," trans. Libby Meintjes, *Public Culture* 15, no. 1 (2003): 39.

64. James Tyner, *Dead Labor: Toward a Political Economy of Premature Death* (Minneapolis: University of Minnesota Press, 2019), x, xi. Tyner asserts that "prema-

ture death is an intrinsic, systemic condition of necrocapitalism" (16). Tyner argues that necrocapitalism is "not simply a matter of who lives, who dies, and who decides; it has become a matter of who profits from the death of living labor . . . [I]n an age of precarity, living laborers are exploited not only in life but in death" (86).

65. Marx, *Capital, Volume 1*, 465.

66. Marx, *Grundrisse*, 296, 272. My ideas about living labor are indebted to Dipesh Chakrabarty, *Provincializing Europe: Postcolonial Thought and Historical Difference* (Princeton, NJ: Princeton University Press, 2000), and Sandro Mezzadra, "How Many Histories of Labour? Towards a Theory of Postcolonial Labor," *Postcolonial Studies* 14, no. 2 (2011): 151–70. Drawing on Chakrabarty's work, Mezzadra writes that living labor "constitutes itself as a necessary excess—as a constitutive outside of capital relation itself" (163). In a slightly different vein, Jason Read asserts that living labor is "the conflictual connection" between abstract and concrete labor; "Marx used the term 'living labor' to primarily foreground the opposition between the worker and the accrued power of capital, of dead labor, but the term also incorporates labor as it is lived." Read, "Conscious Organs: Towards a Political Anthropology of Labor Power," *Philosophy Today* 64, no. 1 (2020): 90. On the distinction between "productive labor," which is labor that is made productive for and objectified in capital, and living labor, see Gulli, *Labor of Fire*, esp. chap. 2.

67. Chakrabarty, *Provincializing Europe*, 66.

68. Sandro Mezzadra puts it this way: "[T]he constitution and composition of living labor are nowadays open processes both from the point of view of capital and from the point of view of the subjectivities that make up living labor itself." "Living in Transition: Toward a Heterolingual Theory of the Multitude," *Transversal*, June 2007, https://transversal.at/transversal/1107/mezzadra/en.

69. Lisa Lowe, *Immigrant Acts: On Asian American Cultural Politics* (Durham, NC: Duke University Press, 1996), 27–28.

70. Aiwa Ong, "The Gender and Labor Politics of Postmodernity," in *The Politics of Culture in the Shadow of Capitalism*, ed. Lisa Lowe and David Lloyd (Durham, NC: Duke University Press, 1997), 65.

71. Harvey, *Spaces of Hope*, 49.

72. Marx, *Capital, Volume 1*, 711.

73. See, for starters, Mariarosa Dalla Costa and Selma James, *The Power of Women and the Subversion of the Community* (Bristol: Falling Wall Press, 1973); Lise Vogel, *Marxism and the Oppression of Women* (London: Pluto Press, 1983). On Black radical theories of reproduction, see Bill Mullen, 'The Russian Revolution, Black Bolshevichki and Social Reproduction,' *Viewpoint*, December 14, 2017, https://www.viewpointmag.com/2017/12/14/russian-revolution-black-bolshevichki-social-reproduction/#fn23-8568.

74. Marx, *Capital, Volume 1*, 724.

75. Tithi Bhattacharya argues that the working class "must be perceived of as everyone in the producing class who has in their lifetime participated in the totality of reproduction of society—irrespective of whether that labor has been paid for by capital or remained unpaid. Such an integrative vision of class gathers together the temporary Latina hotel worker from Los Angeles, the flextime working mother from Indiana who needs to stay home due to high childcare costs, the African-American full-time school teacher from Chicago, and the white, male and unemployed, erstwhile UAW worker from Detroit." Bhattacharya, "How Not to Skip Class: Social Reproduction of Labor

and the Global Working Class," *Viewpoint Magazine*, October 31, 2015, https://viewpoin tmag.com/2015/10/31/how-not-to-skip-class-social-reproduction-of-labor-and-the-gl obal-working-class/.

76. Nikhil Pal Singh and Joshua Clover, "The Blindspot Revisited," *Verso Blog*, October 12, 2018, https://www.versobooks.com/blogs/4079-the-blindspot-revisited.

77. Benjamin Balthaser argues powerfully that "U.S. working-class literature has always been about the production of a class identity through modes of racial looking, identification, and solidarity"; I think it can also be argued that gender divisions, differences, and structures have likewise always been central elements and preoccupations of working-class writing. Balthaser, "The Race of Class: The Role of Racial Identity Production in the Long History of U.S. Working-Class Writing," in *Working-Class Literature(s): Historical and International Perspectives*, ed. J. Lennon and M. Nilsson (Stockholm: Stockholm University Press, 2017), 31. For one compelling attempt to define working-class writing, see Janet Zandy, "In the Skin of Worker, or, What Makes a Text Working Class," in *Hands: Physical Labor, Class, and Cultural Work* (New Brunswick, NJ: Rutgers University Press, 2004), 84–93. Zandy doesn't stipulate collective association or solidarity in her list of qualities that define working-class texts, but she does argue that such texts are deeply focused on "relationality" (86), typically exhibit a "communal sensibility" (90) and "consciousness of connective tissue" (90), and often "takes sides" on "the continuous, larger struggle for economic justice" (92).

78. The literary scholars whose work I have learned and benefited from include, among others, Peter Hitchcock, Janet Zandy, Sherry Linkon, Michael Denning, Lisa Lowe, Amy Schrager Lang, Bill Mullen, Bruce Robbins, Gavin Jones, John Marsh, Kathleen M. Newman, Marcial González, Dennis López, Benjamin Balthaser, Sonali Perera, Pamela Fox, Polina Kroik, Paul Lauter, Clare Callahan, Robin Brooks, Grace Kyungwon Hong, Rachel Rubin, Sara Appel, Lawrence Hanley, and Cora Kaplan.

79. Cora Kaplan, "Introduction: Millennial Class," *PMLA* 115, no. 1 (January 2000): 13.

80. Sonali Perera, *No Country: Working-Class Writing in the Age of Globalization* (New York: Columbia University Press, 2014), 3, 4.

81. Hyman quoted in Kim Moody, *Workers in a Lean World: Unions in the International Economy* (New York: Verso, 1997), 145.

82. Adam Przeworski, "Proletariat into a Class: The Process of Class Formation from Karl Kautsky's *The Class Struggle* to Recent Controversies," *Politics & Society* 7, no. 4 (1977): 372.

83. Goran Therborn argues that class formation is "an *open-ended* process with no fixed destination. Classes must be seen, not as veritable geological formations once they have acquired their original shape, but as phenomena in a constant process of formation, reproduction, re-formation and deformation." Therborn, "Why Some Classes Are More Successful Than Others," *New Left Review* 138 (1983): 37–55. In a related vein, Kim Moody explains that "the recomposition of the working class by industries, occupations, gender, ethnicity, and race is and always has been a recurrent feature of capitalism. And with recomposition comes internal conflict born of inequality." Moody, *Workers in a Lean World*, 144.

84. Antonio Negri, "The Labor of the Multitude and the Fabric of Biopolitics," trans. Sara Mayo and Peter Graefe with Mark Coté, ed. Mark Coté, *Mediations* 23, no. 2 (Spring 2008): 22.

Chapter 1

1. Mike Davis, *Prisoners of the American Dream: Politics and Economy of the U.S. Working Class* (New York: Verso, 1986), 16.
2. Davis, *Prisoners of the American Dream*, vii.
3. Davis, *Prisoners of the American Dream*, 314.
4. Russell Banks, *Continental Drift* (New York: HarperPerennial, 2007), 39. Further citations appear parenthetically by page number in the body of the text.
5. Michael J. Dash, *Haiti and the United States: National Stereotypes and the Literary Imagination* (London: Macmillan, 1997), 148; Michael Shapiro, "Moral Geographies and the Ethics of Post-Sovereignty," *Public Culture* 6, no. 3 (1994): 486.
6. See, among other works, Aimee Bahng, *Migrant Futures: Decolonizing Speculation in Financial Times* (Durham, NC: Duke University Press, 2017); Elizabeth Ammons, *Brave New Words: How Literature Will Save the Planet* (Iowa City: University of Iowa Press, 2010); Kandice Chuh, "Of Hemispheres and Other Spheres: Navigating Karen Tei Yamashita's Literary World," *American Literary History* 18, no. 3 (Fall 2006): 618–37; Caroline Rody, "The Transnational Imagination: Karen Tei Yamashita's *Tropic of Orange*," in *Asian North American Identities: Beyond the Hyphen*, ed. Eleanor Ty and Donald C. Goellnicht (Bloomington: Indiana University Press, 2004), 130–48; Timothy Libretti, "The Other Proletarians: Native American Literature and Class Struggle," *Modern Fiction Studies* 47, no. 1 (Spring 2001): 164–89.
7. Michael Denning, *Culture in the Age of Three Worlds* (New York: Verso, 2004), 153.
8. Fredric Jameson, "Cognitive Mapping," in *Marxism and the Interpretation of Culture*, ed. Cary Nelson and Lawrence Grossberg (Urbana: University of Illinois Press, 1988), 353.
9. Jameson, "Cognitive Mapping," 351. Jameson asserts that cognitive mapping is a pedagogical mode that links personal stories to capitalist totality. But he acknowledges that "'totalizing' process ... often means little more than the making of connections between various phenomena, a process which ... tends to be ever more spatial." I am arguing that, in its attention to historical and contemporary colonialism and racism, as well as class, *Continental Drift* connects individual stories to capitalism, but also to more than capitalism. Fredric Jameson, *Postmodernism, or, The Cultural Logic of Late Capitalism* (Durham, NC: Duke University Press, 1991), 403.
10. Jeff Kinkle and Alberto Toscano, *Cartographies of the Absolute* (Winchester, UK: Zero Books, 2015), 22.
11. See, among other sources, Kathleen R. Arnold, *America's New Working Class. Race, Gender, and Ethnicity in a Biopolitical Age* (State College: Penn State University Press, 2009); Jefferson Cowie, *Stayin' Alive: The 1970s and the Last Days of the Working Class* (New York: New Press, 2010); Denning, *Culture in the Age of Three Worlds*; Joshua Freeman, "Labor During the American Century: Work, Workers, and Unions Since 1945," in *Blackwell Companion to Post-1945 America*, ed. Jean-Christophe Agnew and Roy Rosenzweig (Malden, MA: Blackwell Publishers, 2002), 192–210; David Harvey, *A Brief History of Neoliberalism* (Oxford: Oxford University Press, 2005).
12. James Atlas, "A Great American Novel," *The Atlantic* 255, no. 2 (Feb. 1985): 94; Davis, *Prisoners of the American Dream*, viii.
13. Cowie, *Stayin' Alive*, 369.

14. Cowie, *Stayin' Alive*, 368.

15. Of course, Bob also dies as the novel ends, but his death signifies in quite different ways than the death of Claude and the other migrants. Bob's death literalizes his own personal decline, which is traced across the novel (echoing the book's debts to literary naturalism), and also allegorizes the larger demise of the white male North American industrial working class. But his death comes as an exceptional moment, if not exactly a surprising plot twist. Bob may be poor and looked down on by many of his fellow Americans, but he is not subject to the perpetual threat of arbitrary violence and premature death from which Claude and Vanise are never free.

16. Silvia Federici, "The Reproduction of Labor-Power in the Global Economy, Marxist Theory, and the Unfinished Feminist Revolution," *Caring Labor: An Archive*, October 25, 2010, https://caringlabor.wordpress.com/2010/10/25/silvia-federici-the-reproduction-of-labour-power-in-the-global-economy-marxist-theory-and-the-unfinished-feminist-revolution/.

17. Federici, "The Reproduction of Labor-Power."

18. In fact, one of the remarkable features of the novel is its insistence on the heterogeneity of working-class laboring situations and arrangements across the American hemisphere. For more on this dimension of contemporary global capitalism, see Sandro Mezzadra and Brett Neilson, *Border as Method, or, the Multiplication of Labor* (Durham, NC: Duke University Press, 2013).

19. Laura Hapke, "American Proletarian Fiction," in *Encyclopedia of Literature and Politics*, ed. M. Keith Booker (Westport, CT: Greenwood, 2005), 584. See also Barbara Foley, *Radical Representations: Politics and Form in U.S. Proletarian Fiction, 1929–1941* (Durham, NC: Duke University Press, 1993); Paul Lauter, "American Proletarianism," in *The Columbia History of the American Novel*, ed. Emory Elliott and Cathy N. Davidson (Columbia University Press, 1988), 331–56; Paula Rabinowitz, *Labor and Desire: Women's Revolutionary Fiction in Depression America* (Chapel Hill: University of North Carolina Press, 1991).

20. On tourists and vagabonds, see Zygmunt Bauman, *Globalization: The Human Consequences* (New York: Columbia University Press, 1998).

21. Russell Banks and Loïc Wacquant, "Casting America's Outcasts: A Dialogue between Russell Banks and Loïc Wacquant," *Amerikastudien* 53, no. 2 (2008): 214–15.

22. Stuart Hall, "Race, Articulation, and Societies Structured in Dominance," *Sociological Theories: Race and Colonialism* (Paris: UNESCO, 1980): 305–45.

23. Freeman, "Labor During the American Century," 205.

24. Robin Kelley, *Yo' Mama's DisFunktional!: Fighting the Culture Wars in Urban America* (Boston: Beacon Press, 1997), 128.

25. On the intertextual dynamics of Banks's novel, see Andrea Dimino, "'The Planet Survives... Through Heroism': Florida as the New World in Russell Banks's *Continental Drift*," in *Florida Proceedings*, ed. C. Slate (Cambridge: Cambridge Scholars Press, 2008): 132–53.

26. Trish Reeves, "Interview with Russell Banks," in *Contemporary Literary Criticism*, vol. 72, ed. Thomas Voeller (Detroit: Gale, 1992), 9.

27. Christopher Douglas, *Reciting America: Culture and Cliché in Contemporary U.S. Fiction* (Urbana: University of Illinois Press, 2001), 56.

28. For this insight, I'm indebted to a former student, Cameron McLinden.

29. Dash, *Haiti and the United States*, 149.

30. Dash, *Haiti and the United States*, 149.
31. On the poetics of relation, see Édouard Glissant, *Poetics of Relation*, trans. Betsy Wing (Ann Arbor: University of Michigan Press, 1997).
32. Paul Gilroy, *The Black Atlantic: Modernity and Double-Consciousness* (Cambridge, MA: Harvard University Press, 1993).
33. Peter Linebaugh and Marcus Rediker, *The Many-Headed Hydra: Sailors, Slaves, Commoners, and the Hidden History of the Revolutionary Atlantic* (Boston: Beacon Press, 2001), 172.
34. Tillie Olsen, *Tell Me a Riddle* (New York: Delta, 1989), 109.
35. I am indebted to Aarthi Vaade for this formulation, which comes originally from Dipesh Chakrabarty, who contends, "European thought is at once both indispensable and inadequate in helping us to think through the experiences of political modernity in non-Western nations." Chakrabarty, *Provincializing Europe: Postcolonial Thought and Historical Difference* (Princeton, NJ: Princeton University Press, 2007), 16.
36. Iris Marion Young, "Gender as Seriality: Thinking Women as a Social Collective," *Signs* 19, no. 3 (1994): 728.
37. Jean-Paul Sartre, *Critique of Dialectical Reason Volume 1: Theory of Practical Ensembles* (London: Verso, 1991), 267. Fred Jameson notes that seriality "can be defined as a collective situation in which the center is always elsewhere." Jameson, *Archaeologies of the Future: The Desire Called Utopia and Other Science Fictions* (New York: Verso, 2007), 243–44.
38. Sartre, *Critique of Dialectical Reason*, 260.
39. Sartre, *Critique of Dialectical Reason*, 263, 265.
40. Sartre, *Critique of Dialectical Reason*, 256.
41. Sartre, *Critique of Dialectical Reason*, 312.
42. Young, "Gender as Seriality," 727.
43. Sartre, *Critique of Dialectical Reason*, 311, my emphasis.
44. Sartre, *Critique of Dialectical Reason*, 267.
45. Young, "Gender as Seriality," 726–67.
46. Sonya Rose, "Class Formation and the Quintessential Worker," in *Reworking Class*, ed. John Hall (1997), 154.
47. Davis, *Prisoners of the American Dream*, ix.
48. See Mezzadra and Neilson, *Border as Method*.
49. My thinking here is indebted to Aníbal Quijano and Immanuel Wallerstein, "Americanity as a Concept, or the Americas in the Modern World-System," *International Social Science Journal* 63, no. 4 (1992): 549–57.
50. Jameson, *Postmodernism*, 51.
51. Jameson, *Postmodernism*, 51.
52. Russell Banks, *Continental Drift* (New York: HarperPerennial, 1994), 114. This passage was excised from the 2007 edition of the novel, presumably due to a printing error.

Chapter 2

1. Karen Tei Yamashita, *Tropic of Orange* (Minneapolis: Coffee House Press, 1997), 35. Further references appear parenthetically by page number in the body of the text.

2. I am drawing on the notion of the CIO working class from Michael Denning, *The Cultural Front: The Laboring of Twentieth-Century American Culture* (New York: Verso, 1996), 7–9.

3. Denning, *The Cultural Front*, 280. See also Erin Battat, *'Ain't Got No Home': America's Great Migrations and the Making of an Interracial Left* (Chapel Hill: University of North Carolina Press, 2014).

4. As labor historian Joshua Freeman explains, the "typical American worker of the 1950s—a male 'breadwinner' in a blue-collar union job supporting a family—has virtually ceased to exist." "The shift away from manufacturing," he explains, "often meant a move from secure, high-paid, unionized jobs to insecure nonunion jobs that sometimes paid little more than minimum wage and lacked benefits." Freeman, "Labor in the American Century," in *A Companion to Post-1945 America*, ed. Jean-Christophe Agnew and Roy Rosenzweig (Malden, MA: Blackwell Publishers, 2002), 205, 204. See also Aiwa Ong, "The Gender and Labor Politics of Postmodernity," in *Politics of Culture in the Shadow of Capital*, ed. Lisa Lowe and David Lloyd (Durham, NC: Duke University Press, 1997); Hong, *The Ruptures of American Capital: Women of Color Feminism and the Culture of Immigrant Labor* (Minneapolis: University of Minnesota Press, 2006); and Sandro Mezzadra and Brett Neilson, *Border as Method, or, The Multiplication of Labor* (Durham, NC: Duke University Press, 2013).

5. Walter Benn Michaels, "Going Boom," *Book Forum*, Feb/March 2009, available at http://www.bookforum.com/inprint/015_05/3274. Michaels offers an extended version of this argument in *The Trouble with Diversity: How We Learned to Love Identity and Ignore Inequality* (New York: Metropolitan Books, 2006).

6. Kim Moody, *Workers in a Lean World: Unions in the International Economy* (New York: Verso, 1997), 35.

7. See Polina Kroik, "Introduction," *Working USA* 15, no. 1 (March 2012).

8. Rachel Adams, *Continental Divides: Remapping the Cultures of North America* (Chicago: University of Chicago Press, 2009), 246.

9. For more on the ways that attention to labor can complicate critical narratives of cultural and social flow, see Augustine Sedgewick, "Against Flows," *History of the Present: A Journal of Critical History* 4, no. 2 (Fall 2014): 143–70.

10. Christa Grewe-Volpp, "'The oil was made from their bones': Environmental (In) Justice in Helena Maria Viramontes's *Under the Feet of Jesus*," *Interdisciplinary Studies in Literature and Environment* 12, no. 1 (Winter 2005): 61–78; Sonia Saldivar-Hull, "Political Identities in Contemporary Chicana Literature: Helena María Viramontes's Visions of the U.S. Third World," in *Writing Nation, Writing Region: European Contributions to American Studies*, ed. Theo D'haen (Amsterdam: Netherlands American Studies Association, 1996), 156–65; Arianne Burford, "Cartographies of a Violent Landscape: Viramontes's and Moraga's Remapping of Feminisms in *Under the Feet of Jesus* and *Heroes and Saints*," *Genders*, no. 47 (2008), http://www.genders.org/g47/g47_burford.html.

11. For a superb discussion of the novel along these lines, with which my own reading very much agrees, see Dennis López, "Ghosts in the Barn: Dead Labor and Capital Accumulation in Helen María Viramontes's *Under the Feet of Jesus*," *Twentieth-Century Literature* 65, no. 4 (December 2019): 307–42.

12. Sassen quoted in Kroik, "Introduction," 6.

13. Helena Maria Viramontes, *Under the Feet of Jesus* (New York: Plume, 1995), 4. Further references appear parenthetically by page number in the body of the text.

14. Don Mitchell notes the deadly conditions of U.S. agricultural labor: "farm labor is deadly both in the short and long term. Mortality rates for agricultural workers are more than five-and-a-half times the national average, and the average life-span for farm workers is 49 years compared to the average." Mitchell, "Work, Struggle, Death, and Geographies of Justice: The Transformation of Landscape in and beyond California's Imperial Valley," *Landscape Research* 32, no. 5 (2007): 567.

15. For a powerful argument about how racialized populations and "illegal aliens" are criminalized and thereby made ineligible for personhood and humanity, see Lisa Cacho, *Social Death: Racialized Rightlessness and the Criminalization of the Unprotected* (New York: New York University Press, 2012).

16. Mae Ngai, *Impossible Subjects: Illegal Aliens and the Making of Modern America* (New York: Columbia University Press, 2004), 128–29.

17. The changing composition of the predominant farm labor population in California—from Chinese and then Japanese workers in the late nineteenth and early twentieth centuries, to Filipinos, Mexicans, and white Dust Bowl refugees during the 1920s, 30s and 40s, to immigrants from across Central America and Mexico since midcentury—tells much of the story of immigration to and migration in the western United States over the past century. U.S. immigration policy has been designed to provide a steady supply of impoverished, unorganized, and socially precarious workers—many of them stateless, stripped of civil and political rights—for corporate interests in agriculture and other labor-intensive industries. And while the ethnic and racial composition of the farm workers community has fluctuated over the past one hundred years, labor conditions have remained consistent: farm workers are, in the words of one historian, "the poorest, most disadvantaged, and most underprivileged class of laborers in the United States." Emily Plec, "The Rhetoric of Migrant Farmworkers," in *Who Says?: Working Class Rhetoric, Class Consciousness, and Community*, ed. William DeGenaro (Pittsburgh: University of Pittsburgh Press, 2007), 113, 107. Significantly, farm workers were excluded from the New Deal–era labor laws that provided American workers with certain basic rights and standards, including unemployment insurance, Social Security, and minimum wage rates. Moreover, the social invisibility of farm work and the highly exploitative and contingent conditions of such labor are linked to race and citizenship; that so many farm workers are people of color and non-U.S. citizens facilitates their economic exploitation. As a result, farm labor looks today much as it did a century ago: physically demanding, poorly paid, and performed by workers who are disenfranchised due to racial, ethnic, or citizenship status. The unprotected, contingent, low-pay-and-no-benefit conditions that characterize farm labor are becoming increasingly common for other American workers, who are losing the standards of economic stability and job security that characterized a great deal of industrial and other blue-collar work during the long New Deal era. As the author of the award-winning study of contemporary farm labor, *With These Hands*, Daniel Rothenberg, explains: "American workers providing basic services and manual labor are increasingly employed under conditions that strongly resemble the farm labor system—working in uncertain, shifting, temporary jobs that provide no benefits and often do no pay enough to keep workers and their families above the poverty line." Rothenberg, *With These Hands: The Hidden World of Migrant Farmworkers Today* (Berkeley: University of California Press, 2000), 325. Other industries, from manufacturing to medicine to education, are now adopting the strategies of subcontracting and part-time, casualized employment that agricultural employers have long

used to keep farm workers at such remarkably low levels of subsistence. Rather than representing an exception to the working-class experience in the U.S. outside agriculture, as they did for much of the twentieth century, farm workers are coming more and more to epitomize it.

18. Burford, "Cartographies."

19. See Marx, *Capital, Volume 1* (London: Penguin, 1990); Elaine Scarry, *The Body in Pain* (New York: Oxford University Press, 1985); John Holloway, *Crack Capitalism* (London: Pluto Press, 2010).

20. See Bruno Gulli, *Labor of Fire: The Ontology of Labor between Economy and Culture* (Philadelphia: Temple University Press, 2005).

21. Carlos Gallego argues that Estrella's political consciousness and action flow from her capacity for cognitive mapping: "Estrella's agency and the interventionist politics it gives rise to emerge from her capacity to map her situatedness within a late capitalist geopolitical totality." Gallego, "Topographies of Resistance: Cognitive Mapping in Chicano/a Migrant Literature," *Arizona Quarterly: A Journal of American Literature, Culture, and Theory* 70, no. 2 (Summer 2014): 42.

22. López, "Ghosts in the Barn," 325.

23. Janet Zandy, *Hands: Physical Labor, Class and Cultural Work* (New Brunswick, NJ: Rutgers University Press, 2004), 153.

24. Ong, "The Gender and Labor Politics of Postmodernity," 86.

25. In describing her writing, Viramontes refers to her mother's nopalitos, products of her mother's creativity and inventiveness: "She would always make nopales, just cactus, put a little here and there, a bit of chile, with one pork chop or two to feed a whole family. That is what I try to do with my work. Take what you think is ugly or useless and make something beautiful." Isabel Dulfano, "Some Thoughts Shared with Helena María Viramontes," *Women's Studies: An Interdisciplinary Journal* 30, no. 5 (September 2001): 659.

26. Ana Patricia Rodríguez, "Refugees of the South: Central Americans in the U.S. Latino Imaginary," *American Literature* 73, no. 2 (June 2001): 387–412; Marta Caminero-Santangelo, "Central Americans in the City: Goldman, Tobar, and the Question of Panethnicity," *LIT: Literature, Interpretation, Theory* 20, no. 3 (July–September 2009): 173–95; Kirsten Silva Gruesz, "Utopía Latina: *The Ordinary Seaman* in Extraordinary Times," *Modern Fiction Studies* 49, no. 1 (Spring 2003): 54–83.

27. Michael Templeton, "Becoming Transnational and Becoming Machinery in Francisco Goldman's *The Ordinary Seaman*," *Symploke* 4, nos. 1–2 (2006): 279.

28. Rodríguez, "Refugees of the South," 404.

29. Marcel van der Linden, *Workers of the World: Essays toward a Global Labor History* (Leiden: Brill, 2008).

30. My reading of this scene is indebted to Walter Benn Michaels, "Model Minorities and the Minority Model—the Neoliberal Novel," in *The Cambridge History of the American Novel*, ed. Leonard Cassuto, Clare Eby, and Benjamin Reiss (Cambridge: Cambridge University Press, 2011), 1029.

31. Peter Linebaugh and Marcus Rediker, *The Many-Headed Hydra: Sailors, Slaves, Commoners, and the Hidden History of the Revolutionary Atlantic* (New York: Verso, 2000), 151.

32. Linebaugh and Rediker, *The Many-Headed Hydra*, 164.

33. Linebaugh and Rediker, *The Many-Headed Hydra*, 172.

34. Kirsten Silva Gruesz argues that "the crew of the Urus—a crew of migrants, exiles,

and stowaways—relives and transcends the movement toward class consciousness begun in the Pequod." Gruesz, "Utopía Latina," 74.

35. Interview with the *Boston Phoenix*, March 1997.

36. As Ana Rodríguez argues, "Goldman explores the plight of Central American refugees who leave the economic disparity of their home countries only to encounter similar conditions in the North [and] the stranded ship comes to represent the modern economic machinery of the North." Rodríguez, "Refugees of the South," 405. Floating in Brooklyn, the *Urus*, Marta Caminero-Santangelo observes, "distills perfectly the liminal positioning of immigrants with respect to an economic system to which they contribute their 'hard labor,' but which fails to fully extend to them the reach of its protections or opportunities." Caminero-Santangelo, "Central Americans in the City," 178–89.

37. Gruesz, "Utopía Latina," 70.

38. Luis Guarnizo and Michael Peter Smith, quoted in Templeton, "Becoming Transnational," 274.

39. My focus on the abyss and the resonance of histories of harm accords with Rodrigo Lazo's brief reading of the novel. Rodrigo Lazo, "Hemispheric American Novels," in *The Cambridge History of the American Novel*, ed. Leonard Cassuto, Clare Eby, and Benjamin Reiss (Cambridge: Cambridge University Press, 2011), 1084–95.

40. I use the term "homeless" because that is the word the novel uses to describe unhoused persons, although I do on occasion use the term "unhoused," which has come into more widespread usage since the novel was published to suggest that although a person may not have adequate housing, they may still have a home.

41. Elisabeth Mermann-Jozwiak, "Yamashita's Post-National Spaces: 'It All Comes Together in Los Angeles,'" *Canadian Review of American Studies* 41, no. 1 (Spring 2011): 1–24; Caroline Rody, "The Transnational Imagination: Karen Tei Yamashita's *Tropic of Orange*," in *Asian North American Identities: Beyond the Hyphen*, ed. Eleanor Ty and Donald C. Goellnicht (Bloomington: Indiana University Press, 2004): 130–48; Sue-Im Lee, "'We Are Not the World': Global Village, Universalism, and Karen Tei Yamashita's *Tropic of Orange*," *Modern Fiction Studies* 53, no. 3 (Fall 2007): 501–27.

42. One critic who does make labor central to a reading of *Tropic of Orange* is Aimee Bahng, who insists, "Whereas much of the rhetoric surrounding the border wall discussion revolves around national security, threat of terrorist attack, and 'alien invasion,' Yamashita's *Tropic of Orange* returns focus to the issue of labor—most notably: the labor that goes into building walls and other technologies that regulate border permeability; the labor rendered invisible by neoliberal discussions of free trade and unencumbered movement across borders; and the laborers who must cross the border 'illegally' in order to sustain the contradictory demands for cheap labor on the one hand, and a racially consolidated national identity on the other." Aimee Bahng, *Migrant Futures: Decolonizing Speculation in Financial Times* (Durham, NC: Duke University Press, 2018), 62.

43. For a different reading of mapping in *Tropic of Orange*, which also focuses on Buzzworm and Manzanar but through Henri Lefebvre's notion of "differential space," see Cristina M. Rodriguez, "'Relentless Geography': Los Angeles' Imagined Cartographies in Karen Tei Yamashita's *Tropic of Orange*," *Asian American Literature: Discourses and Pedagogies* 8 (2017): 104–30.

44. Edward Said, *Culture and Imperialism* (New York: Vintage, 1993), 332.

45. Henry Yu, "Los Angeles and American Studies in a Pacific World of Migrations," *American Quarterly* 56, no. 3 (September 2004): 540.

46. Don Mitchell, "Working-Class Geographies: Capital, Space, and Place," in *New Working-Class Studies*, ed. Sherry Linkon and John Russo (Ithaca, NY: Cornell University Press, 2005), 85.

47. Michael Hardt and Antonio Negri, *Multitude: War and Democracy in the Age of Empire* (New York: Penguin, 2004), 134.

48. See the introduction to Amy Lang and Cecelia Tichi, *This Is What Democracy Looks Like: A New Critical Realism for a Post-Seattle World* (New Brunswick, NJ: Rutgers University Press, 2006), and Rob Nixon, *Slow Violence* (Cambridge, MA: Harvard University Press, 2012).

49. Sedgewick, "Against Flows."

50. Lazo, "Hemispheric American Novels," 1084.

51. "It is the perpetuation and further pauperization of the transnational labor force that explains U.S. immigration policy," Dixon, Martínez, and McCaughan argue. The state's tactics of "repression, terror, and selective deportation" are "all designed to assure capital a supply of unorganized, submissive labor stripped of any and all civil and political rights." Marlene Dixon, Elizabeth Martínez, and Ed McCaughan, "Theoretical Perspectives on Chicanas, Mexicanas and the Transnational Working Class," *Contemporary Marxism*, no. 11 (Fall 1985): 57–58. See also William Robinson and Xuan Santos, "Global Capitalism, Immigrant Labor, and the Struggle for Justice," *Class, Race and Corporate Power* 2, no. 3 (2014), available at https://digitalcommons.fiu.edu/classracecorporatepower/vol2/iss3/1.

52. See Ngai, *Impossible Subjects*.

53. Cedric Robinson, *Black Marxism: The Making of the Black Radical Tradition* (Chapel Hill: University of North Carolina Press, 1983), 4.

54. Quoted in Nathan Brown, "The Proletariat," *Trans-Scripts* 3 (2013): 63.

55. Brown, "The Proletariat," 64.

56. Brown, "The Proletariat," 65.

57. On literature as a form of spatial and political mapping, see Robert Tally, "On Literary Cartography: Narratives as Spatially Symbolic Act," in *NANO: New American Notes Online* (January 2011), https://nanocrit.com/issues/issue1/literary-cartography-narrative-spatially-symbolic-act.

58. Saskia Sassen, *Globalization and Its Discontents* (New York: New Press, 1998), xxxiv.

59. Fredric Jameson, *Postmodernism, or, The Cultural Logic of Late Capitalism* (Durham, NC: Duke University Press, 1991), 54.

Chapter 3

1. Jackie Wang, *Carceral Capitalism* (South Pasadena, CA: Semiotext(e), 2018).

2. By biopolitics, I refer to the administration of life and populations, the determination and management of who lives, who dies, and under what circumstances and conditions. I am adapting the term "necrocapitalism" from James Tyner, who describes it as "a new political economy of premature death . . . in which the valuation and vulnerability of life itself is centered on two overlapping criteria: productivity and responsibility. . . . Those individuals who are deemed nonproductive or redundant, based on economic bioarithmetic, are disproportionately vulnerable and increasingly disallowed life to the

point of premature death." Tyner, *Dead Labor: Toward a Political Economy of Premature Death* (Minneapolis: University of Minnesota Press, 2019), xiii. As explained in the introduction, my conception of necrocapitalism is also indebted to the work of Ruth Wilson Gilmore, Manning Marable, Cedric Robinson, Achille Mbembe, and others who have argued that capitalism's governing logics of life and death are highly racialized.

3. In the year *Gran Torino* and *Frozen River* were released, and in which *Fruitvale Station* was set, Stephen Greenhouse argued that there had been a steady erosion of working-class livelihoods since the 1970s, even as productivity, corporate profits, and incomes for the wealthy had continued to rise. The previous thirty years, he asserted, had witnessed "a profound, overarching shift in the American economy—corporations have been steadily shredding the post-World War II social contract in which they shared their increased prosperity with their workers." Between 1979 and 2005, wages for workers in the bottom fifth of the income spectrum rose just 6 percent after inflation; nearly thirty-three million workers, he noted, earn less than ten dollars an hour. In addition, the social protections and provisions of the New Deal welfare state have been steadily dismantled under a neoliberal regime of privatization, leaving workers more vulnerable to an increasingly antiunion public sphere and a job market in which outsourcing, downsizing, and contingent labor are increasingly prevalent. Contemporary workers, Greenhouse argued, faced low-paying, casualized, deeply exploitative and often dangerous job options that undercut the prospects for prosperity that had been available to many workers in the previous generation. Greenhouse, *The Big Squeeze: Tough Times for the American Worker* (New York: Anchor Books, 2009), 28. Historian Lizabeth Cohen describes the period as "an historic reign of prosperity, lasting longer and more universally enjoyed than ever before in American history." Cohen, *A Consumers' Republic: The Politics of Mass Consumption in Postwar America* (New York: Vintage, 2003), 121. Of course, the much-vaunted era of rising wages and working-class prosperity did not apply to all workers, by any means. African Americans, immigrants, and women were most often relegated to less desirable, lower-paying jobs—and most women were locked out of the wage labor force.

4. Sandro Mezzadra and Brett Neilson, *Border as Method, or, The Multiplication of Labor* (Durham, NC: Duke University Press 2013).

5. Christina Sharpe, *In the Wake: On Blackness and Being* (Durham, NC: Duke University Press, 2016), 106.

6. Benjamin Balthaser argues, "U.S. working-class literature has always been about the production of a class identity through modes of racial looking, identification, and solidarity." Balthaser, "The Race of Class: The Role of Racial Identity Production in the Long History of Working-Class Writing," in *Working-Class Literature(s): Historical and International Perspectives*, ed. J. Lennon and M. Nilsson (Stockholm: Stockholm University Press, 2017), 31.

7. See Jodi Melamed, "Racial Capitalism," *Critical Ethnic Studies* 1, no. 1 (Spring 2015): 76–85; and Ruth Wilson Gilmore, "Fatal Couplings of Power and Difference: Notes on Racism and Geography," *Professional Geographer* 54, no. 1 (2002): 15–24.

8. Steven Ross, *Working-Class Hollywood: Silent Film and the Shaping of Class in America* (Princeton, NJ: Princeton University Press, 1998), 7.

9. Ross, *Working-Class Hollywood*, 9. On the rise of the movie palaces as a form of class discipline, see also David Nasaw, *Going Out: The Rise and Fall of Public Amusements* (New York: Basic Books, 1993).

10. Emmett Winn, *The American Dream and Contemporary Hollywood Cinema* (London: Continuum Publishing, 2007), 12.

11. Winn, *The American Dream and Contemporary Hollywood Cinema*, 128.

12. John Bodnar, *Blue-Collar Hollywood: Liberalism, Democracy, and Working People in American Film* (Baltimore: Johns Hopkins University Press, 2003).

13. Linda Dittmar, "All That Hollywood Allows: Film and the Working Class," *Radical Teacher* 46 (Spring 1995): 39.

14. Fredric Jameson, "Reification and Utopia in Mass Culture," in *Jameson, Signatures of the Visible* (New York: Routledge, 1990), 29.

15. Jameson, "Reification and Utopia in Mass Culture," 30.

16. Kim Nicolini, "Class, Race and Clint," *Counterpunch*, August 14–16, 2009, http://www.counterpunch.org/2009/08/14/class-race-and-clint/.

17. Robert Alpert, "Clint Eastwood's *Gran Torino*: The Death of America's Hero," *Jump Cut: A Review of Contemporary Media* 51 (Spring 2009), http://www.ejumpcut.org/archive/jc51.2009/granTorino/index.html.

18. Mike Rose, *The Mind at Work: Valuing the Intelligence of the American Worker* (New York: Penguin, 2005), xvii.

19. Nicolini, "Class, Race and Clint."

20. Adrienne Davis, "Masculinity and Interracial Intimacy in *Star Trek* and *Gran Torino*," *New Political Science Journal* 32 (2010): 166.

21. On "conservative" as a cover for reactionary responses to claims for social justice, see Corey Robin, *The Reactionary Mind: Conservatism from Edmund Burke to Sarah Palin* (New York: Oxford University Press, 2011).

22. Louisa Schein and Va-Megn Thoj, "*Gran Torino*'s Boys and Men with Guns: Hmong Perspectives," *Hmong Studies Journal* 10 (2009): 13.

23. Jerry Herron, "Detroit: Disaster Deferred, Disaster in Progress," *South Atlantic Quarterly* 106, no. 4 (Fall 2007): 670. See also Dan Georgakas and Marvin Surkin, *Detroit: I Do Mind Dying: A Study in Urban Revolution* (Chicago: Haymarket Books, 2012).

24. Tania Modleski, "Clint Eastwood and Male Weepies," *American Literary History* 22, no. 1 (2009): 153.

25. Schein and Thoj, "*Gran Torino*'s Men and Boys with Guns," 771. "More specifically," they note, the film "sets up good Asians and bad Asians, coded in predictably gendered ways such that those worthy of being saved are feminine, vulnerable, unable to defend themselves" (771).

26. Modleski, "Clint Eastood and Male Weepies," 152.

27. Ly Chong Jalao, "Looking *Gran Torino* in the Eye: A Review," *Journal of Southeast Asian American Education and Advancement* 5, no. 1 (2010), available at http://docs.lib.purdue.edu/cgi/viewcontent.cgi?article=1016&context=jsaaea.

28. Schein and Thoj, "*Gran Torino*'s Boys and Men with Guns," 6–7.

29. On Mohawk sovereignty and the refusal of U.S. and Canadian citizenship, see Audra Simpson, *Mohawk Interruptus: Political Life Across the Borders of Settler States* (Durham, NC: Duke University Press, 2014).

30. Wilfred Raussert, "Inter-American Border Discourses, Heterotopia, and Translocal Communities in Courtney Hunt's Film *Frozen River*," *Norteamérica* 6, no. 1 (2011): 21.

31. Jolene Rickard, "Visualizing Sovereignty in the Time of Biometric Sensors," *South Atlantic Quarterly* 110, no. 2 (Spring 2011): 473–74.

32. Sara Appel makes a similar observation about the visual portrait of Ray in this opening sequence. Appel argues for reading Ray as a "'borderland' subject" whose privileges as a white person with U.S. citizenship the film both acknowledges and questions. Appel, "A Turn of the Sphere: The Place of Class in Intersectional Analysis," in Nicholas Coles and Paul Lauter, *A History of American Working-Class Literature* (Cambridge: Cambridge University Press, 2017), 418.

33. It is worth noting that Thompson was born to two Cherokee parents in what was at the time designated Indian Territory in what is now Oklahoma.

34. Michael Shapiro, "Moral Geographies and the Ethics of Post-Sovereignty," *Public Culture* 6 (1994): 482.

35. Courtney Hunt, "On *Frozen River*," *Script Magazine* 14, no. 4 (July–August 2008), 60.

36. Lisa Hinrichsen, "Canadian Crossings: Exploring the Borders of Race and Class in Courtney Hunt's *Frozen River*," in *Blue Collar Pop Culture Volume 1*, ed. Keith M. Booker (New York: Praeger Publishers, 2012), 64.

37. Starting in 2007, some Mohawk tribal police officers were authorized to enforce New York State law. See https://www.nyspnews.com/article_display.cfm?article_id=3812, accessed December 19, 2012.

38. Raussert, "Inter-American Border Discourses," 29.

39. Raussert, "Inter-American Border Discourses," 29.

40. A. O. Scott, "Neo-Neo Realism," *New York Times Magazine*, March 22, 2009, http://www.nytimes.com/2009/03/22/magazine/22neorealism-t.html, accessed December 19, 2012.

41. See Mezzadra and Neilson, *Border as Method*.

42. Esther Zuckerman, "Ryan Coogler on Humanizing a Movement for 'Fruitvale Station,'" *The Atlantic*, July 12, 2013, available at https://www.theatlantic.com/entertainment/archive/2013/07/ryan-coogler-humanizing-movement-fruitvale-station/313366/.

43. Mychal Denzel Smith, "Rewriting Black Manhood: A Conversation With 'Fruitvale Station' Director Ryan Coogler," *The Nation*, July 18, 2013, available at https://www.thenation.com/article/rewriting-Black-manhood-conversation-fruitvale-station-director-ryan-coogler/.

44. Wesley Morris argues, "To present Grant this way—as a son who loves his mother, as a father who loves his daughter, as the sort of person who comforts a dying dog and pleads with a shop owner to permit a pregnant woman to use his restroom—is to remove the stigma. He's a lower-middle-class kid who got mixed up with crime. But most of the narrative belongs to a charming, charismatic, devoted young man, someone striving to better himself. It's not only that this Grant is a person. It's that, to a fault, he's made to be more than Black male pathology." Wesley Morris, "Strange Fruitvale: The Eerie Intersection of Trayvon Martin and *Fruitvale Station*," *Grantland*, July 23, 2013, available at: https://grantland.com/features/fruitvale-station-trayvon-martin/.

45. Critic Philip Conklin argues: "But because of the tragic portrayal of Oscar, and the focus on his attempt to turn his life around, Coogler loses sight of the bigger point he's trying to make. The depiction of Oscar as a reformed criminal, a noble, caring man and an attentive father on the path to righteous, legal living, obfuscates the real struggle. Of course, all these things make Oscar's story much more tragic and emotional for the viewer because we identify with him, we're rooting for him. But the real injustice in the killing of Oscar Grant lies not in the fact that the better life he'd vowed to live had been taken away from

him, but in the fact that we live in a society of deeply entrenched, systematic racism, in which an event like this, no matter the circumstances of the victim, could happen at all. In short, by accentuating the tragedy of this single event, we lose a sense of context, a sense of the mechanisms of society that created the conditions of this horrible event." "We live in a profoundly unequal society, and the illegal or morally ambiguous behavior of those on the wrong end of it should not be a determining factor in their right to life or sympathy." Conklin, "The Struggle of Representation: *Fruitvale Station*," *The Periphery*, April 2014, available at http://www.theperiphery.com/fruitvale-station.

46. Alicia Garza, a Black Lives Matter cofounder, observed, "I would say for those of us who created Black Lives Matter, it really does start with Oscar Grant as our Rodney King moment—where the violence our communities experience every day was actually captured on video and circulated around the world." Quoted in Natia Voynovskaya, "After Oscar Grant, Oakland Artists Inspired a New Generation of Activists," available at https://www.kqed.org/arts/13847704/after-oscar-grant-oakland-artists-inspired-a-new-generation-of-activists.

47. For more on the activism, protest, and unrest after Grant's death, see Thandisizwe Chimurenga, *No Doubt: The Murder(s) of Oscar Grant* (Scotts Valley, CA: CreateSpace Independent Publishing Platform, 2014); George Ciccariello-Maher, "Oscar Grant Was Our Spark," *Commune* (Summer 2019), available at https://communemag.com/oscar-gr ant-was-our-spark/; David Id, "A Celebration of the Justice for Oscar Grant Protesters," *IndyBay*, December 31, 2018, available at: https://www.indybay.org/newsitems/2018/12/31/18820046.php.

48. See Greenhouse, *The Big Squeeze*.

49. Ruth Wilson Gilmore notes that, as of 2007, "African Americans and Latinos comprise two-thirds of [California's] 160,000 prisoners." Gilmore, *Golden Gulag: Prisons, Surplus, Crisis, and Opposition in Globalizing California* (Berkeley: University of California Press, 2007), 7.

50. Morris, "Strange Fruitvale."

51. James Tyner argues that Marx is clear that "as long as capitalism exists, structural violence is both necessary and unavoidable and that capitalism causes unnecessary and avoidable premature death." Tyner, *Dead Labor*, 49.

52. The film thus seems to be in accord with Jackie Wang's argument in *Carceral Capitalism*: "Black racialization, then, is the mark that renders subjects as suitable for—on the one hand—hyperexploitation and expropriation, and on the other hand, annihilation." Wang, *Carceral Capitalism*, 122.

53. Charisse Burden-Stelly, "Modern U.S. Racial Capitalism: Some Theoretical Insights," *Monthly Review*, July 1, 2020, https://monthlyreview.org/2020/07/01/mode rn-u-s-racial-capitalism/.

54. See Julilly Kohler-Hausmann, "Guns and Butter: The Welfare State, the Carceral State, and the Politics of Exclusion in Postwar United States History," *Journal of American History* 102, no. 1 (June 2015): 87–99. Loïc Wacquant argues that the post-1970s prison expansion in the United States represented a fourth regime of racial management, after slavery, Jim Crow, and the development of the modern ghetto. All four systems, he argues, are designed to support both "*labor extraction*" and "*ethnoracial enclosure*." Wacquant, *Punishing the Poor: The Neoliberal Government of Social Insecurity* (Durham, NC: Duke University Press, 2009), 202–203. Gilmore notes that "as a class, convicts are deindustrialized cities' working or workless poor." Gilmore, *Golden Gulag*, 7.

55. Manning Marable, *How Capitalism Underdeveloped Black America: Problems in Race, Political Economy, and Society* (Chicago: Haymarket Books, 2015 [1983]), 222, 114.
56. Marable, *How Capitalism Underdeveloped Black America*, 225.
57. Jesmyn Ward, *Sing, Unburied, Sing* (New York: Scribner, 2017), 283.
58. Hardt and Negri describe the multitude as the collective singularities of all those who labor under capitalism, "an open and expansive concept" that "gives the concept of the proletariat its fullest definition." Hardt and Negri, *Multitude: War and Democracy in the Age of Empire* (New York: Penguin, 2004), 107.
59. James Tyner argues that "one's exposure to death is . . . conditioned by one's position in capitalism. Stated differently, the relations between labor and capital necessarily inform the relations between life and death." Tyner, *Dead Labor*, x. See also Don Mitchell, who argues that "what we need to do . . . is see that violence of various sorts is a *foundation* of the economy." Mitchell, "Dead Labor: The Geography of Workplace Violence in America and Beyond," *Environment and Planning A* 32 (2000): 764. Taking *Fruitvale Station* as an ur-text, I argue—following the work of Cedric Robinson, Ruth Wilson Gilmore, Jodi Melamed, Jackie Wang, Lisa Cacho, and many other scholars of racial capitalism—that exposure to premature death under capitalism is crucially shaped by race and is in fact a key factor in processes of racialization as well as labor discipline.
60. Lisa Cacho, *Social Death: Racialized Rightlessness and the Criminalization of the Unprotected* (New York: New York University Press, 2012).
61. Sean Hill, "Precarity in the Era of #BlackLivesMatter," *WSQ: Women's Studies Quarterly* 45, no. 3–4 (Fall–Winter 2017): 94–109.
62. Saidiya Hartman, "Venus in Two Acts," *Small Axe* 26 (June 2008): 4.
63. Brad Evans and Henry Giroux, *Disposable Futures: The Seduction of Violence in the Age of Spectacle* (San Francisco: City Light Books, 2015), 50.

Chapter 4

1. For box office earnings, see www.IMDb.com.
2. Sherry Ortner has recently argued that independent film often serves as a form of cultural critique, challenging dominant ideas about how society is structured. While she acknowledges the charge, made by a range of commentators and critics, that independent cinema is in fact no longer independent from Hollywood but has largely been incorporated into the established filmmaking system, she holds out the possibility that the production, circulation, and meaning of many independent films embody oppositional potential that can contest dominant values of neoliberal capitalist society. "Many independent films," she contends, "embrace a kind of harsh realism, making films that display the dark realities in contemporary life, and that make demands on the viewer to viscerally experience and come to grips with those realities." "Dark and violent films about the misery of work in the new economy," she contends, "or about the dysfunctionality of families in a world of absent parents, among others, tell stories that Hollywood is almost never willing to tell, about the fraying social fabric of American society today." She acknowledges, however, that "'Cultural critique' in [American] indie features is almost always implicit, embedded in the stories and mise-en-scènes of the films," rather than driven home in an overtly agit-prop fashion. Sherry Ortner, "Against Hollywood: American Independent Film as a Critical Cultural Movement," *HAU: Journal of Ethnographic Theory* 2, no. 2 (2012): 4, 18.

3. A. O. Scott, "Neo-Neo Realism," *New York Times Magazine*, March 22, 2009, http://www.nytimes.com/2009/03/22/magazine/22neorealism-t.html?pagewanted=all&_r=0.

4. Lauren Berlant, *Cruel Optimism* (Durham, NC: Duke University Press, 2011), 201. The literature on neoliberalism is extensive; for starters, see David Harvey, *A Brief History of Neoliberalism* (Oxford: Oxford University Press, 2005); Lisa Duggan, *The Twilight of Equality? Neoliberalism, Cultural Politics, and the Attack on Democracy* (Boston: Beacon Press, 2004); Wendy Brown, "Neoliberalism and the End of Liberal Democracy," *Theory and Event* 7, no. 1 (2003): 1–25.

5. While precarity as a term and concept has come into widespread usage in recent decades, it is nothing new. It is to some extent the basic condition of life under capitalism, in which, as Marx put it, "everything that is solid melts into air." And yet, while precarity may be endemic to capitalism, the volatile energy of which tends to challenge stability of all kinds, the current regime of neoliberal, post-Fordist globalization expands conditions of precarity in unprecedented ways and dimensions. On neoliberalism, see, for starters, the work of David Harvey, Lisa Duggan, and Wendy Brown. The literature on precarity is fairly large, and growing. Among the texts that I have found helpful are (in addition to Berlant, *Cruel Optimism*) Brett Neilson and Ned Rossiter, "From Precarity to Precariousness and Back Again: Life, Labor and Unstable Networks," *The Fibreculture Journal* 5 (2005), available at http://five.fibreculturejournal.org/fcj-022-from-precarity-to-precariousness-and-back-again-labour-life-and-unstable-networks/; Brett Neilson and Ned Rossiter, "Precarity as Political Concept, or Fordism as Exception," *Theory, Culture and Society* 25, nos. 7–8 (2008): 51–72; Vassilis Tsianos and Dimitris Papadopoulos, "Precarity: A Savage Journey to the Heart of Embodied Capitalism," *Transversal* (2006), available at http://eipcp.net/transversal/1106/tsianospapadopoulos/en. Judith Butler uses the term not in reference to the instability of the post-Fordist economy, but to describe the innate vulnerability of human beings to one another. See Butler, *Precarious Life: The Powers of Mourning and Violence* (New York: Verso, 2006).

6. Berlant, *Cruel Optimism*, 192.

7. Michael Denning, "Wageless Life," *New Left Review* 66 (November–December 2010): 79–97.

8. Berlant, *Cruel Optimism*, 169.

9. David Harvey, "The Right to the City," *New Left Review* 53 (September–October 2008), available at https://newleftreview.org/II/53/david-harvey-the-right-to-the-city.

10. Immanuel Ness, *Immigrants, Unions, and the New U.S. Labor Market* (Philadelphia: Temple University Press, 2005), 25.

11. On the political imposition of immigration restriction in the United States, starting in the 1920s, and the creation of the "illegal alien as a new legal and political subject, whose inclusion within the nation was simultaneously a social reality and a legal impossibility—a subject barred from citizenship and without rights," see Mae Ngai, *Impossible Subjects: Illegal Aliens and the Making of Modern America* (Princeton, NJ: Princeton University Press, 2004), 4.

12. Ngai, *Impossible Subjects*, 15.

13. Harvey, "The Right to the City."

14. Saskia Sassen, *Globalization and its Discontents* (New York: The New Press, 1998), xx.

15. Sassen, *Globalization and its Discontents*, xxi.

16. Sassen, *Globalization and its Discontents*, xxxii.

17. Sassen, *Globalization and its Discontents*, xxxii, my emphasis.

18. For an extended version of this argument, see Polina Kroik, "Neoliberal Labour in Ramin Bahrani's Films: Uneven Development, Entrepreneurial Governmentality, and Political Resistance," *Canadian Review of American Studies* 46, no. 2 (Summer 2016): 223–44. Kroik's astute analysis argues that the films' focus on entrepreneurial stories "point[s] to individual rather than political solutions to oppression"; I argue that the tension between individual and potentially collective responses to precarity, and between the emphasis on metaphorical and material modes of representation, is a constitutive feature of the films' precarious realism. Kroik, "Neoliberal Labour," 241.

19. Hyman quoted in Kim Moody, *Workers in a Lean World* (New York: Verso, 1997), 145. On the tension between "competition" and "association," see Marx and Engels, *The Communist Manifesto*, https://www.marxists.org/archive/marx/works/1848/communist-manifesto/.

20. Michael Atkinson, "Night Watch," *Village Voice*, August 29, 2006, http://www.villagevoice.com/2006-08-29/film/night-watch/. J. J. Murphy contends that *Man Push Cart* is a "meditation on the streets of New York City at night, as Bahrani emphasizes the cinematic details of this milieu over plot in order to create a kind of poetic realism." Available at http://www.jjmurphyfilm.com/blog/2008/03/.

21. Jason Anderson, "Spotlight/Chop Shop," in *Cinema Scope*, https://cinema-scope.com/spotlight/spotlight-chop-shop-ramin-bahrani-us/; Samuel Wigley, Review of *Man Push Cart*, *Sight & Sound* 16, no. 10 (October 1, 2006): 66.

22. Wigley, Review of *Man Push Cart*.

23. Sukhdev Sandhu, "A Hymn to New York's Invisibles," *The Telegraph*, September 29, 2006, https://www.telegraph.co.uk/culture/film/3655606/A-hymn-to-New-Yorks-invisibles.html.

24. Sandhu, "A Hymn to New York's Invisibles."

25. David Walsh, "An Interview with Ramin Bahrani, director of *Chop Shop*," World Socialist Web Site, September 26, 2007, http://www.wsws.org/en/articles/2007/09/rbah-s26.html.

26. http://filmmakermagazine.com/1305-ramin-bahrani-chop-shop/.

27. "I think both these films are about immigrant-type characters: in *Chop Shop*, Ale is young enough that he maybe could have been born here, or if he and Isamar immigrated they were very young, that was left deliberately ambiguous—but I don't think that's the essential issue of the film. I just feel like I'm tired of seeing the same independent films being made over and over again ... about these really attractive white kids, and their really attractive friends, and their problems." http://blog.moviefone.com/2007/09/11/tiff-interview-ramin-bahrani-director-chop-shop/.

28. Karl Marx, *Capital, Volume 1* (London: Penguin, 1990), 798.

29. Ramin Bahrani, interview by Nick Dawson, *Filmmaker Magazine*, February 27, 2008, http://filmmakermagazine.com/1305-ramin-bahrani-chop-shop/.

30. In another interview, Bahrani explained the craft required to construct the feeling of reality he wanted: "*Push Cart* and *Solo* are 95 percent on tripod. *Chop Shop* is more deceptive because it's handheld, but even then, it's incredibly planned. It's 30 takes minimum. And not 30 takes figuring it out. It's 30 takes doing the same damn thing. It's hard to make someone think it's real. It's really hard." Sam Adams, "Interview with Ramin Bahrani," *The A.V. Club*, May 20, 2009, http://www.avclub.com/articles/ramin-bahrani,28248/.

31. Although noting that the film "never lapses into sentimentality," film critic J. J. Murphy argues that Bahrani and cinematographer Michael Simmonds "are much more interested in capturing the look and texture of this underground economy with closely observed poetic images, such as a blue rubber sandal floating down a flooded street or a black pit bull attacking a car jack with menacing ferocity." J. J. Murphy, review of *Chop Shop*, available at http://www.jjmurphyfilm.com/blog/2008/03/. Extending this argument, Kevin Fujishima contends that while the film challenges conventional cinema by showcasing immigrant workers, it fails to offer a hard-hitting statement about contemporary political economy. "Anyone who goes into *Chop Shop* expecting some kind of stealth statement about class divisions in American society will probably be disappointed," he insists, "because Bahrani, unlike those Italian neorealist directors of old, isn't all that interested in social criticism. Poverty and loneliness, he seemingly acknowledges at the outset, is a fact of life; his focus is more specifically on how poor individuals try, don't try, or fail to work out of it. In other words, he's more interested in universals than in topical relevance, and it is on that universal level that both [*Man Push Cart* and *Chop Shop*] gain their emotional resonance." Kevin Fujishima, "In Dreams Begin . . . : *Chop Shop*," *Slant Magazine: The House Next Door*, February 27, 2008, http://www.slantmagazine.com/house/2008/02/in-dreams-begin-chop-shop/.

32. Berlant, *Cruel Optimism*, 172.

33. On Hine's photographs of young people, see Sarah Chinn, *Making American Adolescence* (New Brunswick, NJ: Rutgers University Press, 2008).

34. As Jason Francisco contends, "Hine spurned pity and other forms of belittling sympathy, and embraced the full human agency of those he photographed: he showed people who are wronged but not incapacitated, exploited but not deficient." Francisco, "Review of Laurence Salzmann's *Écheleganas: A Life Left Behind*," http://jasonfrancisco.net/jason_francisco_photoworks_%26_writings/Echeleganas_by_Laurence_Salzmann___Jason_Francisco.html.

35. Kroik, "Neoliberal Labor in Ramin Bahrani's Films," 232. Kroik contends that while Bahrani avoids the "paternalism implied in the cinema of the 'other,'" his "directorial choices lessen *Chop Shop*'s political impact." "Kroik, "Neoliberal Labor in Ramin Bahrani's Films," 242, 240.

36. Jack Conroy, *The Disinherited* (Columbia: University of Missouri Press, 1991), 225.

37. Lauren Berlant, "A Properly Political Concept of Love: Three Approaches in Ten Pages," *Cultural Anthropology* 26, no. 4 (2011): 688.

38. David Riker, interview with PBS, http://www.pbs.org/itvs/thecity/film_interview.html.

39. Riker explained, "And I made a point in this film not to invent anything and there is really only one exception to it, which is the role of the street puppeteer. Other than his character, everything in the film is based on someone's experience in New York City today. And all of the elements of the stories are based on someone's experience. What they are is composited together, so that in the end the characters are amalgams of many different immigrant lives." "David Riker and the People of *La Ciudad*," *Revolutionary Worker* 1048 (March 26, 2000), http://www.revcom.us/a/v21/1040-049/1048/riker.htm.

40. Robert Smith, *Mexican New York: Transnational Lives of New Immigrants* (Berkeley: University of California Press, 2005).

41. Smith, *Mexican New York*, 19, 20.

42. "David Riker and the People of *La Ciudad*."
43. See Karl Marx and Friedrich Engels, *The Communist Manifesto* (New York: Penguin Books, 2002), 233 passim.
44. "David Riker and the People of *La Ciudad*."
45. Laura Hapke, *Sweatshop: The History of an American Idea* (New Brunswick, NJ: Rutgers University Press, 2004), 105.
46. On seriality, see chapter 1.
47. Marx, *Capital, Volume I*, 916, 926.

Coda

1. Russell Banks, *Continental Drift* (New York: HarperPerennial, 2007), 43.
2. On solidarity as "precarious alliances," see Sara Appel, "A Turn of the Sphere: The Place of Class in Intersectional Analysis," in *A History of American Working-Class Literature*, ed. Nicholas Coles and Paul Lauter (Cambridge: Cambridge University Press, 2017), 406–23; on "emergent solidarity," see Rick Fantasia, *Cultures of Solidarity: Consciousness, Action, and Contemporary American Workers* (Berkeley: University of California Press, 1988), 26.
3. This paragraph is indebted to Rubén Gaztambide-Fernández, "Decolonization and the Pedagogy of Solidarity," *Decolonization: Indigeneity, Education & Society* 1, no. 1 (2012): 41–67; and David Roediger, "Making Solidarity Uneasy: Cautions on a Keyword from Black Lives Matter to the Past," in David Roediger, *Class, Race, and Marxism* (New York: Verso, 2017), 157–88.
4. Sandro Mezzadra and Brett Neilson, *Border as Method, or, The Multiplication of Labor* (Durham, NC: Duke University Press, 2013), 91.
5. Mezzadra and Neilson, *Border as Method*.
6. Richard Hyman, "Where Does Solidarity End?," https://www.iwm.at/transit-online/where-does-solidarity-end
7. Hannah Arendt, *On Revolution* (London: Penguin Books, 1990), 88.
8. Michael Hardt and Antonio Negri, *Commonwealth* (Cambridge: Belknap Press, 2011), 159.
9. Richard Dienst, "Feeling Like a Communist," https://bondsofdebt.wordpress.com/2012/03/08/feeling-like-a-communist/.
10. Mezzadra and Neilson, *Border as Method*, 301.
11. Gaztambide-Fernández, "Decolonization and the Pedagogy of Solidarity," 44.
12. Chandra Mohanty, *Feminism without Borders: Decolonizing Theory, Practicing Solidarity* (Durham, NC: Duke University Press, 2003), 6; Roediger, "Making Solidarity Uneasy."
13. Gaztambide-Fernández notes that solidarity "always operates in tension with logics of domination." Gaztambide-Fernández, "Decolonization and the Pedagogy of Solidarity," 47.
14. Fantasia, *Cultures of Solidarity*, 17.
15. Marcel Paret, "Precarious Class Formations in the United States and South Africa," *International Labor and Working-Class History* 89 (Spring 2016): 85.

Index

abandonment, 5–6, 66, 103, 108, 123, 145
absence of labor, 9
   See also unemployment
abstract labor, 16–18, 62, 70, 84, 162
accumulation, 73, 84
   capitalist, 76, 81, 85, 88, 122, 124, 141
   flexible, 52, 88, 161, 164
   primitive, 61
acquisitive individualism, 48
Adams, Rachel, 54
affiliation and collectivity, 35, 44, 83, 101–3, 130–31, 151–53, 162–63
   seriality, 45–49, 158, 176n37
   See also belonging; interdependencies; solidarity
affinities, 8, 67
Agamben, Georgio, 31
agency, 104, 120, 129, 130, 146–47
agricultural labor, 10, 36, 178n14, 178n17
   in *Under the Feet of Jesus* (Viramontes), 21–22, 50, 55–64
Agwé, 43
Akwesasne (Mohawk) Reservation. *See Frozen River* (Hunt)
Alberta Federation of Labor, 161–62
Algren, Nelson, 147
alienation, 35, 96, 166n5
Almanac of the Dead (Silko), 26
Alpert, Robert, 95
alterity, 11, 35, 41–42, 73, 85, 136
Amazon unionization drive, 3
America Is in the Heart (Bulosan), 56
American Dream, 34, 40, 43–44, 48, 91, 105
Amexicano (film), 92

Angel of History, 75
annihilation, 60, 124, 185n52
antagonistic reciprocity, 46
anti-apartheid movement, 161
anti-Blackness, 89, 98, 100, 115, 121–22
anti-imperialism, 95–96
   See also imperialism and empire
Appel, Sara, 184n32
Arendt, Hannah, 162
Asian American workers, 13, 38, 72, 77–78, 79–80, 155–56
   feminization of Asian men, 99–100, 183n25
   Hmong, 22–23, 86–90, 93–102, 113–15, 123–24, 125, 126
   as model minority, 99
   See also Frozen River (Hunt)
assimilation, 98–99
association, 20, 130
asymmetry of positions, 33
The Atlantic (journal), 29, 116
Atlas, James, 29
auto industry, decline of, 12

Bahrani, Ramin
   Chop Shop, 23, 125–26, 129–31, 137, 141–49, 188n27, 188n30, 189n31
   Man Push Cart, 23, 125, 126, 129–41, 188n20, 188n30
Baker, Sean
   The Florida Project (film), 4–5
banks, demonization of, 34, 79
Banks, Russell. *See Continental Drift* (Banks)
bare life, 31, 66

191

192 • Index

Bauman, Zygmunt, 80–81
Bay Area Rapid Transit (BART), 22–23, 86–90, 115–24, 126
being with (Jean-Luc Nancy), 163
belonging, 11, 19, 23, 59, 73, 83, 94, 101, 130–31, 160
  See also affiliation and collectivity; interdependencies; solidarity
Benjamin, Walter, 75
Berlant, Lauren, 12, 126–27, 145, 148
The Bicycle Thief (film), 139, 157
bildungsroman, 51, 90, 148
biopolitics, 23, 31, 86–87, 89, 90, 122–24, 181n2
Birth of a Nation (film), 100
Black Lives Matter movement, 3, 118, 161, 185n46
Black Panther (Coogler), 115
Black workers, 13, 14, 30–31, 37–38, 43–44, 66–67, 72
  anti-Blackness, 89, 98, 100, 115, 121–22
  Black unemployment, 22–23, 86–90, 115–24, 126, 170n47, 171n52
  in *Fruitvale Station* (Coogler), 22–23, 86–90, 115–24, 126
  Haitian migrants/immigrants, 25, 30–33, 34, 40–43, 44, 47
Blake (Delaney), 31
The Bluest Eye (Morrison), 122–23
Bodnar, John, 91
Bonifacio, Matthew, 92
border crossings, 7, 85, 90, 103–5, 109, 111–12, 114–15, 184n32
  See also transnationalism
Bordwell, David, 144
Bourdieu, Pierre, 10
Breaking Away (film), 91
Breaking Bad (TV series), 29–30
Brown, Nathan, 84
built environment, inequalities in, 76
Bulosan, Carlos, 56
Burden-Stelly, Charisse, 121

Cacho, Lisa, 122–23
Camus, Albert, 135
Canadian border. See *Frozen River* (Hunt)

Cannes Film Festival, 115
Capital (Marx), 18, 158, 167n12, 169n31
capitalism, 10, 15–18, 42, 46–47, 53, 84, 123–24, 174n9
  capitalist accumulation, 76, 81, 85, 88, 122, 124, 141
  carceral, 22–23, 86–90, 115–24, 126, 185n52
  consumer, 35–36, 68–69, 78
  crisis, 147
  global, 11, 22, 121, 126–31, 136
  labor-capital conflict, 166n10
  late, 5–8, 13, 22, 48, 51–52, 65, 107, 127, 161–62, 179n21
  multinational, 51
  necrocapitalism, 16, 23, 31, 35, 86, 123–24, 172n64, 181n2, 185n51, 186n59
  neocolonial, 48, 51, 73
  neoliberal, 103, 144, 148–49, 186n2
  service-sector, 36
  slave, 79
  welfare, 28
  See also racial capitalism
carceral capitalism, 22–23, 86–90, 115–24, 126, 185n52
  See also criminalization; mass incarceration; police violence
Caribbean economy, 28, 30–33
Chakrabarty, Dipesh, 17–18, 84, 172n66, 176n35
child labor, 58, 107
  in *Chop Shop* (Bahrani), 23, 125–26, 129–31, 137, 141–49, 188n27, 188n30, 189n31
Choking Man (film), 92
Chop Shop (Bahrani), 23, 125–26, 129–31, 137, 141–49, 188n27, 188n30, 189n31
cinema of precarity, 126
  See also independent films: migrant labor in
citizenship
  planetary labor citizenship, 59–60, 81, 151
  See also immigrants; undocumented workers
class formation, 11, 26–27, 55, 64, 83, 88–89, 115, 160–64, 173n83

precarious, 163
  See also Continental Drift (Banks)
Clinton administration, 53–54
Coalition of Immokalee Workers, 2
cognitive mapping, 6, 27–28, 32, 48–49, 74, 85, 174n9, 179n21
  See also maps
colonialism, 6, 31–33, 38, 42, 46–47, 51, 78–79, 83, 100, 174n9
  neocolonialism, 22, 48, 51, 65, 69, 70–71, 73
  settler, 103, 109–10
commodity circulation, 106–7, 128
commodity fetishism, 57
community-in-becoming, 71
competition, 20, 130, 151–53
Comte, August, 161
Congress of Industrial Organizations (CIO) working class, 51, 88, 90, 177n2
Conroy, Jack, 147
consumer capitalism, 35–36, 68–69, 78
contested space, metaphors of, 42
Continental Drift (Banks), 21, 24–49, 160, 176n52
  post-Fordism in, 28–35
  racial anxieties in, 35–39
  See also deterritorialization in *Continental Drift* (Banks)
Coogler, Ryan
  Black Panther, 115
  Fruitvale Station, 22–23, 86–90, 115–24, 126
countermodernities, 42
Covid-19 pandemic
  essential workers during, 3
Cowie, Jefferson, 30
creativity, 12, 51, 58, 61, 106, 127, 148, 170n46
criminalization, 58–60, 120
  See also carceral capitalism; mass incarceration
crisis capitalism, 147
cultural difference, 81, 98, 109–10
  as substitute for class, 52–53
Cultures of Solidarity (Fantasia), 163

Dafoe, Willem, 4
Dardenne, Jean-Pierre and Luc, 92
Dash, J. Michael, 26, 41
Davis, Adrienne, 97
Davis, Mike, 24–25, 29, 46–47
dead labor, 15–16, 23, 31, 83–84, 88, 107, 122–24, 171n64, 172n66, 186n59
  in *The Ordinary Seaman* (Goldman), 65–66, 69, 71
  in *Under the Feet of Jesus* (Viramontes), 57, 62
  See also living labor: description of; necrocapitalism; premature death
Delaney, Martin, 31
Denning, Michael, 1, 26, 51, 165n1, 167n13, 177n2
Depression era, 51, 105, 147
desperation, of workers, 4, 19, 56, 65, 81, 127, 136
  in *Continental Drift* (Banks), 29–30, 33
  in *Frozen River* (Hunt), 102–3, 105–6, 109, 113, 115
detective noir, 71
deterritorialization in *Continental Drift* (Banks), 39–49
  seriality, 45–49
Detroit, Michigan, 22–23, 86–90, 93–102, 113–15, 123–24, 125, 126
dialogic tensions, 20
Dienst, Richard, 162
Dirty Pretty Things (film), 92–93
The Disinherited (Conroy), 147
Disney World, 4–5
displacement, 4, 7, 27–28, 59, 63, 83, 92, 126, 129, 134, 153–54
dispossession, 6–10, 22, 33, 81, 85, 103, 108, 113, 126
Dittmar, Linda, 91–92
Douglas, Christopher, 40
downward mobility, 160
  See also Continental Drift (Banks)
Durkheim, Emile, 161

Eastwood, Clint
  Gran Torino, 22–23, 86–90, 93–102, 113–15, 123–24, 125, 126
  The Outlaw Josey Wales, 100
  Unforgiven, 100

Index

Ebert, Roger, 103, 105–6
economic recession of 2008, 182n3
   in *Fruitvale Station* (Coogler), 22–23, 86–90, 115–24, 126
   in *Gran Torino* (Eastwood), 22–23, 86–90, 93–102, 113–15, 123–24, 125, 126
   See also Frozen River (Hunt)
emergent solidarities, 161, 190n2
Engels, Friedrich, 16, 130
entrapment, sense of, 153–54
environmental racism, 56
epic poetry, 55
Equiano, Olaudah, 31
era of compression, 96
essential workers, 3
ethnic literature, 21–22, 84
exclusion, 11, 26, 109, 122–23, 163, 165n3, 170n47
ex-lege proletariat, 14
exploitation, 13–14, 18, 82–83, 105, 138, 146, 147, 178n17, 182n3
   in *Continental Drift* (Banks), 23, 44
   flexploitation, 12
   in *Gran Torino* (Eastwood), 88, 124
   hyperexploitation, 31–33, 66, 121–22, 127, 129, 185n52
   in *The Ordinary Seaman* (Goldman), 65, 69, 71
   in *Under the Feet of Jesus* (Viramontes), 53, 56–58, 61
expropriation, 88, 185n52

Falling Down (film), 29
Fantasia, Rick, 163
fantasy of common being, 162
Federici, Silvia, 13–14, 33, 84
feminism
   feminist literature, 18, 21–22, 50, 55–64
   feminist working-class cooperation, 86
feminization
   of Asian men, 99–100, 183n25
   of labor, 29–30, 37
Fight for Fifteen campaign, 3, 129
Filmmaker (magazine), 137
film noir, 112–13
films with wide distribution, labor in, 86–124
   cinema and the working class, 90–93
   Fruitvale Station (Coogler), 22–23, 86–90, 115–24, 126
   Gran Torino (Eastwood), 22–23, 86–90, 93–102, 113–15, 123–24, 125, 126
   See also Frozen River (Hunt); independent films
First International, 161
flag of convenience registration, 68–69
flexible accumulation, 52, 88, 161, 164
flexploitation, 12
Florida
   Department of Children and Families, 5
   depictions of race and capitalism in, 35–39
The Florida Project (film), 4–5
Florida, Richard, 127
fluidity, 4, 11, 22, 54, 81–82, 163
food truck labor, 23, 125, 126, 129–41, 142, 188n20, 188n30
Ford, Henry, 98
Fordist depictions of working class, 1–2, 6–10, 28–29, 52, 87, 96, 114, 168n15, 177n4
   See also post-Fordism
Francisco, Jason, 189n34
Freeman, Joshua, 12, 15, 37, 177n4
Frozen River (Hunt), 22, 86–90, 102–15, 123–24, 125–26
   border crossings in, 103–5, 109, 111–12, 114–15
   comparison to *Gran Torino* (Eastwood), 113–15
   ice, as metaphor in, 104–5
   Fruitvale Station (Coogler), 22–23, 86–90, 115–24, 126

Galeano, Eduardo, 78
Gaztambide-Fernández, Rubén, 162, 163, 190n3, 190n13
gender
   heteropatriarchy, 19, 99, 103, 111, 114
   masculinity, 34, 95, 97, 98–100, 109, 113, 114
   sexism, 100, 108
   See also feminism; feminization; women workers

generational transition, 94
gentrification, 23, 87, 88, 119
gig economy, 3, 13
Gilmore, Ruth Wilson, 16, 171n51, 185n49, 185n54
Gilroy, Paul, 42
The Girl (Le Sueur), 147
globalization, 3, 19–20, 27, 35, 47–49, 50–51, 53–54, 113–14
  global capitalism, 11, 22, 121, 126–31, 136
  global city, 127–31, 144
  global labor, 150–51
  neoliberal, 65, 66, 81, 84, 125
  post-Fordist, 11–15
Global North, 12, 14–15, 30–31, 33, 51, 53, 79, 84
  See also hemispheric political economics
Global South, 12, 29, 51, 79
  See also hemispheric political economics
Goldman, Francisco
  The Ordinary Seaman, 21–22, 50, 64–71
Gómez-Peña, Guillermo, 78
Good Will Hunting (film), 91
Grant, Oscar, 22–23, 86–90, 115–24, 126
Gran Torino (Eastwood), 22–23, 86–90, 93–102, 113–15, 123–24, 125, 126
The Grapes of Wrath (Steinbeck), 51, 56, 83, 91
Gruesz, Kirsten Silva, 70, 71, 179n34
Grundrisse (Marx), 15, 17, 170n46

Haitian migrants/immigrants, 25, 30–33, 34, 40–43, 44, 47
Hall, Stuart, 7, 37
Hapke, Laura, 157
Hardt, Michael, 33, 81–82, 122, 162, 186n58
Hartman, Saidiya, 123
Harvey, David, 13, 17–18, 128, 129
Le Havre (film), 92
hemispheric literature, 21–22, 26, 50–51, 54–55, 71–80, 82
hemispheric political economics, 68, 70, 180n36

uneven development, 32, 47, 68, 128, 149, 154
  See also Global North; Global South
Hernandez, Esther, 57
heterogeneity, of working populations, 33, 53, 84, 85, 88–89, 113–14, 158–59, 175n18
heteropatriarchy, 19, 99, 103, 111, 114
Hine, Lewis, 145–46, 148–49, 189n34
Hinrichsen, Lisa, 110
Hmong immigrants, 22–23, 86–90, 93–102, 113–15, 123–24, 125, 126
homelessness, 66, 71–80, 150, 154–55, 180n40
human trafficking, 31
Hung (TV series), 29–30
Hunt, Courtney. *See Frozen River*
Hyman, Richard, 20, 130, 161–62
hyperexploitation, 31–33, 66, 121–22, 127, 129, 185n52
hyperprecarity, 123

identity, 22–23, 45, 50, 53, 89–90, 96–97, 114–15, 182n6
  identity politics, 19, 73, 129–30
  unmooring of, 129–30
immaterial labor, 33, 78
immigrants, 2, 7, 10–14, 37–38, 78–79, 128–29, 165n1, 171n49
  as essential workers, 3
  Haitian, 25, 30–33, 34, 40–43, 44, 47
  Hmong, 22–23, 86–90, 93–102, 113–15, 123–24, 125, 126
  Immigrant Freedom Rides, 2–3
  "new," 51
  Pakistani, 23, 125, 126, 129–41, 188n20, 188n30
  See also Latinx workers; migrant and itinerant workers; undocumented workers
immigration policy (US), 83, 181n51, 187n11
Immigration Act of 1965, 26, 29
imperialism and empire, 22–25, 38, 40, 42, 46–47, 69–70, 100, 176n49
  See also anti-imperialism; warfare, US-sponsored

independent contractors, 138
independent films, migrant labor in, 125–59, 186n2
   Chop Shop (Bahrani), 23, 125–26, 129–31, 137, 141–49, 188n27, 188n30, 189n31
   focus on migrant workers of color in global city, 125–31
   La Ciudad/The City (Riker), 23, 125, 126, 129–31, 149–58, 189n38
   Man Push Cart (Bahrani), 23, 125, 126, 129–41, 188n20, 188n30
Indigenous workers, 86, 134n37
   See also *Frozen River* (Hunt)
Industrial Workers of the World (IWW), 161
interdependencies, 26–27, 42, 46–47, 52, 160, 162–63
   See also affiliation and collectivity; belonging; solidarity
international cinema, 92–93
International Labor Office, 170n36
International Monetary Fund (IMF), 79
invisibility, of labor, 30, 32, 75, 83–84, 98, 136–37
isolation, 45–46, 83, 130–36, 141, 146, 151–53, 154–56

James, C. L. R., 68
Jameson, Fredric, 6, 27, 48–49, 74, 85, 93, 101, 168n14, 174n9, 176n37
Jump Cut (journal), 95

Kaplan, Cora, 19
Kaurismaki, Aki, 92
Kelley, Robin D. G., 13, 37–38, 84
King, Rodney, 77, 185n46
Kinkle, Jeff, 27
knowledge workers, 78, 127
Korean War, 93, 94, 95–96
Kroik, Polina, 130, 147, 177n7, 188n18

labor-as-cognition, 61–62
labor-in-motion, 7, 52, 78, 107, 112, 124
   See also migrant and itinerant workers; transnationalism
labor power, 16, 83–84

La Brea tar pits, 60–61
La Ciudad/The City (Riker), 23, 125, 126, 129–31, 149–58, 189n38
class, 140
class consciousness, 6, 19–21, 24–27, 53, 59, 62–63, 147, 157, 180n34
class struggle, 18–19, 81, 157
class warfare, 54
   coherence of, 27
   contingency of, 157
   cultural difference as substitute for, 52–53
   as inseparable from race, 37–38, 44–45
   obscured as personal issues, 91–92
   politics of, 19
   as relation rather than identity, 8, 17, 44–45, 88, 158–59, 163–64, 172n75, 172n77
   seriality, 45–49, 158, 176n37
   as unity-in-dispersal, 19–20
   See also working class
Lange, Dorothea, 105
La Promesse (film), 92
late capitalism, 5–8, 13, 22, 48, 51–52, 65, 107, 127, 161–62, 179n21
   See also *Continental Drift* (Banks)
Latinx workers, 13, 14, 38, 72, 78–80
   in *Chop Shop* (Bahrani), 23, 125–26, 129–31, 137, 141–49, 188n27, 188n30, 189n31
   in *Fruitvale Station* (Coogler), 22–23, 86–90, 115–24, 126
   in *La Ciudad/The City* (Riker), 23, 125, 126, 129–31, 149–58, 189n38
   in *The Ordinary Seaman* (Goldman), 21–22, 50, 64–71
   in *Under the Feet of Jesus* (Viramontes), 21–22, 50, 55–64
Lazo, Rodrigo, 82, 180n39
Legba, 39–40
Le Sueur, Meridel, 147
liberal guilt, 34
liberal humanism, 115–18
Linebaugh, Peter, 42, 67–68, 84
Lipsitz, George, 84
literature, labor in, 147
   literary assemblage, 55

literary imperialism, 40
migration narratives, 50–55, 80–85
  in *The Ordinary Seaman* (Goldman),
    21–22, 50, 64–71
  in *Tropic of Orange* (Yamashita), 21–22,
    26, 50, 71–80
  in *Under the Feet of Jesus* (Viramontes),
    21–22, 50, 55–64
  See also Continental Drift (Banks)
living labor
  description of, 15–21, 53, 60, 84, 123,
    157, 163–64, 168n17, 172n66, 172n68
  See also dead labor
logic of inevitability, 124
logic of possibility, 123
López, Dennis, 62
Los Angeles, California, 21–22, 26, 50,
  71–80
Lowe, Lisa, 17

magical realism, 9, 48, 51, 55, 71, 80, 92
Maid in Manhattan (film), 91
Man Push Cart (Bahrani), 23, 125, 126,
  129–41, 188n20, 188n30
maps, as metaphor, 74–76, 85, 180n43
maps of labor, 21–22, 50–85
  migration narratives, 50–55, 80–85
  in *The Ordinary Seaman* (Goldman),
    21–22, 50, 64–71
  in *Tropic of Orange* (Yamashita), 21–22,
    26, 50, 71–80
  in *Under the Feet of Jesus* (Viramontes),
    21–22, 50, 55–64
Marable, Manning, 16, 121–22, 170n47,
  171n52
Martin, Trayvon, 115
Marx, Karl, 15–20, 61, 66–67, 84, 121, 123,
  130, 140, 172n66, 187n5
  Capital, 18, 158, 167n12, 169n31
  Grundrisse, 15, 17, 170n46
"Marxism and the Interpretation of Culture" conference (University of Illinois), 27
masculinity, 34, 95, 97, 98–100, 109, 113,
  114
mass culture, 93, 101
mass incarceration, 14, 33, 102, 110–11,

116–22, 171nn51–52, 185n49, 185n54
  See also carceral capitalism; criminalization; police violence
materiality, 63, 82, 139, 151
Mbembe, Achille, 16
Mehserle, Johannes, 115, 118, 124
Melville, Herman
  Moby-Dick, 42, 67–68
Mesa, Sophina, 87, 88
metaphor, 135–36
  of contested space, 42
  ice as, 104–5
  maps as, 74–76, 85, 180n43
  ships as, 42–44, 66
Meyerson, Harold, 14
Mezzadra, Sandro, 12, 161, 169n31, 172n66,
  172n68
Michaels, Walter Benn, 52–53, 179n30
migrant and itinerant workers, 7, 10, 11, 37,
  43–44, 50–51
"Migrant Mother" (Lange), 105
migration narratives, 50–55, 80–85
migratory ideas and art, 80–81
  in *The Ordinary Seaman* (Goldman),
    21–22, 50, 64–71
  in *Tropic of Orange* (Yamashita), 21–22,
    26, 50, 71–80
  in *Under the Feet of Jesus* (Viramontes),
    21–22, 50, 55–64
  See also Continental Drift (Banks); independent films, migrant labor in;
    transnationalism
Mitchell, Don, 81, 178n14, 186n59
mobility, 42–43, 81, 103, 105, 112
  upward, 34, 40–41, 65, 73, 91, 99, 130,
    140
  See also downward mobility
Moby-Dick (Melville), 42, 67–68
model minority, 99
modernity, 42, 66, 115, 176n35
Modleski, Tania, 99, 100
Mohanty, Chandra, 163
Moody, Kim, 13, 54, 173n83
moral economy, 41, 48, 117, 120,
  184nn44–45
Morris, Wesley, 119, 184n44
Morrison, Toni, 122–23

multiplication of labor, 12, 88–89
mutuality, 62–63

Nancy, Jean-Luc, 162–63
Narrative (Equiano), 31
National Child Labor Committee, 145–46
national exceptionalism, 47
nationalism, racial, 97
National Taxi Workers Alliance, 2, 129
Native Son (Wright), 122–23
naturalism, 39, 140, 175n15
necrocapitalism, 16, 23, 31, 35, 86, 123–24, 172n64, 181n2, 185n51, 186n59
See also dead labor; premature death
necropolitics, 16
Negri, Antonio, 20, 33, 81–82, 122, 162, 186n58
Neilson, Brett, 12, 126–27, 161, 169n31
neocolonialism, 22, 65, 69, 70–71
neocolonial capitalism, 48, 51, 73
neoliberalism, 3, 7, 10, 14, 26–28, 50–51, 71, 126–30, 145, 171n52, 182n3
neoliberal capitalism, 103, 144, 148–49, 186n2
neoliberal globalization, 65, 66, 81, 84, 125
neoliberal novel, 52
neoliberal policy, 53–54, 79
neorealism, 9, 23, 112, 116, 125–26, 130, 139–40, 142–43, 150, 157
neo-neorealism, 126
Neruda, Pablo, 78
Ness, Immanuel, 13, 128–29, 151
new claims, formation of, 129
New Deal, 24, 30, 178n17, 182n3
New York City, New York
in *Chop Shop* (Bahrani), 23, 125–26, 129–31, 137, 141–49, 188n27, 188n30, 189n31
in *La Ciudad/The City* (Riker), 23, 125, 126, 129–31, 149–58, 189n38
in *Man Push Cart* (Bahrani), 23, 125, 126, 129–41, 188n20, 188n30
in *The Ordinary Seaman* (Goldman), 21–22, 50, 64–71
New York Times (newspaper), 1

Ngai, Mae, 59
Nicolini, Kim, 96
Norma Rae (film), 91
North American Free Trade Agreement (NAFTA), 79–80

Obama, Barack, 115
Occupy Wall Street, 3, 118
Olsen, Tillie, 4, 43, 56
On Earth We're Briefly Gorgeous (Vuong), 10–11
Ong, Aiwa, 63
On Revolution (Arendt), 162
On the Waterfront (film), 91
The Ordinary Seaman (Goldman), 21–22, 50, 64–71
OUR Walmart campaign, 3
The Outlaw Josey Wales (Eastwood), 100

Pakistani immigrants, 23, 125, 126, 129–41, 188n20, 188n30
Palestine, social movements in, 161
Palme D'Or, 92
Paret, Marcel, 163
Paris Commune, 161
partition and confinement, 90
Patterson, Orlando, 123
Perera, Sonali, 19–20
photography, labor in, 145–46, 148–49, 157–58, 189n34
physical labor, 56–58, 64, 66, 68, 78, 96–97, 149, 151–53
pity, 146–47, 148, 162
planetary labor citizenship, 59–60, 81, 151
PMLA (journal), 19
poetic realism, 143–44, 188n20
police violence, 22–23, 86–90, 115–24, 126
See also carceral capitalism; mass incarceration; violence
post-Fordism, 11–15, 28–35, 114–15, 168n18, 178n17
postmodern metafiction, 71
poverty, 13, 56, 79, 82, 92, 101–6, 121, 128, 178n17
in *Chop Shop* (Bahrani), 148
in *Continental Drift* (Banks), 37, 47–48
in *Man Push Cart* (Bahrani), 131, 139

practico-inert reality, 45
praxis, 45
precarious realism, 9–10, 55, 85, 112, 120–21, 131, 140, 168n15
   in *Chop Shop* (Bahrani), 125, 147
   in *Continental Drift* (Banks), 48
   La Ciudad/The City (Riker), 151, 158–59
   See also realism
precarious work and precarity of labor and laboring peoples, 3, 12–14, 22–23, 40, 51, 89, 118–19, 126–27, 170n34, 187n5
   cinema of precarity, 126
   hyperprecarity, 123
   precariat, 3, 11, 158, 166n5
   precarious class formation, 163
   See also solidarity, precarious forms of
premature death, 15–16, 31, 82, 90, 122–23, 135, 181n2, 185n51
   in *Fruitvale Station* (Coogler), 22–23, 86–90, 115–24, 126
   See also dead labor; necrocapitalism
Pretty Woman (film), 91
primitive accumulation, 61
Prisoners of the American Dream (Davis), 24–25, 29, 46–47
proletarian literature, 8–9, 11, 25, 26, 27–28, 30, 34–35
   bildungsroman, 51, 90, 148
   migration narratives as, 50–55, 56, 59
proletariat, 13, 66, 84, 160
   definition of, 8–9, 52, 167n13, 186n58
   ex-lege, 14
   global, 13
   lumpenproletariat, 67
   persons without reserves, 76
Przeworski, Adam, 20
Pulitzer Prize, 26

race, 4, 7, 44, 109–10
   anti-apartheid movement, 161
   Black Lives Matter movement, 3, 118, 161, 185n46
   essential workers, people of color as, 3
   gentrification, 23, 87, 88, 119
   as inseparable from class, 37–38, 44–45

"Race, Class and Societies Structured in Dominance" (Hall), 37
racial nationalism, 97
screen of, 38–39
slave labor, 31, 47–48, 66, 69–70, 79
   See also Asian American workers; Black workers; colonialism; immigrants; Indigenous workers; Latinx workers; whiteness; White workers
racial capitalism, 3, 16, 20–21, 31–33, 73, 118–22, 123, 186n59
   in *Fruitvale Station* (Coogler), 22–23, 86–90, 115–24, 126
racialization, 14–16, 52, 82–83, 120–21, 185n52, 186n59
   in *Continental Drift* (Banks), 28–31, 35–37, 46
   in *Frozen River* (Hunt), 124
   in *Gran Torino* (Eastwood), 86
   in *Under the Feet of Jesus* (Viramontes), 59
racism, 16, 19, 22, 38–39, 83, 117–19, 120, 174n9
   anti-Blackness, 89, 98, 100, 115, 121–22
   environmental, 56
   of police state, 22–23, 86–90, 115–24, 126
   slurs, 93–96, 98
rags to riches narratives, 91
Raussert, Wilfred, 111–12
Reagan era, 24–25, 28, 47–49, 121–22
realism, 40, 65, 101, 105–6, 132–33, 167n14, 186n2
   magical, 9, 48, 51, 55, 71, 80, 92
   neo-neorealism, 126
   neorealism, 9, 23, 112, 116, 125, 130, 139–40, 142–43, 150, 157
   poetic, 143–44, 188n20
   social, 55, 56, 58
   surrealism, 9
   vernacular, 48
   See also precarious realism
reality television, 71, 72
redemption, 94, 97, 100
Rediker, Marcus, 42, 67–68, 84
reserve army of labor, 121–22, 127
"The Right to the City" (Harvey), 128

Riker, David
 La Ciudad/The City, 23, 125, 126, 129–31, 149–58, 189n38
Rivera, Tomás, 56
Robinson, Cedric, 84
Robinson, William, 7
Rodríguez, Ana, 66, 180n36
Rose, Mike, 96
Rose, Sonya, 45, 46
Ross, Andrew, 12
Ross, Steven, 90–91
Rossiter, Ned, 126–27
rust belt, 12

Said, Edward, 80
Salt of the Earth (film), 156
Sandhu, Sukhdev, 135–36
San Francisco, California, 22–23, 86–90, 115–24, 126
Santos, Xuan, 7
Sartre, Jean-Paul, 45–49
Sassen, Saskia, 13, 56, 85, 127, 129
Schein, Nancy, 98, 99, 183n25
Schenk, Nick, 93
Scott, A. O., 112, 126, 142–43
seafaring labor, 21–22, 50, 64–71
second shift of labor, 135, 143–44
seriality, 45–49, 158, 176n37
service-sector capitalism, 36
settler colonialism, 103, 109–10
sexism, 100, 108
sexual violence, 31, 40, 93, 98, 100
sex work, 10, 14, 23, 30–31, 40, 142, 148
Shapiro, Michael, 26, 109
Sharpe, Christina, 89
Silko, Leslie Marmon, 26
Simmonds, Michael, 133, 188n31
Sing, Unburied, Sing (Ward), 122
slave labor, 31, 47–48, 66, 69–70, 79
Smith, Neil, 32
Smith, Robert, 150
social control, 119–20
social death, 16, 120, 122–23
socialism, 161, 165n1
social realism, 55, 56, 58
social reproduction, 18–19, 22, 58, 63–64, 75, 81, 89, 157, 172n75

solidarity, possibility of, 5, 10, 65, 81–82, 87–90, 97–98, 109–15, 158–59
 in *Chop Shop* (Bahrani), 130–31, 141, 146, 148–49
 in *Continental Drift* (Banks), 21–28, 42, 47–49
 in *Gran Torino* (Eastwood), 101–3, 113–15, 124
 in *Under the Feet of Jesus* (Viramontes), 59, 63
 See also affiliation and collectivity; belonging; interdependencies
solidarity, precarious forms of, 23, 160–64, 182n6, 190n2, 190n13
 emergent solidarity, 161, 190n2
 emotional, 86
 specter of, 43
Somebody in Boots (Algren), 147
Sony Pictures Classics, 125–26
Starbucks unionization drive, 3
Steinbeck, John, 56, 83
stereotypes, 98, 101, 116
A Streetcar Named Desire (Williams), 87
stress, 4, 23, 95, 135, 137–38, 139, 140
Strike for Black Lives (2020), 3
subjectivity, labor as, 17, 18
Sun Belt economy, 26, 28, 30, 35–39
Sundance Film Festival, 103, 115
Sun Maid raisins, 57
"surplus" populations, 8–9, 15–17, 76, 81, 90, 121–23, 141, 167n12
surrealism, 9
survival circuits, 56
sweatshops, 150, 155–57

Templeton, Michael, 65, 71
thinking beyond state sovereignty, 109
third space, 104
Thoj, Va-Megn, 98, 99, 183n25
Thompson, Florence, 105, 184n33
threads of routine, 144
Toscano, Alberto, 27
transnationalism, 5–6, 13, 14–15, 24–25
 approaches to cultural study, 81
 from below, 71
 border crossings, 7, 85, 90, 103–5, 109, 111–12, 114–15, 184n32

transnational life, 150–51, 153–54
transnational slave narratives, 31
transnational migrations, 13, 47, 151, 164, 170n36
　See also *Continental Drift* (Banks); migrant and itinerant workers
transnational proletarian encounter, narratives of, 41–42, 48, 89–90
　Gran Torino (Eastwood), 22–23, 86–90, 93–102, 113–15, 123–24, 125, 126
　See also *Frozen River* (Hunt)
Tropic of Orange (Yamashita), 21–22, 26, 50, 71–80
Trump, Donald, 1, 2
Tsing, Anna, 11
Tyner, James, 16, 171n64, 181n2, 185n51, 186n59

Under the Feet of Jesus (Viramontes), 21–22, 50, 55–64
undocumented workers, 10, 14, 33, 43–44, 129, 171n50
　in *The Ordinary Seaman* (Goldman), 21–22, 50, 64–71
　See also *Frozen River* (Hunt)
unemployment, 75, 86, 170n47, 171n52
　absence of labor, 9
　among Black people, 22–23, 86–90, 115–24, 126, 170n47, 171n52
　reserve army of labor, 121–22, 127
uneven development, 32, 47, 68, 128, 149, 154
　See also hemispheric political economics
Unforgiven (Eastwood), 100
unhoused workers, 66, 71–80, 150, 154–55, 180n40
unionization and labor movements, 3, 14, 53–54, 98, 129, 165n1
United Students against Sweatshops, 2
University of Illinois, 27
unofficial workers, 32–33
unwaged or coerced labor, 9–10, 31–33, 42–43, 76–77, 83–84, 105, 167n13
　mass incarceration, 14, 33, 102, 110–11, 116–22, 171nn51–52, 185n49, 185n54
　slave labor, 47–48, 66, 69–70, 79

UPS strike (1997), 2
upward mobility, 34, 40–41, 65, 73, 91, 99, 130, 140
urban renewal, 75
utopian elements, 64–65, 71, 93–94, 101–2

vagabonds, 80–81
vernacular realism, 48
Vietnam War, 99, 100
violence, 51, 57, 61–62, 72, 82, 101–2, 138–39, 147
　by police, 22–23, 86–90, 115–24, 126
　sexual, 31, 40, 93, 98, 100
　vigilantism, 95–96, 98, 100
　warfare, US-sponsored, 64, 65, 69, 93, 94, 95–96, 99, 100
Viramontes, Helena María, 179n25
　Under the Feet of Jesus, 21–22, 50, 55–64
visual poetics, 132–33
Vodun, Haitian, 39–40, 43
Vuong, Ocean, 10–11, 168n21

wage labor, 14, 46, 83–84
Ward, Jesmyn, 122
warfare, US-sponsored, 64, 65, 69, 93, 94, 95–96, 99, 100
Warner Brothers, 125
Weinstein Company, 115, 126
welfare capitalism, 28
whiteness
　presumed innocence of, 48
　white flight, 94, 96
　white masculinity, 98–99
　white privilege, 102, 110, 184n32
　white saviorism, 93–94, 96, 99–100
White workers, 14, 29–30, 33–35, 86, 165n3, 175n15
　in *Gran Torino* (Eastwood), 22–23, 86–90, 93–102, 113–15, 123–24, 125, 126
　racial anxieties of, 22, 35–39, 40–41, 46
　See also Fordist depictions of working class; *Frozen River* (Hunt)
Williams, Tennessee, 87
Winant, Gabriel, 6, 170n34
Winn, Emmett, 91
witness, 148–49, 163

women workers, 2, 4, 13, 26, 150, 155–57, 182n3
   double labors of, 58, 63–64, 107–8, 179n25
   as essential workers, 3
   feminization of labor, 29–30, 37
   in film, 91
   sexism, 100, 108
   sexual violence against, 31, 40, 93, 98, 100
   sex work, 10, 14, 23, 30–31, 40, 142, 148
   See also feminism; *Frozen River* (Hunt)
working class
   changing literary and cinematic depictions of, 3–11, 166n10
   Congress of Industrial Organizations (CIO), 51, 88, 90, 177n2
   feminist working-class cooperation, 86
   Fordist depictions of, 1–2, 6–10, 28–29, 52, 87, 96, 114, 168n15, 177n4
   post-Fordism, 11–15, 28–35, 114–15, 168n18, 178n17
   See also class
Working Girl (film), 91
World Bank, 79
world market, 84
World Trade Organization, 2
Wright, Richard, 122–23

Yamashita, Karen Te
   Tropic of Orange, 21–22, 26, 50, 71–80
   . . . y no se lo tragó la tierra / . . . And the Earth Did Not Devour Him (Rivera), 56
Yonnondio (Olsen), 4, 56
Young, Iris Marion, 45, 46
Yu, Henry, 81

Zandy, Janet, 62, 173n77
Zimmerman, George, 115